FIELD GUIDE TO THE ANIMA

Tristan da

and Gough Island

Edited by Peter G Ryan
Percy FitzPatrick Institute, University of Cape Town
Honorary Conservation Officer, Tristan da Cunha

Contributing authors
Tim Andrew, Marthán Bester, James Glass, Niek Gremmen, Christine Hänel,
Gerhard Jakubowsky, Koos Roux, Peter Ryan and Sue Scott

James Glass
RockHOPPER Giftshop
tristan.trading@gmail.com
1/4/2013
-5/4/2013

OTEP is a joint programme of the Foreign and Commonwealth Office
and the Department for International Development to support the implementation of the
Environment Charters and environmental management more generally in the UK Overseas Territories.

The Royal Society for the Protection of Birds
is the United Kingdom Partner of BirdLife International
supporting bird and biodiversity conservation in the UK Overseas Territories

RSPB registered charity England & Wales no 207076, Scotland no SC037654

To the Saga Ruby Library

piscespublications

Published by
Pisces Publications, Newbury, 2007 for the Tristan Island Government

10-digit ISBN: 1 874357 33 1   13-digit ISBN: 978 1 874357 33 9

British Library-in-Publication Data
A catalogue record for this book is available from the British Library

Designed by
NatureBureau, Newbury, UK (www.naturebureau.co.uk)
Pisces Publications is the imprint of NatureBureau

Printed by
CTP Book Printers, Parow, South Africa

Author addresses

Tim Andrew, Enviro-Fish Africa, 22 Somerset Street, Grahamstown 6139, South Africa
(t.andrew@ru.ac.za)

Marthán Bester, Mammal Research Institute, University of Pretoria, Pretoria 0002, South Africa
(mnbester@zoology.up.ac.za)

James Glass, Agriculture and Natural Resources Department, Tristan da Cunha, TDCU 1ZZ, South Atlantic
(jamesglass@gmail.com)

Niek Gremmen, Data-Analyse Ecologie, Hesselsstraat 11, 7981 CD Diever, The Netherlands
(gremmen@wxs.nl)

Christine Hänel, PO Box 829, Stellenbosch 7599, South Africa
(chrishanel@yahoo.com)

Gerhard Jakubowsky, Department of Botany and Zoology, University of Stellenbosch, Matieland 7602, South Africa
(gerhardj@sun.ac.za)

J P Roux, South African National Biodiversity Institute, Compton Herbarium, Private Bag X7, Claremont 7735, South Africa (roux@sanbi.org)

Peter Ryan, Percy FitzPatrick Institute, University of Cape Town, Rondebosch 7701, South Africa
(peter.ryan@uct.ac.za)

Sue Scott, Strome House, North Strome, Lochcarron, Ross-shire, IV54 8YJ, Scotland
(suescott153@btinternet.com)

Contents

Foreword

The Tristan da Cunha islands, because of their isolation, represent some of the least disturbed temperate island systems in the world. As well as supporting the most remote human community, they are also home to many endemic plant and animal species, some of which are globally threatened by extinction. Although some 44% of the group's land area is set aside as nature reserves, with both Gough and Inaccessible Islands inscribed as World Heritage Sites, there is a limited awareness of the global importance of this area, of the rich diversity of species they contain and of the threats they face.

Although the community is small (currently some 270 people) and resources limited, Tristanians are doing what they can to recognise and to conserve this special heritage. Measures have included adoption of a Biodiversity Action Plan as a strategy to support conservation efforts, one objective of which is to raise awareness both locally and more widely about the importance of the biodiversity of the islands.

The publication of this field guide serves to contribute to this and is designed both as an educational resource for children and adults here, and also for the increasing number of visitors to the Islands, many on cruise ships. Revenue from the sale of field guides will go to the Tristan Environment Fund to support future conservation work on the Islands.

Our grateful thanks to everyone involved in the field guide project, particularly to editor Peter Ryan and his fellow contributors, James Glass, Niek Gremmen, Gerhard Jakubowsky, Koos Roux, Christine Hanel, Marthán Bester, Sue Scott and Tim Andrew. Thanks also to Sarah Sanders and her RSPB colleagues for devising, implementing and part-funding the project, and to the UK Government's Overseas Territories Environment Programme for financial support.

Mike Hentley
Administrator
Tristan da Cunha
November 2006

South Hill, Inaccessible Island, is a spectacular trachyte plug

v

Authors' acknowledgements and dedication

All the authors of this book have had the privilege of visiting Tristan and experiencing the unique hospitality of the island community. We are extremely grateful to the people of Tristan, through their Island Council and Administrator, for permission to conduct research at the islands. We hope that this book will help to increase awareness of the importance of Tristan for biodiversity conservation globally, and further efforts to conserve the islands' unique natural heritage.

We thank our colleagues, many of whom have provided invaluable assistance in the field, as well the South African Department of Environmental Affairs and Tourism, Ovenstone Fishing and Tristan's Natural Resources Department for logistic support during visits to the islands. Peter Ryan is especially grateful to Coleen Moloney, John Cooper, Richard Cuthbert, Erica Sommer, Barry Watkins, Sue Milton, Richard Dean, Ross Wanless, Andrea Angel, Cliff Dorse and Mike Fraser; Sue Scott thanks Paul Tyler and Alison Rothwell; Marthán Bester thanks Allan Seabrook and Gideon Rossouw. Most photographs were taken by the authors, but several other people kindly supplied images, especially Ross Wanless and Cliff Dorse.

The section on non-vascular plants would not have been possible without the contributions of Ryszard Ochyra and Jiri Vana (bryophytes), Dag Øvstedal (lichens) and Bart van de Vijver (diatoms), who identified most of the specimens collected by Niek Gremmen. Phil Heemstra and the South African Institute for Aquatic Biodiversity provided some of the illustrations of fish and sharks. Much information in the chapter on terrestrial invertebrates resulted from the efforts of numerous experts who identified specimens recently collected at the islands: David Barraclough (University of Natal), Maurizio Biondi (University of L'Aquila, Italy), Stephen Compton (University of Leeds), Ansie Dippenaar, Elizabeth Grobbelaar, Riaan Stals and Eddie Ueckermann (Plant Protection Research Institute, Pretoria), Henry Disney and Richard Preece (Cambridge University), Vladimir Gusarov (University of Oslo Natural History Museum), Heloise Heyne (Onderstepoort Veterinary Institute, Pretoria), Ashley Kirk-Spriggs (Albany Museum, Grahamstown), Hiromu Kurahashi (National Institute of Infectious Diseases, Tokyo), Laurence Mound (CSIRO Entomology, Canberra), Ricardo Palma (Museum of New Zealand Te Papa Tongarewa, Wellington), John Reynolds (Oligochaetology Laboratory, Kitchener), Hamish Robertson and Simon van Noort (Iziko South African Museum, Cape Town), Rüdiger Schmelz (Universidad de A Coruña, Spain), Maitland Seaman (University of the Free State, Bloemfontein), Sandra McInnes (British Antarctic Survey, Cambridge), Mark Shaw (National Museums of Scotland, Edinburgh) and Martin Villet (Rhodes University, Grahamstown).

Peter Creed and Barbara Creed from NatureBureau worked tirelessly to select images and design the book. The final product is as much their achievement as the authors. As editor, this project has been an ambition of mine ever since I spent a summer on Inaccessible Island in 1989/90. However, it wouldn't have come to fruition without the support and enthusiasm of Sarah Sanders from the RSPB. Sarah made sure the funding was in place, and provided vital support in proof reading the text. Finally, I would like to thank all the authors and photographers for their contributions.

We dedicate this book to the memory of Nigel Wace (1929–2005), who played a pivotal role in the conservation of the Tristan islands. Nigel started his 50-year love affair with Tristan as botanist on the Gough Expedition of 1955–56. Together with Sir Martin Holdgate, he led the Conservation Survey of the islands in 1968, resulting in the Tristan Conservation Ordinance of 1976 and the monograph *Man and Nature in the Tristan da Cunha Islands*, widely recognised as a classic of conservation science. Nigel visited the islands in each decade from the 1950s to the 1990s, and at the time of his death was planning a revision of the Tristan flora; we hope he approves of this book.

Peter Ryan
Cape Town
November 2006

Northern Rockhopper Penguins rest
on the boulder beach at Salt Beach,
Inaccessible Island

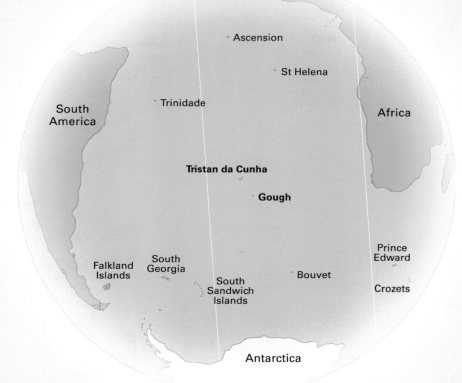

Ascension
· St Helena
· Trinidade
South America
Africa
Tristan da Cunha
Gough
Prince Edward
Falkland Islands
South Georgia
South Sandwich Islands
· Bouvet
Crozets
Antarctica

THE ISLAND SETTING

The Tristan da Cunha archipelago is a group of mountainous islands in the central South Atlantic Ocean, mid-way between the southern tip of Africa and South America. Gough Island, 350 km south-southeast, is the nearest other land. The main island of Tristan has been inhabited since the early 1800s, and currently has a permanent population of some 270 people. Accessible only by sea, and more than 2,400 km from the nearest human settlement at St Helena, it is widely regarded as the most isolated human community. Much has been written about the people of Tristan, their history and culture, but there is less information about the islands' natural history, despite their global importance for biodiversity. Many species have evolved at the islands, and are found nowhere else. What makes Tristan particularly important is that human impacts have been limited, especially at the uninhabited islands. This book provides an identification guide to many of the animals and plants found there.

The book is arranged along taxonomic lines, dealing first with the terrestrial biota, and then briefly covering marine diversity. The level of information provided varies between groups, partly because of our greater knowledge of groups such as birds and mammals, but partly because it reflects the likely interests of the majority of readers. The weevils and lichens of Tristan are fascinating, but their identification is by no means easy. Given limited space, we can only provide an overview of the diversity of these lesser-known groups.

Before describing the species found at Tristan, it is necessary to understand something about the islands' natural history. This first chapter sets the scene for the species accounts, describing the origins of the islands and the major habitats found there. Because of the impacts humans have had on the islands, we also provide a brief human history and an overview of human activities at the islands.

Island structure and origins

Tristan and Gough are oceanic islands that have never been linked to a continental land mass. The islands are the summits of massive shield volcanoes that rise up from the abyssal depths of the South Atlantic Ocean, more than 3,000 m deep. They lie a little to the east of the mid-Atlantic Ridge, where the African and South American tectonic plates are slowly pulling apart. The Tristan archipelago comprises three main islands: Nightingale and Inaccessible roughly 20 km apart, and Tristan 30–32 km from the other islands. Given their mountainous structure, all are visible from each other on a clear day. Gough Island, 350 km south-southeast of the Tristan group, is alone apart from the numerous stacks that surround the island. There are other volcanic peaks in the general area, but they are not tall enough to reach the sea-surface, instead forming sea mounts.

Tristan is associated with a 'hotspot', where a fault in the earth's crust allows volcanism over a long period. Potassium-Argon dating of rocks shows that Nightingale Island is up to 18 million years old, whereas the oldest rocks on Tristan are only some 200,000 years old. Compared to other archipelagos such as Hawaii or the Galapagos, Tristan is unusual in having islands of such disparate ages so close together. However, the main island is on a different volcanic plinth, separated from the two other islands by water some 2,000 m deep. The sea between Nightingale and Inaccessible reaches more than 500 m deep. The islands were built by a series of volcanic eruptions and intrusions, resulting in complex geological structures. Most lavas are basaltic, but many intrusive features such as dykes and plugs are tougher, erosion-resistant trachytes. There are some layers of tuff, often orange-brown, which resemble sedimentary rocks. The most recent lavas are relatively cool *aa* flows or small cinders and scoria that solidified as they were ejected into the air from spatter cones.

Despite protracted periods of volcanism, each island's size and structure is determined by its age. Older islands are smaller and lower-lying due to erosion of the more superficial lavas. Marine erosion typically outstrips fluvial erosion, resulting in steep coastal cliffs and fairly shallow river valleys ending in waterfalls. This is best illustrated at Inaccessible Island, where slumping driven by marine erosion is clearly visible above Blenden Hall and has resulted in the few small areas of coastal lowlands. Only along the north and east coasts of Gough Island are there deeply-incised river valleys. The following points summarise the main features of the islands:

Tristan
- The largest island (96 km²), roughly circular 12 km across.
- Highest point: Queen Mary's Peak, 2060 m.
- Age: 200,000 years. Most recent eruption at the settlement (1961). Other recent eruptions include Stony Hill (1,000 years) and Big Green Hill (10,000 years ago).
- Classic volcanic shape, with steep-sided gulleys radiating from the central peak and steep cliffs caused by marine erosion. Coastal lowlands are confined to the settlement plain (north-west), Caves-Stony Beach (south) and Sandy Point (east). Numerous cinder cones dot the lower slopes or 'Base'; some contain crater lakes.

Nightingale
- The smallest island (4 km²), with two large islets, Stoltenhoff and Alex.
- Highest point: High Ridge, approximately 400 m.
- Age: 18 million years; most recent eruption: Ned's Cave (<200,000 years ago).
- Highly eroded; mainly trachyte rocks remain, forming low cliffs with sea caves. Boggy ponds have developed in shallow depressions on the western plateau.

Inaccessible
- Intermediate-sized (14 km²), rhomboidal 5 by 4 km, highest in the west.
- Highest point: Swale's Fell, approximately 600 m.
- Age: 3–4 million years; most recent eruption: Round Hill (<50,000 years ago).
- Remnant of a Tristan-type volcano (estimated 16 km across and 2,200 m high), eroded mainly from the west, resulting in the highest cliffs in the west and a plateau sloping down to the east. The outline of the original island remains as a shallow shelf mainly to the west of the current island.

Gough
- The second largest island (65 km²), 13 km long and 5 km across.
- Highest point: Edinburgh Peak, 910 m.
- Age: 3–5 million years; most recent eruption: Edinburgh Peak (100,000 years ago).
- West coast characterised by marine erosion and convex slopes, but fluvial erosion has cut a series of deeply incised valleys or 'glens' along the north and east coasts. Erosion-resistant trachyte plugs form numerous sea-stacks and peaks (eg Hag's Tooth, Pummel Crag); dykes form wall-like structures.

Tristan

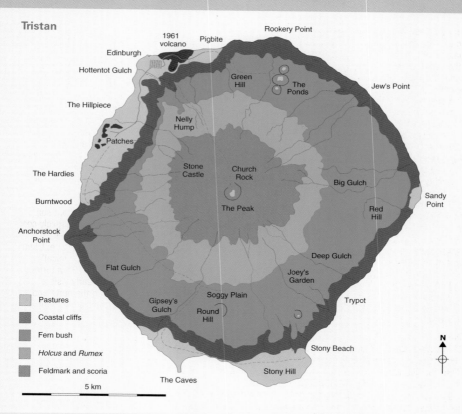

- Pastures
- Coastal cliffs
- Fern bush
- *Holcus* and *Rumex*
- Feldmark and scoria

5 km

1961 volcano
Pigbite
Rookery Point
Edinburgh
Hottentot Gulch
Green Hill
The Ponds
Jew's Point
The Hillpiece
Nelly Hump
Patches
Stone Castle
Church Rock
Big Gulch
The Hardies
The Peak
Red Hill
Sandy Point
Burntwood
Anchorstock Point
Deep Gulch
Flat Gulch
Joey's Garden
Trypot
Soggy Plain
Gipsey's Gulch
Round Hill
Stony Beach
The Caves
Stony Hill

N

Nightingale

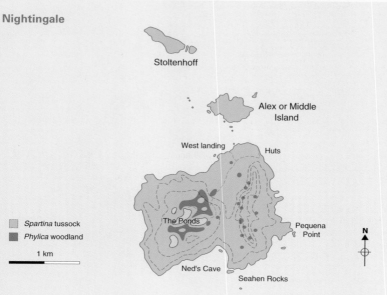

- *Spartina* tussock
- *Phylica* woodland

1 km

Stoltenhoff
Alex or Middle Island
West landing
Huts
The Ponds
Pequena Point
Ned's Cave
Seahen Rocks

N

Inaccessible

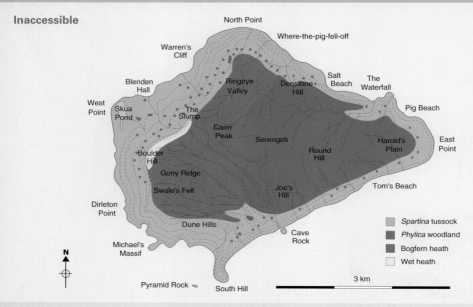

North Point
Where-the-pig-fell-off
Warren's Cliff
Blenden Hall
Salt Beach
The Waterfall
Ringeye Valley
Denstone Hill
West Point
Skua Pond
The Slump
Pig Beach
Cairn Peak
Serengeti
Harold's Plain
East Point
Boulder Hill
Round Hill
Gony Ridge
Swale's Fell
Joe's Hill
Tom's Beach
Dirleton Point
Dune Hills
Cave Rock
Michael's Massif
N
Pyramid Rock
South Hill

Spartina tussock
Phylica woodland
Bogfern heath
Wet heath

3 km

Gough

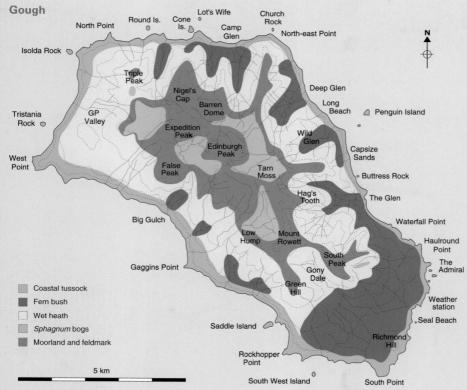

Lot's Wife
Round Is.
Cone Is.
Church Rock
North Point
Camp Glen
North-east Point
Isolda Rock
N
Triple Peak
Nigel's Cap
Deep Glen
Long Beach
Penguin Island
Tristania Rock
GP Valley
Barren Dome
West Point
Expedition Peak
Wild Glen
Edinburgh Peak
Capsize Sands
False Peak
Tarn Moss
Buttress Rock
Hag's Tooth
The Glen
Big Gulch
Waterfall Point
Low Hump
Mount Rowett
Haulround Point
Gaggins Point
South Peak
The Admiral
Gony Dale
Green Hill
Weather station
Coastal tussock
Fern bush
Wet heath
Saddle Island
Seal Beach
Sphagnum bogs
Moorland and feldmark
Richmond Hill
Rockhopper Point
5 km
South West Island
South Point

▲ (1) Tristan from the west   ▼ (2) Nightingale from the west, with Stoltenhoff and Alex islands on the left

▲ (3) The south-east coast of Inaccessible Island   ▼ (4) The east coast of Gough Island, between the Glen and North-east Point

▲ (1) Hag's Tooth on Gough. Snow is frequent on the higher ground in winter

Cold, wet and windy?

The islands' climate is classified as cool temperate. They lie on the edge of the roaring forties, and have a reputation for being rather cold, wet and windy. This is well deserved for Gough Island, but is misleading for Tristan. It is often windy, but Tristan is only 250 km south of the southern tip of Africa, and is often decidedly warm in summer. Pack some sunscreen if you visit the islands. For the record, the average air temperature near sea level is 15°C at Tristan (range 2 to 25°C) and 12°C at Gough (-3 to 25°C), with relatively little daily or annual variation due to the moderating effect of the ocean. It gets considerably colder at higher elevations, with snow regular on the peaks of Tristan and Gough in winter (sometimes as late as December at Tristan). Also, wind chill lowers the apparent temperature substantially, so it is wise to carry a thermal top and windbreaker when walking on the islands.

Rain falls throughout the year, linked to the passage of cold fronts. Sometimes these dump up to 180 mm in a few hours, causing flash floods and peat slips. Fronts are most frequent in winter, resulting in a slight winter peak in rainfall, but more than 40% of rain falls in summer. On average, at least some rain falls 250 days per year at the Settlement on Tristan, where the annual average rainfall is 1,670 mm. At the weather station on Gough it rains almost 300 days per year, with an annual average of around 3,000 mm. The daily rain counts are misleading, however, because the weather is often quite variable, with sunny spells between showers. The weather also varies considerably around the islands. The peaks are often wreathed in orographic cloud, formed when moist, maritime air cools as it is forced to rise. As a result, precipitation is up to 50% higher on the peaks than at the coast. The taller islands also create sheltered 'holes' on their down-wind sides, resulting in warm, sunny pockets that shift with wind direction.

The prevailing winds are from the west, but veer to the north-east prior to the passage of a cold front, then back steadily to the south or south-west as the front moves through. Average wind speed is 36 km/h at Tristan and 44 km/h at Gough, with a tendency for stronger winds in winter. At Tristan, gales blow on 2% of days in summer and 10% in winter (5 and 15%, respectively, at Gough). Wind strength typically increases with altitude, and can be exceptionally strong on exposed ridges.

The climate at Tristan has remained relatively constant during at least the last 20,000 years. The islands were not glaciated during the last ice-age. However, global change is already affecting the islands' climate. Over the last 40 years, average air temperatures at Gough Island have increased by 0.6°C, and climate change models predict further increases of 1–5°C over the next century. The long-term impacts of these changes are unknown, but a warmer climate is likely to favour alien, introduced species that compete with the native fauna and flora.

The tyranny of distance

The most important factor shaping the biota at Tristan is the volcanic origin of the islands in the middle of a vast ocean. All terrestrial animals and plants, and indeed the shallow-water marine biota, have had to disperse across several thousand kilometres of ocean. Some groups of organisms are well adapted to long-distance dispersal and come to dominate island ecosystems, whereas other groups that are abundant elsewhere are absent from islands. Most terrestrial species arrived in one of four ways: blowing on the wind

▲ (2) Orographic clouds frequently occur over the islands, such as at Blenden Hall on the west coast of Inaccessible Island

▲ (3) Storm seas from the north-west make it impossible to land even in the harbour at Tristan

(eg lightweight seeds and spores, spiders on silk 'parachutes'), flying (eg birds, moths, butterflies), hitching a ride on or in another animal (eg seeds stuck to birds' feathers or stored in their stomachs), or drifting there on a log or a raft of vegetation. The prevailing winds and currents are from the west, resulting in most immigrants arriving from southern South America, the Falklands and adjacent islands. However, some species have arrived from southern Africa, and many species are shared with Amsterdam and St Paul, oceanic islands at a similar latitude in the central Indian Ocean.

Vagrants usually arrive in small numbers, bringing with them only a subset of the genetic diversity found in their source populations. Most find conditions at the islands quite different from those to which they are adapted, and as a result, only a small proportion survive. But those that do succeed tend to flourish. They have few predators or competitors, and the islands are home to vast populations of seabirds and seals that import nutrients and energy in the form of guano, eggs, placentas, carcasses, etc. Provided there isn't a continuous stream of new arrivals maintaining a link to the source population, the colonists can adapt to local conditions, evolving rapidly due to strong selective pressures and relatively small population sizes. This results in a high proportion of species found nowhere else. In some cases, the new colonists respond to the many vacant niches by evolving into a variety of different species in a process termed adaptive radiation. At Tristan, the best-studied example is among the endemic buntings, with small-billed dietary generalists and large-billed specialists evolving to exploit the woody fruits of *Phylica* trees. Other radiations have occurred among *Scaptomyza* flies, *Tristanodes* weevils, *Balea* land snails, *Agrostis* grasses and *Nertera* fowl berries.

The tyranny of distance causes differential immigration, speciation and adaptive radiations. It results in the ecosystems at oceanic islands being 'disharmonic', lacking many of the elements usually found in continental systems. This is part of what makes islands such special places for biologists, but it also makes their biota highly susceptible to extinction. The arrival of humans introduced new species both accidentally and deliberately. Many native species struggle to cope, having evolved in the absence of humans and their commensals. Tristan has been fortunate that only a few species have become extinct to date, but preventing the arrival of further alien species is crucial to conserve the many endemic species.

Terrestrial habitats

Terrestrial habitats are defined by their plant communities. Descriptions of the species characteristic of each habitat are given in the following section on terrestrial plants; this merely gives an overview of the composition, structure and distributions of the main habitats. Vegetation types tend to be segregated by altitude, although where they replace each other varies depending on the level of exposure, and is generally at lower elevations at Gough Island than at the milder, northern islands. Starting from the coast, the major habitats are as follows:

Tussock grassland: Most of Nightingale Island and the coastal lowlands and cliffs up to 200–500 m at Inaccessible are covered with tussocks of *Spartina arundinacea*, forming an almost uniform carpet up to 3 m high, broken only by occasional Island Trees and small patches of shorter vegetation dominated by ferns such as *Blechnum penna-marina* and *Rumorha adiantiformis*. Similar vegetation once occurred on the lowlands of Tristan, but has been removed by grazing livestock, and replaced by pastures dominated by an array of introduced grasses and clovers. The few surviving *Spartina* plants on Tristan are confined to steep slopes, inaccessible to even the most adventurous sheep. At Gough, *Spartina* tussock is less well developed, and largely confined to offshore stacks, sea cliffs, and adjacent slopes. The smaller tussock grass *Parodiochloa flabellata* is more abundant, forming dense stands especially along the western cliffs. Well-developed tussock grassland is excluded from areas with frequent slumps and rockslides as well as areas heavily trampled by seals. These disturbed sites support a greater diversity of plants, including Pig Dock *Rumex frutescens*, brass button daisies *Cotula* spp. and numerous introduced species.

Fern bush: Fern bush is a diverse community found above coastal tussock grassland up to around 800 m at Tristan and 500 m at Gough, where it is best developed at more sheltered sites along the east and south coasts. It covers most of the plateau of Inaccessible, but is confined to the area around the Ponds at Nightingale. Fern bush is characterised by two large and distinctive species: Bog Ferns *Blechnum palmiforme* and Island Trees *Phylica arborea*. Bog Ferns are endemic to the islands, and are one of the more charismatic plants, resembling cycads with their broad trunks and terminal arrays of stiff fronds. Despite their common name, they are not typically associated with boggy areas. In sheltered sites they grow up to 2 m high, but they usually are shorter, and in more exposed areas their stems often sprawl over the ground, making walking tiresome. One early visitor to Tristan likened it to walking over a pile of tangled ships' hawsers.

Island Trees are more aptly named, as they are virtually the only tree native to the islands. They grow 5–8 m high in sheltered sites, but become increasingly stunted in exposed sites. In some areas, where trees are densely-packed, they form a closed-canopy with a relatively open understorey, whereas in others the trees are more scattered, with a dense ground cover between the trees dominated by ferns including Bog Ferns, *Ctenitis aquilina*, Bracken *Histiopteris incisa*, *Elaphoglossum laurifolium* and *Asplenium obtusatum*, as well as flowering plants including Dog Catcher *Acaena sarmentosa*, Berry Bush *Empetrum rubrum* and fowl berries *Nertera* spp. In places, such as around the Ponds on Nightingale, there are small areas dominated by tussocks of Small Bog Grass *Scirpus bicolor*. Both Island Trees and Bog Ferns often support many other plants on their stems and branches, notably the filmy ferns *Hymenophyllum* and various lichens. Dense growths of Old Man's Beard lichen *Usnea* occur in areas where orographic mist is frequent.

Fern bush often comprises two rather distinct communities, *Phylica* woodland and Bog Fern heath, segregated by altitude or exposure. Bog Fern heath occurs at higher and more exposed sites where Island Trees are excluded. At Gough, large areas are dominated by dense stands of Bracken. The rhizomes of this deciduous fern form a dense mat, which, together with the smothering effect of dead fronds dropped in autumn and the rapid growth of new fronds in spring, prevents other plants germinating. Recruitment of new Island Trees in particular appears to require some form of disturbance, such as a bird burrow or peat slip. Slips are triggered by heavy rainfall, and generally strip off the vegetation and underlying peat layer to the bedrock. Fresh slips are colonized by various mosses, sedges, grasses, fowl berries, Dog Catcher and Devil's Fingers *Lycopodium diaphanum*, as well as Island Tree and Bog Fern seedlings. Dominance by Bracken is unusual at the northern islands, although it occurs locally, such as on Harold's Plain at Inaccessible.

Wet heath: Wet heath is a transitional vegetation type, containing elements of other vegetation types. It is fairly short (<0.5 m high), and contains fewer ferns than fern bush, with a higher proportion of mosses, grasses, sedges and other flowering plants. Wet heath occurs from the upper limit of fern bush to above 800 m in sheltered locations at Gough Island. It is localised along the highest western rim of the plateau at Inaccessible, and doesn't occur at Nightingale, which is too low-lying. At Tristan, meadows dominated by two alien species, Farm Grass *Holcus lanatus* and Sorrel Dock *Rumex acetosella*, occur above the Bog Fern zone in what was originally wet heath. Typical plants include Dog Catcher, Tristan Cranberry, fowl berries, Celery *Apium australe*, the endemic *Ranunculus carolii*, *Agrostis* and *Deschampsia* grasses, *Carex* and *Scirpus* sedges and various ferns including dwarf Bog Ferns, *Ctenitis aquilina*, *Blechnum penna-marina* and various *Elaphoglossum* species.

Feldmark and alpine habitats: At higher elevations and on more exposed ridges, wet heath gives way to feldmark, an assemblage of dwarf, cushion-forming plants, including Celery, Tristan Cranberries, *Acaena stangii*, several *Agrostis* grasses and *Scirpus* sedges, the lycophytes *Lycopodium magellanicum* and *Huperzia insularis*, as well as numerous mosses and lichens. Plant diversity and cover is related to soil depth and stability, with few plants where there is little soil, and virtually no macrophytes on the loose scoria that characterise much of the upper slopes of Tristan. Only a few hardy lichens and mosses reach the peak of Tristan.

▲ (1) *Parodiochloa flabellata* tussock grassland on Gough Island

▲ (2) *Phylica* woodland, dominated by Island Trees *Phylica arborea*

▼ (3) Bog Fern *Blechnum palmiforme* heath

▼ (4) Wet heath above 400 m on Gough Island

▼ (5) *Sphagnum* bog on the plateau of Gough Island

▼ (6) Feldmark near the summit of Tristan

▲ (1) A cottage on Tristan in the 1980s showing the roof thatched with Flax *Phormium tenax*

▲ (2) Edinburgh of the Seven Seas nestles under the cliffs on Tristan

Bogs and other wetland habitats: Bogs are widespread at the islands, forming in hollows where drainage is impeded. There are two main types of bogs. At lower elevations, they are dominated by floating mats of Big Bog Grass *Scirpus sulcatus*, that are usually dense enough to support a person's weight. Typical examples are the Ponds at Nightingale as well as Skua Pond at Inaccessible. Spectacled Petrel colonies on the plateau of Inaccessible typically are associated with small Scirpus bogs, which are created and maintained by the birds' burrowing activities. Open patches of water and mud are home to Christensen's Starwort *Callitriche christensenii*, whereas the edges of the bogs support other sedges such as *Carex insularis* as well as Pig Dock and *Hydrocotyle capitata*.

Sphagnum bogs typically occur at higher elevations, being found locally on the plateau of Inaccessible and on the Base of Tristan (eg Soggy Plain), and more extensively on the uplands at Gough. They form on top of peat layers up to 5 m deep and are dominated by the moss *Sphagnum recurvum*, although they also contain a variety of other mosses and liverworts. *Scirpus* sedges are the only flowering plants regularly found in these bogs at the northern islands, but the peculiar, sedge-like *Tetroncium magellanicum* is common in the bogs at Gough.

Stream banks lack a distinct plant community, but many species are found most commonly either along water courses or on their shaded banks. These include the distinctive *Glyceria insularis* as well as various native *Agrostis* grasses. Introduced plants also disperse along streams, with floods creating openings for them to become established. The Broad-leaved Dock *Rumex obtusifolius* is probably the most widespread alien, but Farm Grass and Creeping Bentgrass *Agrostis stolonifera* are a more serious problem as they exclude native vegetation.

Human history

The islands were first discovered by Portuguese explorers pioneering an efficient sailing route around Africa. The northern islands are named after Admiral Tristao d'Acunha, who discovered them in May 1506. Gough Island was first sighted by Goncalo Alvarez in 1505, but later 're-discovered' by Captain Gough of the British ship *Richmond* in 1731. The Portuguese apparently showed little interest in the islands. The first recorded landings were made during the 17th century by the Dutch, who considered using the islands as a stopover on the route to the east. British and French exploration followed, when the smaller islands acquired their current names: Nightingale named after British Captain Gamaliel Nightingale in 1760, and Inaccessible (L'ile Inaccessible) named by French Captain d'Etchevery in 1767, alluding to the near vertical cliffs that prevent access to the island's interior. Stoltenhoff, off Nightingale, was named after the two Stoltenhoff brothers who lived on Inaccessible from 1871 to 1873 in a failed attempt to make their fortunes sealing.

Despite plentiful water, fish, seals and seabirds, the islands remained uninhabited for almost three centuries after their discovery because they lacked safe anchorages. The lobby to establish a British penal colony on Tristan rather than in Australia failed, and it was only when commercial sealing started in the late 18th century that protracted visits were made to the islands. Gangs of sealers were left on the islands from 1790, killing thousands of seals for their skins and oil. Vegetable gardens were established at Tristan, and

▲ (3) The Potato Patches on Tristan

▲ (4) Sealer caves cut into the base of the cliffs at the Glen on Gough Island

goats, pigs and poultry were introduced. The Yankee whaler Jonathan Lambert settled in 1810, and in July 1811 published a proclamation in the Boston Gazette claiming the islands for himself and his heirs, naming them 'The Islands of Refreshment'. Lambert drowned in 1813, but one of his colleagues, Thomas Currie, remained at Tristan until the islands were annexed by Britain in 1816.

A British garrison was stationed at Tristan to prevent the French from using the islands as a base from which to free Napoleon from his exile on St Helena. When the garrison withdrew in November 1817, Corporal William Glass, his wife and two children, and two colleagues were given permission to remain at Tristan. They formed the nucleus of the present community, which was augmented in the male line by castaways and crew from passing ships. The seven surnames on the island all date to the 19th century. In addition to Scot William Glass, Thomas Swain arrived in 1826 from England, Peter Green (formerly Groen) in 1836 from Holland, Americans Thomas Rogers in 1836 and Andrew Hagan in 1849, and Italians Andrea Repetto and Gaetano Lavarello in 1892. Males initially outnumbered females, but this was rectified to some extent in 1827, when five women from St Helena arrived to marry some of the island's bachelors. A more recent addition to the island community was the two Smith sisters from Ireland who arrived in 1908.

Sealing foundered as seal populations were over-exploited, but the small community flourished from 1830–1870, thanks to the large numbers of vessels, especially whalers, calling to trade for fresh produce. From the 1870s, the switch to steam ships, the opening of the Suez Canal, and dwindling whale stocks saw a marked reduction in the numbers of ships visiting Tristan. The economy gradually switched from trading to subsistence crofting. Then the already struggling community was dealt two blows in the 1880s. First, rats arrived from a shipwreck in 1882. They multiplied rapidly, causing extensive damage to crops and native bird populations. Then in 1885, a boat with 15 men aboard was lost after it put to sea to trade with a passing ship. Many islanders left to settle in South Africa and New England, and the population fell by almost half to only 50 people.

Tristan's isolation was greatest during the early 20th century, when there was often more than a year between ships. This period saw an increasing reliance on the outer islands for food and guano as seabird populations on the main island decreased under the combined impacts of people and rats. Missionaries played a large role in guiding island life during this period, including promoting a failed attempt to set up a farming community at the Waterfall on Inaccessible Island in 1936. Links with the outside world increased in the 1940s. A small naval garrison was stationed at Tristan in 1942, bringing the first radio link to Cape Town. After the Second World War, commercial fishing for rock lobster started in 1949, and an expatriate Administrator was appointed.

The island community was rudely thrust into the limelight in 1961, when a volcanic eruption right next to the settlement caused the entire community to flee to Nightingale and then on to the United Kingdom. For most islanders it was their first time off Tristan, and many longed to return. After intensive lobbying, an advance party went back to the island in 1962, and most of the rest of the community returned towards the end of 1963. A harbour was built to compensate for the loss of the main landing beach under the new lava flow. Today, the islands form the UK Overseas Territory of Tristan da Cunha, led by an Administrator and elected Island Council.

▲ (1) House Mice are serious predators of seabird chicks at Gough Island, especially winter-breeding species like this Atlantic Petrel chick

▲ (2) Eradication of alien species, such as this exercise to remove Flax from Nightingale Island, is crucial for the long-term conservation of native species

The community of some 270 people is largely self-sufficient, generating revenue mainly from fishing, and meeting most of their food needs from potatoes and other crops, various products from sheep, cows and poultry, and fishing. All other supplies come from Cape Town. The gradual development of a cash economy has reduced dependence on seabirds. As a result, careful stewardship of marine resources is crucial to Tristan's economy and its conservation.

Scientific exploration

Apart from the visit by Captain Dugald Carmichael during the British occupation in 1816–17, the initial scientific collections were made during brief calls by research and exploration vessels, such as the *Challenger* in 1873, *Scotia* in 1904 and *Quest* in 1922. The first comprehensive study of the northern islands was made by the Norwegian Scientific Expedition in 1937–38. Further observations were made by Bertus and Bunty Rowan, who investigated the potential for a lobster fishery at the islands in the late 1940s, and Sir Hugh Elliott, Administrator from 1950–52. Following the 1961 volcanic eruption and subsequent evacuation, the Royal Society Expedition visited the islands to assess the possibility of the island community returning, and a Conservation Survey was conducted in 1968. The outer islands also were visited during these surveys, but the first proper exploration of Inaccessible Island only took place in 1982–83, when Michael Swales led the Denstone Expedition to the island. The expedition's hut at Blenden Hall has provided the stimulus for further research at Inaccessible.

The first significant scientific study at Gough Island was made by the Gough Island Scientific Survey in 1956–57. The expedition hut at The Glen on the east coast of Gough was maintained as a South African weather station until 1963, when the station was moved to its current site on the south coast, farther from the influence of the island's mountainous interior. The presence of the weather station has facilitated research at the island, and for some groups of organisms, more is known about their status at Gough than at the northern islands.

Human impacts and conservation

Although the Tristan group has some of the least disturbed temperate islands in the world, humans have impacted the islands directly, through exploitation and habitat transformation, and indirectly, through the many species introduced to the islands. Historically, large numbers of whales, seals, fish, and seabirds and their eggs and chicks were killed for food, oil and skins. Seal populations collapsed at all the islands, and although Subantarctic Fur Seals have bounced back, Southern Elephant Seals have failed to recover, despite the cessation of hunting for many years. Human impacts on seabirds were most severe at the main island of Tristan, where Tristan Albatrosses and Southern Giant Petrels disappeared, and populations of other seabirds were greatly reduced, helped along by rat predation. Introduced mice and rats probably accounted for the extinction of the Tristan Moorhen and the local extirpation of Tristan Buntings from Tristan. The bunting's demise may have been helped along by the loss of most of the island's tussock grassland. The coastal lowlands have been almost entirely transformed by grazing livestock and introduced

▲ (3) Tristan Albatrosses and other seabirds are threatened by accidental mortality on long-lines and other fishing gear

▲ (4) Ratting day allows teams to show their prowess at catching rats on the main island of Tristan. Black Rats have serious economic and ecological impacts. There are plans to eradicate them from Tristan

pasture species. In the past, collection of wood from Island Trees *Phylica arborea* also had a significant impact close to the settlement.

At Inaccessible Island, feral pigs almost managed to wipe out the only known breeding population of Spectacled Petrels, and coupled with human exploitation, reduced the sole surviving population of Tristan Albatrosses breeding at the northern islands to just a few pairs. Fortunately the pigs died out before they managed to finish the job. At Gough Island, recent research has shown that House Mice, introduced inadvertently by sealers, are serious predators of seabird chicks, especially in winter. The mice nibble holes into the bodies of their unwitting prey, killing unsustainably large numbers of Tristan Albatross and Atlantic Petrel chicks. Both are largely confined to Gough as breeding species. Unless something is done about the mice, the seabird populations appear doomed to decrease into the foreseeable future. The mice probably also eat the eggs and chicks of Gough Buntings, explaining the much lower abundance of buntings compared to mouse-free Nightingale and Inaccessible Islands.

Mice and rats also have significant impacts on the islands' invertebrates and plants, by selective predation of invertebrates and seeds. These groups also are affected by the many species of invertebrates and plants introduced by humans over the last few centuries. Some of the invasive plant species have the potential to alter radically the vegetation of the islands. Conservation threats are not confined to the islands. The plight of the albatrosses and several of the larger petrels is exacerbated by ongoing accidental mortality on fishing gear, especially long-lines. And the entire economy of Tristan is threatened by illegal fishing in the islands' waters.

Fortunately, the need for environmental protection was recognised, with the 1976 Conservation Ordinance proclaiming Gough Island a nature reserve and providing some protection for seabirds and Island Trees at Tristan. Since then, Inaccessible Island also has been made a reserve, and together with Gough forms one of only two British Natural World Heritage Sites in the UK Overseas Territories. The traditional harvesting of seabirds is now confined to Nightingale Island, where only Great Shearwaters and Rockhopper Penguin eggs may be collected. Tristan has protected almost half of its land area, far ahead of most other countries, and has taken active steps to conserve its marine heritage. The community recently adopted a Biodiversity Action Plan, to be implemented by the Agriculture and Natural Resources Department, which has appointed for the first time on the island a Conservation Officer. The Conservation Ordinance was updated in 2006, allowing Tristan to join the Agreement on the Conservation of Albatrosses and Petrels. Controls on imported goods are being tightened to reduce the risk of further accidental introductions to the islands, and eradication programmes for invasive alien species are either underway (eg New Zealand Flax *Phormium tenax* at Inaccessible and Nightingale, Procumbent Pearlwort *Sagina procumbens* at Gough) or being planned (eg rats on Tristan, mice on Gough).

Flowers of the endemic
Acaena stangii

PLANTS

Plants define terrestrial habitats at Tristan and Gough; their communities are described in the Introduction. Flowering plants dominate most habitats, but they are less diverse than in equivalent continental environments. Their paucity is linked to their relatively large seeds and fruits, which are less likely to disperse over long distances than the small, lightweight spores of ferns, mosses and other non-vascular plants. Most spore-bearing species probably colonised the islands when their spores were carried in the jet stream. Some flowering plants also are wind dispersed, with plumed seeds (eg many members of the daisy family Asteraceae), but most probably used other means to reach the islands. A few species with buoyant fruits may have drifted on ocean currents or rafted there on driftwood (eg Pig Dock *Rumex frutescens*), but most flowering plants probably reached the islands with the assistance of birds or other animals. Seeds may be carried in birds' feathers, or in mud on their legs, with some plants such as Dog Catcher *Acaena sarmentosa* and hook sedges *Uncinia* spp. having seeds designed to hook onto feathers or fur. Other plants like fowl berries *Nertera* spp. or Berry Bush *Empetrum rubrum* produce fruits that are eaten by birds. The birds later excrete the seeds, possibly promoting dispersal among islands within the archipelago, but this is less likely to account for long-distance transfers because of the fast digestion of birds.

The native plants show affinities to the Magellanic region of southern South America and the Falkland Islands (eg *Nertera, Empetrum*), to sub-Antarctic islands (*Agrostis, Uncinia*) and Australia and New Zealand (*Acaena*). There are relatively few connections to southern Africa, the nearest continental area, due to the rather different climatic conditions and dispersal from Africa being against the prevailing westerly winds. Some species show remarkably disjunct ranges, with isolated populations separated by large distances. The Island Tree *Phylica arborea* and Tussock Grass *Spartina arundinacea* occur on the Tristan group and at Amsterdam and St Paul, islands at a similar latitude in the southern Indian Ocean which share several seabird populations with Tristan and Gough. Petrels retain woody seeds and other indigestible matter in their stomachs for months, which may account for the disjunct range of the Island Tree. More bizarre are the local populations of Pepper Tree *Peperomia berteroana* in one valley on Inaccessible and Sophora Tree *Sophora microphylla* in one valley on Gough. The only other populations of these species are at islands in the South Pacific, raising the possibility that they may have been introduced to the Tristan islands by sealers, although *Peperomia* has evolved into an endemic subspecies.

Only some 50 flowering plants are native to the islands, of which 27 are found nowhere else. There are almost as many ferns (35 species), of which 14 are endemic to Tristan and Gough. Non-vascular plants are more diverse than flowering plants and ferns, but they have been less well-studied, and the total number of species is unknown. Relatively few are endemic because their spores disperse easily. In addition to the native species, more than 140 introduced plants have become naturalised (not counting those grown in gardens). Most are confined to the main island of Tristan, with only eight at Nightingale, 27 at Inaccessible and 25 at Gough. Some species were introduced on purpose, such as the New Zealand Flax *Phormium tenax*, which was brought in for thatching, or various grasses imported to improve pastures or combat erosion. But most alien species were introduced by accident, as seeds in plant soil, in hay and other agricultural products, or in other imported materials.

Some introduced plants such as Kikuyu Grass *Pennisetum clandestinum* are pests in the potato patches and gardens, bringing economic costs. Other aliens invade natural vegetation, threatening the extinction of native species. Widespread alien plants include Farm Grass *Holcus lanatus* and Creeping Bentgrass *Agrostis stolonifera*, which have become dominant in several habitats on the islands, and Sorrel Dock *Rumex acetosella*, which dominates, together with *Holcus*, a vegetation belt at about 700–1,000 m above sea-level on the Peak of Tristan. The current ranges of many alien species are probably restricted by climatic conditions. If climate change alters temperature and rainfall patterns, some species that presently appear to pose little threat could become serious pests.

Once introduced species start to spread, they are difficult to eradicate. It is only feasible for species that are large and easy to find, or have restricted distributions. Eradication programmes have been set up for New Zealand Flax on Nightingale and Inaccessible, and for Procumbent Pearlwort *Sagina procumbens* on Gough. The best approach is to prevent their arrival in the first place. Every possible precaution should be made to ensure that all imported goods are free of seeds, insects, fungal spores, etc. Extra care is needed when moving from Tristan to the other islands, given the much greater number of alien species on Tristan.

FLOWERING PLANTS

Flowering plants are the most successful and diverse plants on earth, but their seeds and fruits are much larger than the spores of ferns and non-vascular plants, making long-distance dispersal more difficult. Only some 50 flowering plants are native to the islands, with 27 found nowhere else. Many more flowering plants have been introduced by humans, some of which threaten native ecosystems. Only the more widespread or important introduced plants are included here, a more comprehensive list is given on page 150. Flowering seasons are only approximate; they vary between islands (generally later at Gough) and with elevation (earlier lower down).

Rhamnaceae

Phylica arborea Island Tree

The common native tree, growing up to 7–8 m in sheltered sites, but often much shorter, forming dense, impenetrable thickets. In exposed areas, it forms a procumbent tangle <1 m tall. Evergreen; leaves are small, narrowly elongated, with white hairs mainly on the underside. Bark pale grey, often heavily festooned with lichens and other epiphytes. Flowers October–March; small, whitish and strongly scented; often visited by flying insects. Woody fruits have three (2–4) locules and take a year to mature, turning purple and then black before opening to release large black seeds (one per locule). The seeds are the main food of Wilkins' Bunting and large-billed Inaccessible Buntings. **Distribution**: Tristan, Nightingale, Inaccessible and Gough. A key species of fern bush, occurring up to 800 m on Tristan and 500 m on Gough; also occurs in scattered copses among *Spartina* tussock. Historically, many trees on Tristan cut for fuel. Also occurs at Amsterdam and St Paul in the southern Indian Ocean; seeds possibly distributed in petrel stomachs. Most *Phylica* species occur in South Africa; *P. polifolia* occurs on St Helena.

Fabaceae

Sophora microphylla Sophora Tree, Kowhai

A localised tree up to 8 m high. Leaves arranged in tufts at the end of branches, compound, with 10–20 leaflets along the sides and one at the end. Flowers yellow tubes, 2–5 cm long, with protruding anthers and stamen. Fruit are bean-like pods 5–20 cm long containing up to 12 seeds. Flowers September–October. **Distribution**: Gough; confined to a small stand of about 20 trees in Sophora Glen; they are all roughly the same age, with no evidence of seedlings; may have been introduced by sealers. Native to New Zealand.

Piperaceae

Peperomia berteroana Pepper Tree

A distinctive perennial shrub up to 1 m high with fleshy, shining leaves; leaves whorled, obovate to oblanceolate, about 5–8 cm long, 2–4 cm wide, dark green above, paler below. The tiny greenish flowers are organised in slender axillary spikes 35 mm long. **Distribution**: Endemic subspecies *tristanensis* is confined to Waterfall Valley, Inaccessible, where it occurs along the stream bank in shaded sites between Pig Beach Hill and the eastern flanks of Denstone Hill at 150–300 m; sometimes grown in gardens on Tristan. The nominate subspecies is found 5,000 km away on the Juan Fernandez Islands off the coast of Chile.

Myrtaceae

Metrosideros excelsa New Zealand Christmas Tree, Pohutukawa

A small tree with aromatic, oblong leaves, 4–10 cm long and 3–5 cm wide, with a dense mat of whitish hairs on their underside. Inflorescences conspicuous because of the long red stamens protruding up to 3 cm out of the flowers, giving the appearance of a bottlebrush. Flowers December–February. Seeds are small and easily dispersed by wind. **Distribution**: Introduced to Tristan, where many seedlings and young trees occur around the Settlement, especially on the lava from the 1961 eruption. Native to New Zealand, it has been imported to many parts of the world as a garden plant, and has become an invasive pest in some areas, including South Africa. **Other tree species**: Numerous other tree species have been planted around the Settlement and at Sandy Point on Tristan, where pine trees *Pinus* spp. are spreading onto the Base. There are three *Pinus caribea* at the site of the old hut at the Waterfall on Inaccessible. Apple trees *Malus domestica* have been planted for their fruit at various sites on Tristan and Inaccessible, and Willow trees *Salix babylonica* were planted to provide wood for longboat spars; the last two trees on Inaccessible recently died.

▲ *Phylica arborea* Island Tree, LEFT (1) flowers RIGHT (2) fruit
◀ (3) *Phylica arborea* Island Tree
▼ (4) *Peperomia berteroana* Pepper Tree

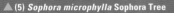

▲ (5) *Sophora microphylla* Sophora Tree
▼ (6) *Sophora microphylla* Sophora Tree, flowers
▼ (7) *Sophora microphylla* Sophora Tree, fruits
▲ (8) *Metrosideros excelsa* New Zealand Christmas Tree
▼ (9) *Metrosideros excelsa* New Zealand Christmas Tree, leaves and buds

Apiaceae

Apium australe Celery
Wild Celery is bright green, with thick, grooved stems and divided leaves with fleshy stalks. It looks, smells and tastes similar to the cultivated celery (*A. graveolens*). Its structure is highly variable, forming low cushions in exposed sites at higher elevations or close to the beach, while plants in sheltered areas may grow up to 1 m or more in height. Small white flowers are produced October–February in umbrella-shaped inflorescences, 10–20 cm across. **Distribution**: Tristan, Nightingale, Inaccessible and Gough; common from sea-level to about 1,000 m on Tristan; occurs at all altitudes and in all vegetation types at the other islands, but is most common in wet heath. Also in South America, Falkland Islands, Australia and New Zealand.

Centella asiatica Asiatic Pennywort
A small, perennial herb with green or purplish creeping stems, rooting at the nodes. Leaves kidney-shaped, or round or heart-shaped, 2–5 cm across, with crenate margins; on glabrous petioles 1–20 cm long. Flowers inconspicuous, whitish or pink, in small groups (reduced umbels) of 2–4 on short stalks rising from the nodes. **Distribution**: Introduced at Tristan; common on Settlement Plain in meadows, gardens and waste ground. Native to Asia, but is a widespread weed. It is cultivated for chemical compounds used in medicine and cosmetics.

Hydrocotyle capitata
Small herb with creeping stems, rooting at the nodes. The leaf-blades are circular to kidney-shaped, 1–5 cm across, shallowly 5–7-lobed with crenate lobes. The flowers are small, whitish-green, on short stalks, not rising above the leaves. *Centella asiatica* is less hairy and lacks lobed leaves. **Distribution**: Endemic to Tristan, Inaccessible and Gough. Common in damp and shaded areas, up to 700 m on Tristan and 500 m on Gough.

Convolvulaceae

Calystegia soldanella Sea Bindweed
A perennial herb with long root system and procumbent stems 15–50 cm long; leaf-blades kidney-shaped and somewhat fleshy. Flower 3.5–5 cm long, pink, with five white stripes; fruit is a capsule. **Distribution**: Tristan; scattered on sandy beaches; occurs worldwide in similar habitats.

Calystegia sepium Hedge Bindweed
A creeper with broad, arrow-shaped leaves 10 cm long and 5 cm wide. Produces large pink flowers, 5–6 cm long with five narrow white stripes. Flowers November–January. **Distribution**: Tristan and Inaccessible; status uncertain, possibly introduced. On Tristan around the Settlement and at the Patches; on Inaccessible it occurs locally mainly at lower altitudes as a creeper on dense *Spartina*, often along drainage lines. **Similar species**: *C. tuguriorum* (New Zealand Bindweed) has smaller (3 × 3 cm), heart-shaped leaves with rounded basal lobes. Flowers white or pale pink, c2.5–3.5 cm long. Status uncertain, possibly introduced; confined to a single site on Inaccessible near the beach at Blenden Hall; occurs elsewhere in New Zealand, Chile and Juan Fernandez Islands.

Ranunculaceae

Ranunculus carolii
A small, creeping perennial with yellow flowers. The leaf-blades are tripinnate, 4–13 mm long and 6–22 mm wide, the petioles are up to 6 cm long. Petals yellow, 4–5.5 mm long, 1.5–1.7 mm wide. Flowers November–February. **Distribution**: Endemic to Tristan, Inaccessible and Gough. Scattered on Tristan from 700–900 m in meadows on the Base and lower parts of the Peak, in damp and shady gullies, but also on steep and rocky slopes; rare on Inaccessible in wet heath above 500 m; more widespread on Gough from near sea-level to 800 m. It is closely related to *R. biternatus* from South America, New Zealand and some sub-Antarctic islands. **Similar species**: *R. repens* (Creeping Buttercup) introduced to Tristan, occurs in gardens and at the Patches.

Asteraceae

Sonchus oleraceus Common Sowthistle, Annual Sowthistle
A large, yellow-flowered herb, 30–80 cm high, with thick, hollow stems; exudes whitish sap when broken. Leaves soft, pinnately lobed, with soft spiny teeth along the margins. Auricles of the leaves (ear-shaped lobes at the base of the leaves) are arrow-shaped, usually with pointed lobes, usually not clasping the stem. Flowers September–March. Seeds have white plumes for wind dispersal. **Distribution**: A cosmopolitan weed introduced to Tristan, Nightingale, Inaccessible and Gough. Scattered mainly in disturbed areas in lowlands, but locally at higher elevations. **Similar species**: *S. asper* (Prickly Sowthistle) resembles *S. oleraceus*, but the leaves are thicker, less deeply lobed, more glossy on top, and with more prickly spines; the auricles of the leaves are rounded and clasp the stem. Introduced at Tristan and Gough, it grows in similar habitats to *S. oleraceus*, but is less common.

▲ (1) *Apium australe* Celery

▲ (2) *Hydrocotyle capitata*

▼ (3) *Calystegia soldanella* Sea Bindweed

▼ (4) *Calystegia sepium* Hedge Bindweed

▼ (5) *Ranunculus carolii*

▼ (6) *Sonchus oleraceus* Common Sowthistle

Chevreulia sarmentosa
A small yellow-flowered, perennial herb with flowerheads about 10 mm across. Leaves in rosettes. Leaf-blade densely covered with white hairs, spatulate, 15–20 mm long. **Distribution**: Probably introduced to Tristan, restricted to lowlands; one old record from Inaccessible. Widely distributed in South America.

Cotula goughensis Gough Brass Buttons
A yellow-flowered perennial herb about 10–30 cm high; leaves deeply incised and somewhat fleshy, often with some long, white hairs. Flowerheads 5–15 mm across; disc-florets yellow, ray-florets absent. Flowers October–April. Closely resembles other *Cotula* spp; differs in being larger with more fleshy leaves than *C. moseleyi*; lacks dense hairs of *C. australis*. **Distribution**: Endemic to Gough. Common in coastal areas, especially where there is moderate trampling by seals and penguins.

Cotula moseleyi Nightingale Brass Buttons
A small herb, about 12–15 cm high. Leaves glabrous and deeply incised. Flowerheads 5–10 mm across; disc-florets yellow, ray-florets absent. Flowers October–March. **Distribution**: Endemic to Nightingale and Inaccessible. Fairly common in disturbed and open habitats on Nightingale up to 350 m along paths, around The Ponds, in *Spartina* tussock and *Phylica* woodland. Scarce at Inaccessible, restricted to around Great Shearwater burrows along western plateau rim and on rocks in the penguin colony at Salt Beach. **Similar species**: *C. australis* (Australian Brass Buttons) is similar to *C. moseleyi*, but the whole plant is densely hairy. Introduced to Tristan and Nightingale; on Tristan scattered from near sea-level to 100 m on Settlement Plain pastures, gardens and roadsides; on Nightingale occurs alongside *C. moseleyi*. Native to Australia and is widespread as a weed, it also occurs in South Africa.

Lagenophora nudicaulis
Tiny plants, with dark green, spatulate leaves with crenate margins arranged in flat rosettes 3–5 cm across. Flowers in a single flowerhead on a 5–10 cm high stalk, with whitish disc-florets surrounded by pink-purple ray-florets. **Distribution**: Tristan, Inaccessible and Gough. Occurs mostly in wet areas, growing among mosses and as an epiphyte on the stems of Bog Fern *Blechnum palmiforme*. Also found in the Falkland Islands and southern South America.

Leucanthemum vulgare Oxeye Daisy
Erect perennial herb, growing in loose patches, 30–50 cm high. Leaves ovate to spoon-shaped, up to 15 cm long and 2 cm wide with toothed to pinnately-lobed margins. Flowerheads 3–5 cm across, with tubular yellow disc-florets and white petal-like ray-florets. **Distribution**: Introduced at Tristan; scattered in pastures, as a weed in the Potato Patches, and on lowland slopes.

Conyza sumatrensis Sumatran Fleabane
Tall annual herb, about 0.5 to 1.5 m high, with stems and leaves covered by small, soft hairs. Inflorescence is a loose panicle, with flowerheads 1–2 mm in diameter. Seeds with pappus of feathery hairs, which facilitate wind dispersal. **Distribution**: Introduced to Tristan and Inaccessible (eradicated from Gough); abundant weed of open and disturbed areas, including coastal slips up to 450 m.

Gnaphalium thouarsii Cow Pudding Grass
Silvery perennial herb, up to 30–40 cm high. Leaves oblong, silvery-white because of dense hairs. Flowerheads in small groups in the upper half of the stem, in the axils of the leaves, white to brownish. **Distribution**: Endemic to Tristan, Nightingale, Inaccessible and Gough; common in open vegetation (eg peat slips and along rivers) from sea-level to 500 m, but scarce in dense tussock grass. **Similar species**: Three introduced species superficially resemble *G. thouarsii*, but are smaller and more slender, with flowerheads lacking conspicuous 'petals'. Purple Cudweed **G. purpureum** (Tristan; scattered around the Settlement) has flowerheads situated in the axils of the leaves in the upper part of the stem, as in *G. thouarsii*, but the leaves are not as hairy, with most hairs on the underside of the leaves. The other two species, *Pseudognaphalium luteo-album* (Jersey Cudweed) and *Vellereophyton dealbatum* (White Cudweed), have inflorescences clustered in small groups at the end of the stems and branches. Both have whitish leaves with very dense hairs, but *P. luteo-album* has yellow-white inflorescences, while those of *V. dealbatum* are more purplish.

▲ (1) *Chevreulia sarmentosa*   ▲ (2) *Cotula goughensis* Gough Brass Buttons

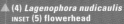
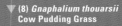

▲ (3) *Cotula moseleyi* Nightingale Brass Buttons   ▲ (4) *Lagenophora nudicaulis*
INSET (5) flowerhead

▼ (6) *Leucanthemum vulgare*
Oxeye Daisy   ▼ (7) *Conyza sumatrensis*
Sumatran Fleabane   ▼ (8) *Gnaphalium thouarsii*
Cow Pudding Grass

Pseudognaphalium luteo-album Muckweed, Jersey Cudweed
Annual herb, 5–30 cm high, stems either unbranched or sparsely branched near the base, with branches ascending. Leaves lanceolate, silvery-white, 2–6 cm long and 0.5–1.2 cm wide. Small flowerheads grouped together at the top of the stem, with small yellow-orange flowers, surrounded by yellowish-white bracts. **Distribution**: A cosmopolitan weed introduced to Tristan and Inaccessible. Scattered on open ground, in pastures, and in rock crevices from sea-level to 1,200 m on Tristan; mainly on coastal slips and relatively dry disturbed areas on Inaccessible.

Vellereophyton dealbatum White Cudweed
Densely white hirsute annual to biennial herb, up to 30 cm high. Leaves oblanceolate to spatulate, 1–5 cm long. 10–40 flowerheads group together in globose terminal clusters. Florets white to yellow; outer female, filiform; inner bisexual, tubular. Flowers November–February. **Distribution**: Introduced to Tristan and Inaccessible from South Africa. Common in pastures of Settlement Plain and on waste ground; possibly also in other parts of the island at lower elevations. Recently introduced to Blenden Hall, Inaccessible.

Chenopodiaceae

Chenopodium ambrosioides Island Tea
Large herb, 50–100 cm high, with branched stems. The leaves have aromatic glands on their underside, giving off a lemon-like smell. The leaf-margins are crenate to shallowly lobed. Oblong, branched inflorescences, with small, greenish flowers. Flowers January–February. **Distribution**: Tristan, Nightingale, Inaccessible and Gough; mainly in dry, sunny sites, including in the lava of the 1961 eruption on Tristan; favours nitrogen-rich soil around penguin colonies or in areas with large numbers of Great Shearwaters. The leaves were used as a tea by the islanders. Plants from Tristan were first collected by Thouars in 1793 and later described as an endemic variety *tomentosum*. However, *C. ambrosioides*, native to Mexico, is widely cultivated and may have been introduced by sailors. **Similar species**: *C. murale* (Nettle-leaved Goosefoot) and *C. album* (Fat Hen) are both introduced to Tristan; both lack the strong smell of *C. ambrosioides*. *Atriplex plebeja* is an enigmatic plant, apparently endemic to Tristan and Nightingale, but now either very rare or extinct. First discovered in 1817 by Carmichael who found it growing along the shore at Tristan, a single plant was found 120 years later on Nightingale. There have been no confirmed records since then.

Solanaceae

Solanum nigrum Tristan Blackberry
An annual herb with a sprawling, open growth form up to 80 cm high. Leaves entire, more or less oval. Flowers white, in small groups. Flowers October–March. Fruit a berry, up to 1 cm across, green when young, turning black when ripe. **Distribution**: Introduced to Tristan and Inaccessible. Locally common in disturbed areas, mainly around the coast at Inaccessible. **Similar species**: *S. tuberosum* (Potato) grows wild locally at Tristan, Inaccessible and Gough, usually near areas of former cultivation.

Brassicaceae

Brassica rapa Turnip
Annual or biennial herb, 20–150 cm high, with broad, cabbage-like leaves and cruciform yellow flowers in a terminal spike. Small black seeds form in long, slender pods that split open length-wise when ripe. **Distribution**: Introduced to Tristan and Inaccessible. Locally common weed around the Settlement and patches at Tristan; confined to the area around the old hut at the Waterfall on Inaccessible, but increasing in abundance, despite repeated weeding efforts.

Cardamine glacialis Scurvy Grass
Perennial herb, up to 30 cm high, but usually rather short and prostrate. Leaves pinnate; leaflets entire, but the top leaflet is larger and often three-lobed. Flowers October–November; flowers white or pinkish, usually in groups at the end of branches. Fruits are 2–4 cm long, narrow capsules, compressed, with seeds in a single row. **Distribution**: Tristan, Inaccessible and Gough. Quite rare, in damp sites such as shady gullies and along stream banks; only found above 500 m on Inaccessible; occurs lower down on Gough. **Similar species**: *Nasturtium officinale* (Watercress) is introduced to Tristan, where it is locally abundant near the Settlement in or alongside streams. Seed capsules are broad and compressed, with seeds in two rows.

▲ (1) *Pseudognaphalium luteo-album* Muckweed

▲ (2) *Vellereophyton dealbatum* White Cudweed

▲ (3) *Chenopodium ambrosioides* Island Tea

▼ (6) *Brassica rapa* Turnip

▲ (4) *Solanum nigrum* Tristan Blackberry INSET (5) flower

▼ (7) *Cardamine glacialis* Scurvy Grass with fruit capsules INSETS (8) flower and (9) leaves

Callitrichaceae

Callitriche christensenii Christensen's Starwort

A distinctive small herb with small, round leaves (<1 cm across), and thin stems, usually forming creeping mats in damp areas or floating on ponds. Flowers are tiny and unisexual; male flowers are reduced to a single stamen, and the female flowers consist of a small ovary with two styles. **Distribution**: Endemic to Tristan, Nightingale, Inaccessible and Gough; usually found in damp and wet areas, especially those enriched by bird faeces. Plants growing in standing water are much more elongated than those on land.

Valerianaceae

Centranthus ruber Red Valerian

Perennial herb, 30–80 cm high. Leaves opposite, ovoid-lanceolate in shape, about 5–8 cm long. Flowers are pink or rarely white in large and showy inflorescences. The fruits are wind-dispersed. **Distribution**: Introduced on Tristan. Possibly brought in as a garden ornamental and escaped. *Centranthus ruber* is native to the Mediterranean region and is a popular garden flower.

Rubiaceae

Nertera depressa Fowl Berry, Hen Berry

A small, creeping, perennial herb, 1–2 cm tall. Easily distinguished from other *Nertera* spp. by its small ovate leaves, usually <5 mm across; leaves glabrous with entire margins, but sometimes the cells are developed into papillae or hairs. Flowers November–February; flowers are yellowish-green, 2–3 mm long. Fruit is orange-red, 3–5 mm across; found on plants year round; commonly eaten by buntings. Each fruit contains two seeds 1.7–2.4 mm long. **Distribution**: Common on Tristan, Inaccessible and Gough from near sea-level to 800 m on Tristan, 600 m on Gough; favours open areas including recent slips; on Tristan even persists in pastures of mainly introduced species. Scarce on Nightingale, where it is largely confined to open areas and rocks. Widespread in South and Central America, the Falkland Islands, South-east Asia, Australia and New Zealand. The Tristan population is genetically closest to those from South America and the Falklands.

Nertera assurgens Fowl Berry, Hen Berry

A creeping, perennial herb, resembling a large form of *N. depressa*, sometimes growing up to 30 cm tall. It is characterised by large, narrow leaves with distinctly undulating margins (unlike *N. holmboei*); leaves narrowly-ovate, 8–16 mm long, 6–12 mm wide. Flowers November–February. Fruits orange-red, 4–6 mm across; seeds 2.1–2.5 mm long. **Distribution**: Endemic to Tristan and Inaccessible. Occurs on coastal cliffs and lower Base at Tristan, 150–710 m; common on Inaccessible plateau, especially in Bog Fern heath.

Nertera holmboei Fowl Berry, Hen Berry

A creeping, perennial herb, resembling a darker green, broad-leaved form of *N. assurgens*. Leaves are broadly ovate, 8–16 mm long, 8–17 mm wide; margins entire (sometimes slightly undulating on Inaccessible). Flowers November–February. Fruit orange-red, 4.5–6 mm long and broad, 2-seeded. Seeds 3.2–3.7 mm long. **Distribution**: Endemic to Nightingale and Inaccessible. Fairly common on the plateau of Inaccessible above 300 m; occurs from sea-level to 300 m on Nightingale. Island populations are genetically distinct, apparently having only recently colonised Nightingale.

Scrophulariaceae

Veronica serpyllifolia Thyme-leaved Speedwell

A small, decumbent perennial herb up to 10 cm high, easily overlooked if not flowering. Leaves broadly ovate, opposite, with leaf-stalks very short or absent. Flowers October–December; flowers 5–8 mm across, whitish or pale blue, with dark blue veins. **Distribution**: Introduced to Tristan and Inaccessible. Locally common in dense groups in grassy places or between rocks; confined to scree slopes and areas with abundant seabird burrows at Inaccessible.

Caryophyllaceae

Cerastium fontanum Common Mouse-ear

A small herb, up to 25 cm tall, with glands on stems and leaves; leaves entire, ovate, distinctly hairy, 10–15 mm long. Flowers November–January; flowers white, about 5 mm across; fruits somewhat curved capsules, up to 12 mm long, containing many seeds. **Distribution**: Introduced to Tristan and Inaccessible, where it is locally common in disturbed areas; one record from Gough. **Similar species**: *C. glomeratum* (Sticky Mouse-ear) is similar, but the flowers are more densely clustered; introduced to Tristan.

▲ (1) *Callitriche christensenii*
Christensen's Starwort

▲ (2) *Centranthus ruber* Red Valerian

▼ (3) *Veronica serpyllifolia*
Thyme-leaved Speedwell

▲ (4) *Nertera depressa* Fowl Berry

▼ (5) *Nertera assurgens* Fowl Berry

▼ (6) *Nertera holmboei* Fowl Berry

▼ (7) *Cerastium fontanum*
Common Mouse-ear

Sagina procumbens Procumbent Pearlwort
A small perennial herb, superficially recalling a dwarf form of Small Bog Grass *Scirpus bicolor*. Grows from a central rosette, with prostrate stems growing in all directions, forming dense cushions or mats. Leaves are narrow, linear, up to 1 cm long; flowers greenish, 2–3 mm across. Fruits are capsules, each containing up to 100 tiny seeds; plants mature within a few months, and seeds survive for many years. **Distribution**: Introduced to Tristan and Gough in the 1990s; spreading rapidly on Tristan, probably helped by human traffic from the Settlement. First found on Gough in 1998 close to the weather station. An eradication programme started in 2000 has prevented its spread, but continued efforts are needed to ensure all seeds are destroyed.
Similar species: *S. apetala* (Annual Pearlwort) also has been introduced to Tristan; it is a much smaller, annual species with ascending stems, and a rosette of leaves at the foot of the stem only in very young plants. It is a common weed in gardens and along road edges.

Stellaria media Chickweed
Annual to biennial herb, up to 30 cm high, with thin stems, with a single row of hairs. Leaves oblong, entire, without hairs. Flowers white, 5–10 mm in diameter. **Distribution**: Introduced to Tristan and Gough; locally common in damp, disturbed areas, including around penguin colonies along the east coast of Gough.

Lamiaceae
Prunella vulgaris Selfheal
A small perennial herb, up to 15 cm high. The stem is square in cross-section, with opposite, entire, oblong leaves. Distinctive purple flowers, up to 2.5 cm long, in a cylindrical inflorescence at the end of the stem.
Distribution: Introduced to Tristan; common around the Settlement and on the coastal scarps up to 400 m.

Oxalidaceae
Oxalis corniculata Procumbent Yellow-sorrel
A small, creeping, perennial herb with tough reddish stems and distinctive trifoliate leaves. Small yellow flowers with five petals. Flowers November–March. Fruits are an oblong capsule, up to 25 mm long, hairy.
Distribution: Introduced to Tristan and Inaccessible; occurs locally in dry, sunny spots, usually on cliffs.
Similar species: *O. pupurea* (Purple woodsorrel), introduced to Tristan, has much larger leaves and is less sprawling; large purple-mauve flowers from September–October; common in lawns and pastures on the Settlement Plain. *Trifolium* spp. (clovers, Fabaceae) also have trifoliate leaves, but have papilionaceous flowers, arranged in dense heads. Clovers are common in lawns and pastures on the Settlement Plain; at least five species have been introduced to Tristan.

Geraniaceae
Pelargonium grossularioides Gooseberry-leaved Pelargonium
An aromatic herb up to 40 cm high. Leaves fairly hairy with long leaf-stalks; leaf-blade round to kidney-shaped, 3–5 lobed, 10–60 mm across. Flowers October–February; 3–20 flowers in umbel-like inflorescences; flowers purplish-pink, up to 1 cm across; easily overlooked. After flowering, develops distinctive 'stork's bill' fruit. **Distribution**: Tristan and Inaccessible; grows mainly in disturbed sites; fairly common on soil slips at Inaccessible and among rocks in *Spartina* tussock. Also occurs in South Africa.

Rosaceae
Acaena sarmentosa Dog Catcher
A herb-like, sprawling shrub with long, procumbent stems, which become woody when older; herbaceous branches, 10–40 cm high, bear compound leaves, each with 4–6 leaflets along either side and one at the end; leaflets grey-green with serrate edges and densely hairy below. Flowers October–February; flowers are small, reddish, in round flowerheads at the end of vertical stalks, raised above the foliage. Each fruit has four spines each ending in recurved barbs; the seed-heads readily attach themselves to animals and people, aiding their dispersal. **Distribution**: Endemic to Tristan, Nightingale, Inaccessible and Gough, where it is common below 750 m on Tristan and 500 m on Gough; scarce near sea-level at the northern islands. Similar to *A. magellanica* which occurs in southern South America and at sub-Antarctic islands.

Acaena stangii Dog Catcher
A dwarf version of *A. sarmentosa*; leaflets are largely hairless, and typically has fewer leaflets per leaf. Fruit spines often lack barbs. Flowers November–February, 2–3 weeks later than *A. sarmentosa* where they co-occur. **Distribution**: Endemic to Tristan, Inaccessible and Gough; mainly found above 500 m.

▲ **(1)** *Sagina procumbens*
Procumbent Pearlwort

▲ **(2)** *Sagina apetala* Annual Pearlwort

▲ **(3)** *Stellaria media* Chickweed

▽ **(4)** *Prunella vulgaris* Selfheal

▽ **(5)** *Oxalis corniculata*
Procumbent Yellow-sorrel

▽ **(6)** *Oxalis purpurea*
Purple Woodsorrel

▽ **(7)** *Pelargonium grossularioides*
Gooseberry-leaved Pelargonium
CLOSE-UP **(8)** flowers

▽ **(9)** *Acaena sarmentosa* Dog Catcher
CLOSE-UP **(10)** fruits

▽ **(11)** *Acaena stangii* Dog Catcher
CLOSE-UP **(12)** flowers

Empetraceae

Empetrum rubrum Berry Bush, Island Berry, Peak Berry
A woody dwarf shrub up to 80 cm tall, with tiny, hard, narrow, bluntly tipped leaves with revolute (rolled back) edges. Flowers minute (<2 mm), pink to purple, on short stalks in between leaves at the ends of branches. Flowers September–October. Fruits berry-like, green when young, turning red-black when ripe in December–March. Fruit eaten by buntings and Tristan Thrushes, especially by fledglings. Habit and shape of leaves variable, resulting in several forms and varieties being described; Peak Berry (variety *tristanitorum*), found at high altitude on Tristan, has a prostrate, matted habit and sweet fruits. **Distribution**: Tristan, Nightingale, Inaccessible and Gough. Common at dry, well-drained sites throughout, but most abundant at higher elevations; occurs up to 1,900 m on Tristan. Also found in the Falklands.

Polygonaceae

Rumex acetosella Sorrel Dock, Sour Grass
A perennial herb, 20–50 cm high, with distinctive arrow-shaped leaves, usually with spreading basal lobes, and small, reddish inflorescences. Dioecious (separate male and female plants). **Distribution**: Introduced to Tristan, Nightingale, Inaccessible and Gough. One of the most abundant alien species on Tristan, forming extensive meadows on the lower parts of the Peak at 700–1,000 m, often with alien grasses such as *Holcus lanatus* and *Agrostis tenuis*. The almost complete replacement of natural vegetation by these species is promoted by sheep grazing. At the other islands it is scarce, local and probably declining in the absence of grazing pressure.

Rumex frutescens Pig Dock
A perennial herb with broad, oblong, glossy, somewhat leathery leaves, rounded at the tip. Small greenish flowers are arranged in globular clusters, and produce fairly large fruits. **Distribution**: Tristan, Inaccessible and Gough; common along shores, in disturbed areas and on floating bog vegetation. Also found in South America; the fruits are buoyant, and may have drifted to the islands from South America.

Rumex obtusifolius Broad-leaved Dock
Up to 120 cm high, erect perennial herb with large, broad, somewhat undulate, but not crisped leaves, which lack the clearly rounded tip of *R. frutescens*. **Distribution**: A cosmopolitan weed, introduced to Tristan, Nightingale, Inaccessible and Gough. It is one of the most widespread aliens on the islands, occurring in disturbed areas in a wide range of habitats up to 800 m; most commonly found along streambeds and on the coast. **Similar species**: *R. crispus* (Curled Dock), introduced to Tristan, has narrower, strongly undulate and crisped leaves.

Plantaginaceae

Plantago major Greater Plantain
A small herb up to 30 cm high with distinctive, broadly ovate, leaves with parallel venation. Flowers small and greenish, arranged in a tall, slender spike up to 30 cm long. **Distribution**: A cosmopolitan weed, introduced to Tristan, Inaccessible and Gough; common in disturbed areas and at seeps, mainly along the coast. **Similar species**: *P. lanceolata* (Narrowleaf Plantain) is another introduced species on Tristan and perhaps Gough; smaller, with long, narrow leaves; flower spike much shorter, elevated on a long, slender stalk.

Euphorbiaceae

Euphorbia peplus Petty Spurge, Milkweed
A small annual up to 30 cm high with erect stems, often branched. Leaves alternate, oval in shape. Flowers green. Like all euphorbias, it contains a milky sap. **Distribution**: Introduced to Tristan, where it is an abundant weed at the Patches.

Araceae

Zantedeschia aethiopica Arum Lily, Calla Lily
Large perennial, evergreen herb, forming 50–100 cm high clumps; leaves large, more or less triangular and somewhat leathery with entire margins. Produces distinctive arum flowers in spring: a yellow rod-like spike, 5–8 cm long, partly enclosed by a large white bract or spathe. Fruits are yellow-green berries. **Distribution**: Introduced to Tristan from South Africa, probably as an ornamental, and has spread into wet and disturbed areas near the Settlement.

▲ (1) *Empetrum rubrum*
Berry Bush, flowers

▲ (2) *Empetrum rubrum*
Berry Bush, fruits

▲ (3) *Empetrum rubrum* Berry Bush

▼ (4) *Rumex acetosella* Sorrel Dock

▼ (5) *Rumex frutescens* Pig Dock

▼ (6) *Rumex obtusifolius*
Broad-leaved Dock INSET (7) flowers

▼ (8) *Plantago major*
Greater Plantain

▼ (9) *Euphorbia peplus*
Petty Spurge

▼ (10) *Zantedeschia aethiopica*
Arum Lily

Agavaceae

Phormium tenax New Zealand Flax

New Zealand Flax is related to the agave. It forms large, dense tufts of thick, 1–3 m high erect grey-green leaves, arranged in flattened fans. Each spring, mature plants produce flower spikes up to 3 m long, bearing tubular red flowers. **Distribution**: Introduced to Tristan, Nightingale and Inaccessible. Native to New Zealand, but is an aggressive invader in many areas (eg St Helena). Introduced to Tristan in the 1800s for thatching; currently used as a windbreak around houses and gardens. It is somewhat invasive, spreading slowly and replacing native vegetation; programmes to remove it from Inaccessible and Nightingale are underway.

Juncaginaceae

Tetroncium magellanicum

A small, sedge-like plant of upland bogs with rigid, folded, grass-like leaves that have reddish bases; grows in loose clonal groups from thick rhizomes, often forming open circles. Flowers are unisexual, arranged in spikes; female flowers reddish; no male flowers have been observed at Gough. **Distribution**: Gough; common in bogs at higher elevations. Also found in southern South America and the Falklands.

Iridaceae

Romulea rosea Onion Grass

A small perennial with a brown corm underground and grass-like leaves which are more or less cylindrical in cross-section. The large solitary flowers are pink-violet. Flowers September–October. Seeds are produced in an oblong capsule, about 1 cm long. **Distribution**: Introduced on Tristan; common in grasslands in the Settlement Plain. Native to South Africa.

Poaceae Grasses

This large group of about 10,000 species in 600 genera worldwide is the most species-rich family of flowering plants at the islands. Grass identification is notoriously difficult, often depending on fine structural details. They are so different from other flowering plants that a special nomenclature is used to describe their parts. The stems (culms) are hollow and usually round in cross-section, with thickened nodes. The leaves are arranged opposite, in two rows but in one plane (you need to look carefully) and differentiated into a lower sheath enclosing the stem and a narrow blade. A membranous appendage (sometimes a ring of hairs) termed a ligule lies at the junction between sheath and blade. The small, wind-pollinated flowers (florets) are highly modified and reduced in comparison to other flowering plants; they are grouped into spikelets which are in turn arranged in a panicle, raceme, spike or head. A spikelet consists of two glumes (bracts) with a lemma (the flower bract), a palea (modified petal), three stamens and two stigmas for each flower. The lemma is sometimes awned. The fruit is called a caryopsis. Grasses are often confused with sedges (Cyperaceae) which have the leaves arranged in three rows and a triangular-sectioned stem. Thirteen species of grasses are endemic to the islands, most of them in *Agrostis*. In addition to the species listed here, there are a large number of introduced grasses (see alien plant list on page 150), mainly found on Tristan, that we cannot illustrate; most European floras provide enough information to identify them.

Spartina arundinacea Tussock Grass, Tussac

A huge grass up to 2.5 m high, usually in large clumps or tussocks, but these coalesce into impenetrable stands in damp areas. Stout stems 5–10 mm across have regularly spaced nodes, giving a bamboo-like impression. Leaves flat and tough, with minutely serrate edges that can inflict nasty cuts. Inflorescences long and compact, at the end of the leafy stems. Flowers October–December. The relatively large seeds are eaten by buntings. **Distribution**: Tristan, Nightingale, Inaccessible and Gough, mainly along coastal scarps up to 500 m. Dominates most of Nightingale and the coastal scarps of Inaccessible, but has been much reduced at Tristan, apparently by grazing and burning. Much less abundant at Gough, where dense stands are restricted to the coastal cliffs. Formerly used to thatch houses on Tristan; also found on St Helena, Amsterdam and St Paul Island.

Parodiochloa flabellata Gough Tussock

A fairly large tussock grass, 40–120 cm high, forming dense clumps, mainly in coastal lowland areas. Stems much smaller than *Spartina arundinacea*; leaves, especially young ones, are folded lengthwise. Inflorescences are dense, compact panicles carried on culms which bear leaves only in their lower part, and usually do not extend much above the leaves. Flowers September–November. Flowers and seeds eaten by introduced mice, even during the day. **Distribution**: Gough, where it is abundant on coastal cliffs up to 300 m, forming dense stands that largely replace *Spartina*. It also occurs on South Georgia, the Falkland Islands and southern South America; has been introduced to the Shetland, Scotland.

▲ **(1)** *Phormium tenax*
New Zealand Flax

▲ **(2)** *Spartina arundinacea* Tussock Grass INSET **(3)** inflorescence

▼ **(4)** *Tetroncium magellanicum*

▼ **(5)** *Parodiochloa flabellata* Gough Tussock

▼ **(6)** *Romulea rosea* Onion Grass

Glyceria insularis
A distinctive grass with broad, pale green, glabrous leaves, usually associated with streams. Rhizomatous perennial, forming small tufts, 25–55(100) cm high. Distinguished from other grasses by the long, many-flowered spikelets. Culms simple, erect or ascending. Leaf-sheaths overlapping; ligules up to 10 mm long; leaves folded and flattened, 6–21(40) cm long, 4–10(15) mm wide. Panicles 12–24(36) cm long. Spikelets 6–10-flowered, 15–23 mm long; glumes one-nerved; lower 3.5–7.5 mm long; upper 5.5–8 mm long; lemmas 6–7.5 mm long. Flowers October–December. **Distribution**: Endemic to Tristan, Inaccessible and Gough. Local on Tristan and Gough along streams, in gullies, crater lakes and damp grassland; scattered on the plateau of Inaccessible along streams and in wet heath, extending down watercourses to about 150 m.

Deschampsia robusta
A large, tufted perennial grass growing 80–110 cm high from a short rhizome; easily distinguished from other *Deschampsia* spp. by the taller, 2–5 noded culms. Culms stout, up to 5 mm across, glabrous. Leaf-sheaths glabrous, up to about 12 cm long; ligules 8–15 mm long; leaf-blades terete, 20–45 cm long and up to 7 mm wide. Panicles 15–25 cm long. Spikelets two-flowered, 8–11 mm long; glumes almost equal, as long as the spikelet, lower one-nerved; upper three-nerved; lower lemma awned, seven-nerved; awn 7.5–8.5 mm long; upper lemma awned, five-nerved; awn up to 5 mm long. **Distribution**: Endemic to Gough, from 200–600 m in wet heath communities, along streams and in wet gullies.

Deschampsia christophersenii
A tufted perennial grass, 15–40 cm high. Culms simple, erect, stiff, two-noded. Leaf-sheaths overlapping, glabrous, up to 7 cm long; ligules 2–5 mm long; leaf-blades terete, stiff, 5–20 cm long, 0.8–1.2 mm wide. Panicles 7–15 cm long with numerous spikelets. Spikelets (1)2-flowered; glumes nearly equal, 7.5–10 mm long, 1–3-nerved; lower lemma awned, 4.5–6 mm long, 5–7-nerved; awn 6–8 mm long; upper lemma awned, 4–5 mm long, 5–7-nerved; awn 4–6.5 mm long. Flowers January–February. **Distribution**: Endemic to Tristan, Inaccessible and perhaps Gough. On Tristan scattered from 600–1,500 m in upland meadows, in *Rumex-Holcus* grassland, in bogs with tree-ferns or *Scirpus* species; on Inaccessible in *Blechnum palmiforme* heath on the plateau; one record from coastal tussock at Gough. **Similar species**: Although placed in another genus *Calamagrostis deschampsiiformis* (endemic; Tristan and Gough) is very hard to distinguish from *D. christophersenii*; it should have 1-flowered spikelets, but *D. christophersenii* also can have one-flowered spikelets; it is possible that the two species are, in fact, conspecific.

Deschampsia mejlandii
A tufted perennial grass, up to 50 cm high; best distinguished from *D. christophersenii* by its flat leaf-blades. Culms simple, erect, with 1–2 nodes. Leaf-sheaths overlapping, glabrous, up to 10 cm long; ligules 7–15 mm long; leaf-blades flat, erect, stiff, linear, prominently ribbed above, linear, with a hard involute tip, up to 22 cm long and 6 mm wide. Panicles 10–25 cm long with numerous spikelets. Spikelets two-flowered, 8–10 mm long; glumes three-nerved; lower 6.5–8.5 mm long; upper to 10 mm long; lower lemma awned, 5–7-nerved, 4–5 mm long; awn 6–6.5 mm long; upper lemma awned, 5–7-nerved; 3–4.5 mm long; awn 4–6.5 mm long. Flowers January–April. **Distribution**: Endemic to Tristan and Inaccessible. On Tristan scattered from 650–1,800 m, sometimes in *Blechnum palmiforme* scrub but more common above the treefern limit in the lower parts of the peak in *Rumex-Holcus* grassland and in *Rhacomitrium* and *Empetrum* heath; on Inaccessible scarce in wet heath along the western edge of the plateau.

Deschampsia wacei
A tufted perennial grass, 6–40 cm high; the short leaf-blades and many leafy innovations give this grass a unique habit, very different from other *Deschampsia* spp. Culms slender, erect, 1–2-noded. Leaf-sheaths glabrous, 1–4 cm long; ligules 2–10 mm long; leaf-blades involute, 1–12 cm long, 0.6–1.3 mm across. Panicles 2.5–15 cm long. Spikelets two-flowered, 9–10 mm long; glumes nearly equal, as long as the spikelet, 1–3-nerved; lower lemma awned, seven-nerved, 5–6 mm long; awn up to 10 mm long; upper lemma awned, seven-nerved, 4–5 mm long; awn 8–9 mm long. Flowers October–January. **Distribution**: Endemic to Gough at 500–600 m, along streams and gullies in wet heath.

Polypogon mollis
A rhizomatous perennial grass, 50–80 cm high, recognised by its long, interrupted and often lobed panicle. Culms simple, several-noded. Leaf-blade flat, up to 25 cm long and 8 mm wide; ligules up to 6 mm long. Panicle 10–23 cm long. Spikelets 5.3–8.3 mm long; glumes one-nerved, extended in a long awnlike tip, 5–7 mm long, hispid mainly on keel; lower glume as long as the spiklet; upper glume 3.8–6.5 mm long; lemma five-nerved, 1.7–2.5 mm long, awned; awn 0.6–1.5 mm long. Flowers January–March. **Distribution**: Endemic to Tristan and Inaccessible, where it is rare; only found twice on Tristan, last in 1816; scarce along watercourses on the plateau of Inaccessible.

▲ **(1)** *Glyceria insularis*

▲ **(2)** *Glyceria insularis* inflorescence

▼ **(3)** *Deschampsia robusta*

▼ **(4)** *Deschampsia christophersenii*

▼ **(5)** *Deschampsia mejlandii*

▼ **(6)** *Deschampsia wacei*

▼ **(7)** *Polypogon mollis*

Agrostis holdgateana

A tufted perennial grass, 10–30 cm high, characterised by densely packed, stiff, upright leaves and culms. Culms terete, glabrous, smooth, (0.3)0.4–0.55 mm across. Leaf-sheaths overlapping, glabrous, 20–40 mm long; ligules (1.2)2–3.4 mm long; leaf-blades terete, stiff, erect or slightly recurved, scaberulous at tip, 4.3–5.5 cm long, 0.5–0.7 mm wide. Panicles dense, spike-like in appearance, 1.5–3.5(4.5) cm long, (15)25–40(50) spiculate, exceeding or not exceeding leaves; pedicels glabrous. Spikelets one-flowered, 4.4–4.8(6) mm long; glumes scabrid on keel, green with white margin, sometimes purplish; lower glume as long as the spikelet; upper glume 3.2–4.2 mm long; lemma awnless, 1.3–1.7 mm long. Flowers December–February. **Distribution**: Endemic to Tristan and Inaccessible; common in Bog Fern scrub and in grassland from 600–1,200 m at Tristan, and on the plateau and upper slopes of Inaccessible, mainly in fern bush and wet heath.

Agrostis magellanica ssp. laeviuscula

A perennial grass, stoloniferous or tufted; very variable in size (10–55 cm high). Culms glabrous, distinctly ribbed in the lower part, 1.2–1.6 mm across. Leaf-sheaths overlapping, ribbed, glabrous; ligules 1.5–6 mm long; leaf-blades flat, upper surface distinctly ribbed, hispid on ribs, lower surface glabrous with prominent white midrib, 2–16 cm long, 1–4 mm wide. Panicles 4–18 cm long with numerous spikelets; pedicels glabrous, exceeding leaves. Spikelets one-flowered, 4.2–5(6) mm long; glumes green with white margin, sometimes purplish, glabrous to scaberulous on keel; lower glume as long as the spikelet; upper glume 4–5 mm long; lemma awned, 1.7–1.8 mm long; awn 1.7–2.5 mm long. Flowers January–February. **Distribution**: Endemic subspecies to Tristan, Inaccessible and Gough. Scattered and locally common on Tristan from 700–1,600 m, and on Inaccessible from about 400 m upwards, mainly in wet heath above the limit of Bog Ferns. The nominate subspecies occurs in southern South America, the Falklands, Prince Edward Islands, Crozet, Kerguelen and New Zealand.

Agrostis goughensis

A stoloniferous, perennial grass forming mats, up to 80 cm high. Culms up to seven-noded, rooting at the nodes. Leaf-sheaths glabrous; ligules up to 10 mm long; leaf-blades flat, narrowly linear, upper surface densely ribbed, scaberulous on the ribs and margins, 8–25 mm long, 4–7.5 mm wide. Panicles up to 23 cm long with numerous spikelets; pedicels scabrid. Spikelets one-flowered, 3.7–4.1(4.5) mm long; glumes yellowish, sometimes purplish, scabrid on keel, lower glume as long as the spikelet, upper glume 3.1–3.5 mm long; lemma awned, 2–2.3 mm long, with long hairs; awn 1.5–2.5 mm long. Flowers December. **Distribution**: Endemic to Gough; erroneously reported from Inaccessible, but the only specimen is the type collected in 1955 from stream banks at The Glen.

Agrostis carmichaelii

A small, tufted, perennial grass, up to 15 cm high. Culms glabrous, finely filiform, 0.15–0.25 mm across. Leaf-sheaths overlapping, glabrous, 8–13 mm long; ligules 0.6–1.2 mm long; leaf-blades terete, involute, filiform, margin glabrous or scaberulous at tip, 2–3 cm long, 0.3–0.4(1) mm wide. Panicles 8–28 mm long, (3)10–23 spiculate, sparsely branched, usually not exceeding leaves; pedicels glabrous. Spikelets one-flowered, (2)2.2–3.2(3.8) mm long; glumes green with white margin, sometimes purplish, glabrous to scaberulous on keel; lower glume as long as the spikelet; upper glume 1.8–2.7 mm long; lemma (1)1.2–1.5 mm long; awn absent or very short (–0.1 mm). Flowers November–February. **Distribution**: Endemic to Tristan, Nightingale, Inaccessible and Gough. Common above 300 m at Tristan (to 1,500 m), Inaccessible and Gough, occurring in *Phylica* woodland, grassland, Bog Fern and *Blechnum penna-marina* heath, and on steep open slopes and rocks. Rare on Nightingale, where it is found on rocks near First Pond.

Agrostis wacei

A small, tufted, perennial grass with a distinctive bluish-green colour, forming moss-like cushions up to 12 cm high. Smaller than *A. carmichaelii*, with purple upper leaf-sheaths and a reduced panicle with rarely more than 1–5 spikelets. Culms branched, finely filiform, terete; leaf-sheaths overlapping, at least uppermost sheath dictitly purple-coloured; ligules up to 1 mm long; leaf-blades finely filiform, terete, 1–1.4 cm long. Panicles 3–7 mm long, not exceeding the leaves, (1)3–5(6) spiculate. Spikelets one-flowered, (1.6)1.8–2.1(2.4) mm long with glumes distinctly scaberulous all over the surface; lower glume as long as the spikelet; upper glume shorter; lemma awnless, 1.2–1.4 mm long. Flowers November–February. **Distribution**: Endemic to Tristan and Inaccessible. On Tristan scattered from 450–760 m in *Blechnum penna-marina* heath, on exposed slopes and ridges, and on rocks.

▲ (1) *Agrostis holdgateana*

▼ (2) *Agrostis goughensis*   ▼ (3) *Agrostis carmichaelii*   ▼ (4) *Agrostis wacei*

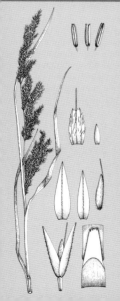

Agrostis media

A tufted, perennial grass, 8–15 cm high (rarely to 30 cm). Distinguished from the other two small endemic Agrostis (*A. carmichaelii* and *A. wacei*) by its awned lemmas and panicles that exceed the leaves. Culms glabrous, filiform, 0.25–0.35 mm across. Leaf-sheaths glabrous, overlapping, (8)14–20 mm long; ligules (1)1.4–1.9 mm long; leaf-blades terete, involute, filiform, scaberulous at tip, 3–4 cm long, 0.3–0.55(1.2) mm wide. Panicles dense, c20–100 spiculate, (19)22–30(43) mm long, usually exceeding leaves; pedicels glabrous. Spikelets one-flowered, 3.1–4.0 mm long; glumes scabrid, green with white margin, sometimes purplish; lower glume as long as the spikelet; upper glume 2.5–3.4 mm long; lemma awned, 1.3–1.6 mm long; awn (0.3)0.7–2 mm long. Flowers October–January. **Distribution**: Endemic to Tristan, Inaccessible and Gough. Locally common on Tristan up to 800 m and on Gough to 500 m. In *Blechnum palmiforme* heath, mosses, grassland, also on bare sand. Reaches the lowest altitude of all endemic *Agrostis* species (on Tristan on slopes of gulches and on rocky places along the road between Potato Patches and Burntwood).

Agrostis trachychlaena

A loosely tufted, blue-grey perennial grass, 15–25 cm high. Culms branched, trailing, ascending from a creeping base, 20–55 cm long. Leaf-sheaths overlapping, distinctly ribbed; ligules 1–3 mm long; leaf-blades flat, prominently ribbed on the upper surface with the ribs scabrid, lower surface glabrous with prominent white midrib, 2–7 cm long, 0.5–2 mm wide. Panicles exceeding the leaves, 1.5–5.5 cm long with c30 to several hundred spikelets; pedicels scabrid. Spikelets one-flowered, 2.8–3(4) mm long with scabrid glumes; lower glume as long as the spikelet; upper glume 1.4–2.6 mm long; lemma awned, 1.2–1.4(1.8) mm long; awn c1.1 mm long. Flowers October–January. **Distribution**: Endemic to Nightingale and Inaccessible. Rare; from 100–275 m in *Spartina* tussock, at albatross nesting sites, on steep rocky slopes at Nightingale; only one record from Inaccessible on dripping rocks above the Waterfall at 150 m.

Agrostis stolonifera Creeping Bent

Slender grass, up to 40 cm high, usually with many stolons (above ground runners), forming loose or dense patches. Inflorescence a loose panicle. **Distribution**: Introduced to Tristan, Inaccessible and Gough; common at Tristan and Gough, often forming dense, monospecific stands along streams and especially alongside waterfalls and seeps on cliffs; rare at Inaccessible, apparently confined to the old hut site at the Waterfall. **Similar species**: *A. gigantea* (Redtop, introduced to Tristan and Inaccessible) looks similar, but plants are considerably larger, but form dense or loose patches by subsurface roots rather than stolons; local on Settlement Plain and at the old hut near the Waterfall at Inaccessible.

Sporobolus africanus Ratstail Grass, Dropseed

Up to 100 cm high grass, growing in loose mats; ligule reduced to a band of short hairs; inflorescence a long and narrow spike-like panicle. **Distribution**: Introduced from Africa to Tristan, where it is abundant in pastures and on waste ground on the Settlement Plain; recently discovered on Inaccessible at Blenden Hall, but all plants were removed.

Anthoxanthum odoratum Vanilla Grass, Sweet Vernalgrass

A tufted perennial grass, 10–40 cm high, with a characteristic vanilla-like smell of coumarin. Culms simple, erect, 1–3-noded. Leaf-blade flat, glabrous or pubescent on both surfaces. The inflorescence is a compact panicle, 4–6 cm long. The spikelets are 7–9.5 mm long and comprise two basal sterile florets and one fertile floret. **Distribution**: A cosmopolitan weed introduced to Tristan. Common in coastal pastures and on the Base (eg at Big Green Hill).

Holcus lanatus Farm Grass, Common Velvet Grass, Yorkshire Fog

Tufted perennial grass, 20–40(80) cm high, characterised by pubescent, grey-green leaves and inflorescences. Culms erect or ascending, 2–5-noded. Leaf-sheaths with many soft hairs; leaf-blades 4–20 cm long, 3–10 mm wide, densely hairy on both sides. Panicles c7–15 cm long, branches pubescent. Spikelets with one fertile floret and one sterile floret at the apex, 4–6 mm long. **Distribution**: Introduced to Tristan, Nightingale, Inaccessible and Gough. One of the most widespread aliens at the islands; at Tristan it occurs in most vegetation types and it is dominant with *Rumex acetosella* in the meadows on the lower part of the Peak; at Inaccessible and Gough it is common along streams and paths, often forming large monospecific stands; at Nightingale it is confined to disturbed places such as along paths. Originally from Europe, it is now globally distributed.

▲ (1) *Agrostis media*

▲ (2) *Agrostis trachychlaena*

▼ (3) *Agrostis stolonifera* Creeping Bent

▼ (4) *Agrostis stolonifera* Creeping Bent

▼ (5) *Sporobolus africanus* Ratstail Grass

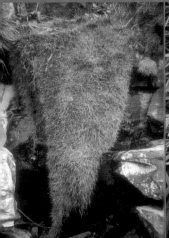

▼ (6) *Anthoxanthum odoratum* Vanilla Grass

▼ (7) *Holcus lanatus* Farm Grass

Pennisetum clandestinum Kikuyu Grass
A tough perennial grass with thick, creeping stolons, which root at the nodes. Leaves straight, up to 1 cm wide and 25 cm long, with a pointed tip, and with ligules consisting of fine, white hairs. The inflorescence is reduced to 2–4 shortly stalked spikelets hidden in the uppermost leaf sheath. Because of the long filaments (up to 50 mm) and stigmas (up to 30 mm), pastures dominated by flowering *P. clandestinum* look like they are covered with spiderwebs. **Distribution**: Introduced to Tristan, where it is widespread, especially in lowland areas around the Settlement. Originally native to North Africa, it has been introduced in many areas, often to limit soil erosion, but it is generally considered a major pest. It usually reproduces from sections of stem, rhizome or stolon that can rapidly grow into thick, dense mats. **Similar species**: *Cynodon dactylon* (Bermuda Grass), introduced to Tristan and Inaccessible, is similar in habit and ligule structure, but smaller (leaves only 2–4 mm wide); inflorescence consists of 3–6 digitate, spike-like racemes, resembling a small set of helicopter blades. Locally common at Tristan; confined to a small patch near the old hut at the Waterfall on Inaccessible.

Poa annua Annual Blue-grass
Small annual or semi-perennial grass, 3–15 (25) cm high. Leaves folded when young. Inflorescence a loose panicle. Flowers October–February. **Distribution**: Introduced to Tristan, Nightingale, Inaccessible and Gough; common in disturbed areas throughout, but most abundant around the coast. **Other introduced grasses**: *P. pratensis* (Smooth Meadow-grass) (Tristan and Gough) is a perennial species, larger than *P. annua*, up to 70 cm high; widespread in lowland areas at Tristan; locally common around the old and new bases at Gough. *Vulpia bromoides* (Squirrel-tail Fescue) (Tristan and Inaccessible) is a slender, annual, erect grass 10–30 cm high; lemma with long awn; inflorescence a narrow panicle, 5–10 cm long; widespread in lowland pastures around Tristan; locally common on coastal slips at Inaccessible. *Aira caryophyllea* (Silvery Hair-grass) (Tristan and Inaccessible), is a tiny, fine-leaved annual grass found growing on boulders and bare areas; inflorescence a loose panicle.

Cyperaceae
Grass-like plants with long, narrow leaves, but the culms (stems) are not hollow and are often triangular in cross section, rather than circular. The leaves are arranged in three rows (two rows in grasses). In some species (eg *Scirpus* spp.) the leaves are reduced to sheaths, without a leaf blade. The flowers are arranged in elongated, unbranched inflorescences (spikes).

Carex insularis
A grass-like perennial up to 80 cm high, generally taller and with broader leaves (10–15 mm wide) than *C. thouarsii*. Culm sharply triangular in cross section with mostly three female and two male spikes. Spikes drooping on long stalks (unlike erect spikes of *C. thouarsii*). Beak of utricle bifid for half or more of its length. Flowers November–February. **Distribution**: Endemic to Tristan, Nightingale, Inaccessible and Gough. Occurs in wetter situations than *C. thouarsii*, from sea-level to 600 m; at Tristan mainly confined to the Base, presumably due to grazing pressure.

Carex thouarsii
A grass-like perennial up to 40 cm high. Smaller than *C. insularis* with narrower leaves, only 5–8 mm wide; leaves V-shaped in cross-section. Culm terete with 3–4 female spikes, and one terminal male spike; spikes crowded or the lowermost one distant. Readily told from *C. insularis* by its erect spikes. Beak of utricle long, bifid only at the tip. Flowers November–February. **Distribution**: Endemic to Tristan, Nightingale, Inaccessible and Gough; widespread in fern bush and wet-heath; local in coastal tussock and at higher elevations.

Cyperus esculentus New Bull Grass, Nutgrass
A 30–40 cm high perennial with thin rhizomes ending in tubers (hard bulbous thickenings 1–2 cm across). Leaves up to 8 mm wide, and are often exceeding the stems. Inflorescence consists of long, narrow spikelets, forming groups at the end of 4–6 thin, 10 cm long stalks that originate from the end of the stem. **Distribution**: Introduced to Tristan, where it is a weed at the Patches. **Similar species**: *C. longus* (Galingale) introduced to Tristan, is similar to *C. esculentus*, but grows up to 60 cm high, has rhizomes up to 1 cm thick, and narrower leaves, which are shorter than the stems; found on stream banks and wet places near the Settlement. *C. tenellus* (Tiny Flat-sedge) introduced to Tristan), is a small tufted annual, up to 10 cm high. The leaves exceed the stems in length, and are thin and bristle-like. The inflorescence usually has two, (1–5), strongly flattened spikelets. It is a weed in the Patches.

▲(1) *Pennisetum clandestinum* Kikuyu Grass

▲(2) *Poa annua* Annual Blue-grass

▲(3) *Aira caryophyllea* Silvery Hair-grass

▲(4) *Carex insularis*

▲(5) *Carex insularis* inflorescence

▼(6) *Carex thouarsii*

▼(7) *Carex thouarsii* inflorescence

Mariscus congestus Old Bull Grass, Clustered Flat-sedge
A tufted perennial, up to 40 cm high, with leaves up to 7 mm wide, shorter than the stems. Inflorescence consists of many spikelets on 15–40 cm long, thin stalks. Seeds are eaten by Inaccessible Buntings. **Distribution**: Introduced from South Africa to Tristan, Nightingale and Inaccessible. Local on the Settlement Plain and new volcano at Tristan; mainly in boggy areas around the hut at Blenden Hall, Inaccessible, and recently introduced to around the huts at Nightingale.

Scirpus bicolor Small Bog Grass
Tufted perennial, usually <10 cm high (rarely up to 20 cm). Usually smaller and more slender than *S. sulcatus*, but growth form highly variable. Leaf-lamina well-developed. Inflorescence a dense terminal or pseudolateral cluster of (1)2 to many spikelets. Spikelets 3–6 mm long; two stigmas. **Distribution**: Endemic to Tristan, Nightingale, Inaccessible and Gough. Abundant in most plant communities from sea-level to about 1,500 m; also one of the first colonisers of lava flows from the 1961 eruption. Forms short, turf-like cushions on exposed rocks and taller isolated tufts in more sheltered sites. Tussocks grow close together in near monospecific stands in some areas of fern bush at Nightingale, Inaccessible and Gough; the tussocks fall over when you walk on them, making for very unstable footing. **Similar species**: *S. chlorostachyus* and *S. verruculosus* are slender annuals; spikelets few and often solitary. Both occur in damp places on the Settlement Plain (Tristan), and probably are introduced.

Scirpus sulcatus Big Bog Grass
Tufted perennial with flowering-stems (5–)20–65 cm high. Usually considerably taller and more robust than *S. bicolor*, and less catholic in its habits. Leaf-lamina much reduced, generally only 2–5 mm long. Inflorescence a dense terminal or pseudolateral cluster of (1)2 to many spikelets; three stigmas. **Distribution**: Tristan, Nightingale, Inaccessible and Gough. Common on all islands up to 1,300 m; usually in damp areas; grows as single tufts among wet heath and in high altitude peat bogs; forms extensive monospecific floating stands in bogs such as The Ponds at Nightingale and Skua Pond at Inaccessible. These mats are so dense that they can be walked on. Also typically forms large mats below Spectacled Petrel colonies on the plateau of Inaccessible.

Uncinia compacta ssp. *elongata* Compact Hook-sedge
A perennial with creeping stolons and grass-like leaves, about 20 cm high. Leaves c2.5 mm wide. Spikes lanceolate-elliptic, up to 4 cm long, with about 10–40 narrowly elliptic utricles. Utricle smooth, 3.2–4.4 mm long. Seeds have hook-tipped spikes that readily attach themselves to animals and plants **Distribution**: Tristan, Inaccessible and Gough. Locally common on the plateau at Inaccessible, growing in shaded situations down to 200 m. This variety is also found at Amsterdam and St Paul Islands; the species also occurs in Tasmania and New South Wales, and on several sub-Antarctic islands. **Similar species**: *U. meridensis* (native to Tristan, Inaccessible and Gough) looks similar, but leaves usually smaller and narrower; utricles ciliate in the upper half, especially on the angles, and the utricles are 5–6 mm long. Spikes generally longer than in *U. compacta*, but shorter than in *U. brevicaulis*. Common in wet heath and fern bush above 300 m, sometimes in dense stands.

Uncinia brevicaulis ssp. *brevicaulis* False Watermeal
A tufted perennial with grass-like leaves, 15–40 cm high. The largest *Uncinia* at the islands, but leaves narrower than *Carex* leaves, c5 mm wide, 10–25 cm long. Spikes linear, 7–12(17) cm long with about 50–150 utricles. Flowers October–December. Seeds have hook-tipped spikes and readily attach themselves to animals and people. **Distribution**: Tristan, Nightingale, Inaccessible and Gough, up to 900 m; in wet places, bogs, gullies, but also in meadows; rare below 300 m on Tristan, presumably due to grazing. This variety is also found at Amsterdam and St Paul Islands; a different variety occurs on the Juan Fernandez Islands off Chile, and at the Falklands.

Juncaceae

Rostkovia tristanensis
A small, glabrous perennial with grass-like leaves up to 16 cm high. Leaves distinctly incurved or circinnate and usually shorter than the stem. A single flower, c1 cm long, stands at the end of the stem, with six brown tepals in two rows, six stamens, and a style with three-parted stigma. Fruit is a many-seeded capsule. **Distribution**: Endemic to Tristan and Gough. Fairly common on Gough, but rarely flowers; only one record from Tristan in *Empetrum* heath above Soggy Plain at 1,100 m. It is closely related to *R. magellanica* which occurs in southern South America, the Falkland Islands and New Zealand.

▲ (1) *Mariscus congestus*
Old Bull Grass

▲ (2) *Scirpus bicolor*
Small Bog Grass, dwarf form

▲ (3) *Scirpus bicolor* Small Bog Grass INSET (4) inflorescence

▲ (5) *Scirpus sulcatus* Big Bog Grass

▼ (7) *Uncinia brevicaulis*
False Watermeal

▼ (8) *Uncinia brevicaulis*
False Watermeal, inflorescence

▲ (6) *Uncinia compacta*
Compact Hook-sedge

▼ (9) *Rostkovia tristanensis*

FERNS Pteridophyta

Ferns are a diverse group of plants characterised by a distinctive vasculature and sperm ultrastructure. There are some 12,000 species worldwide typically arranged into five subgroups, of which only two occur at Tristan and Gough. The ophioglossoid ferns are represented by *Ophioglossum*; all other species are leptosporangiate ferns.

Ophioglossaceae

Ophioglossum opacum

An unusual fern with a single, broadly ovate leaf up to 25 mm long, borne close to the ground at an angle of 45° or less. An erect fertile spike, inserted at the base of the leaf, is up to 65 mm long and contains up to 10 pairs of sporangia. The plant only appears in spring and early summer, persisting at other seasons as an underground, globose tuber-like stem up to 8 mm across. **Distribution**: Tristan and Gough above 600 m on exposed slopes in wet heath. It is also known from St Helena.

Azollaceae

Azolla filiculoides Mosquito Fern

A peculiar pinkish-green fern found floating on water or in wet seeps. It has a symbiotic cyanobacterium that converts ammonia to nitrogen and is widely used as a fertiliser in rice paddies in South-east Asia. The rhizome is horizontal and minutely papillate, bearing single unbranched roots. The leaf lobes are small (about 1 mm long), with the upper lobe green and the lower hyaline. The lower leaf lobe catches the light, giving a jewel-like appearance; it forms a pouch harbouring the bacterium. It is one of the few heterosporous ferns, producing male and female spores in different structures on the same plant, but the sporangia are very small and seldom seen. **Distribution**: Inaccessible, restricted to Skua Pond and seepage areas near sea-level. Widespread throughout the temperate and tropical parts of the world; often introduced.

Hymenophyllaceae

Hymenophyllum aeruginosum

The most common filmy fern, characterised by its brownish to olive-green colour and stalked stellate hairs that are borne along the veins and lamina margin. Fronds linear to ovate, up to 8 cm long; pinnae divided into linear lobes. Minute, shallowly tubular, bivalved sori are formed at the lobe apices. Plants may shrivel up during short dry periods, but recover once wetted again. **Distribution**: Tristan, Nightingale, Inaccessible and Gough, mainly at lower elevations; common on wet cliff faces and the stems of Bog Ferns. Also occurs in South Africa.

Hymenophyllum peltatum

Characterised by relatively long, narrow leaves that lack the hairs of *H. aeruginosum*; pinnae developed on the upper sides only; pinna lobes minutely dentate. Elliptic, bivalvate sori are confined to the lobes closest to the rachis on the lower part of the lamina. The valve lobes are shallowly dentate along the distal margin. **Distribution**: Tristan, Inaccessible and Gough; occurs as an epiphyte on *Phylica arborea* and Bog Ferns, or on damp cliff faces and streambanks, mostly in shaded conditions. Widespread throughout the temperate and tropical parts of the world. **Similar species**: *H. tunbrigense* is a widespread species only recorded once from Tristan, growing on the rhizomes of *Elaphoglossum laurifolium* on a shaded vertical rock face at 300 m. It differs from *H. peltatum* in having a winged rachis. Sori are borne at the lobe apices near the rachis and have deeply cleft serrated involucre outer margins.

Trichomanes angustatum

Easily confused with a *Hymenophyllum*, but has an elongated receptacle extending well beyond the sorus mouth. Fronds are up to 13 cm long; laminae narrowly elliptic in outline; pinnae variously lobed into linear, entire segments. Sori form on the upper side of the pinnae only; deeply cup-shaped; mouth rounded and dilated. **Distribution**: Endemic to Tristan, Nightingale and Inaccessible; rarely encountered; occurs in *Blechnum* scrub and in damp, shady gullies. Reported from rocks in *Spartina* thickets at Inaccessible.

▲ (1) *Ophioglossum opacum*   ▲ (2) *Azolla filiculoides* Mosquito Fern

▼ (3) *Hymenophyllum aeruginosum*   ▼ (4) *Hymenophyllum peltatum*

Adiantaceae

Eriosorus cheilanthoides

A small, delicate fern with long, narrow leaves 2–3 cm wide and 20–30 cm long (rarely up to 50 cm), borne on a thin, creeping rhizome. Lamina closely set with alternate, short-petioled lobed pinnae which have short multicellular hairs on the upper and lower surfaces. Sori form along the veins; lack an indusium. **Distribution**: Tristan, Inaccessible and Gough up to 700 m (500 m on Gough) in wet heath, at the base of rock overhangs and in thick moss in fern bush. At higher elevations only the tips of the fronds are exposed when growing in deep moss. Also found in the Andes of South America.

Adiantum poiretii Maidenhair Fern

A delicate fern that is widely cultivated as an indoor plant. It has erect or arching fronds up to 25 cm long with firm dark brown leaf stalks and branches. Lamina ovate-deltate and up to five-pinnate, with articulated leaflets, thinly herbaceous, glabrous, semicircular to kidney-shaped up to 15 mm long. 3–7 lunate sori occur along the outer margins of the leaflets, covered by a recurved lobe margin. **Distribution**: Tristan, Nightingale, Inaccessible and Gough, from near sea-level to 450 m, mainly in gullies, under rock ledges and on sea-facing cliffs, often with dripping water. Widespread in South and Central America, South-east Asia, and Africa.

Hypolepidaceae

Histiopteris incisa Bracken

One of the commonest ferns in fern bush, often dominating large areas, especially at Gough. It dies back in winter, but rapidly develops new leaves from the dormant rhizomes in spring (September–October). The rhizome is long, creeping and branched, with fronds borne at irregular intervals. Leaves 1–2-pinnate, glabrous, up to 1.5 m long; pinnules are variously lobed. Sori occur along lobe margins; indusium membranous and continuous. **Distribution**: Tristan, Nightingale, Inaccessible and Gough from near sea-level to 650 m, but most abundant at 50–300 m. At Gough it is especially common in fern bush along the south and east coasts, and appears to limit recruitment of other species such as Island Trees to disturbed areas such as peat slips. It is widespread in the southern hemisphere.

Hypolepis villoso-viscida

A finely-divided, grey-green fern with distinctive ginger, needle-shaped glandular hairs which make the frond slightly sticky when touched. Fronds grow from a creeping rhizome that is mostly subterranean and densely set with reddish-brown hairs, rather than scales. Fronds are arching, up to 1.2 m long. Sori are near-marginal at a vein ending and proximal on the ultimate segments. The indusium is a modified lobe margin. The name *H. rugosula* was formerly misapplied for this species. **Distribution**: Tristan, Nightingale, Inaccessible and Gough, from near sea-level to 500 m; often in areas where breeding seabirds are abundant, and more tolerant of salt-spray than many other ferns. Confined to streambeds and penguin colonies in dense coastal tussock grassland. Also found on St Helena and in South Africa.

Aspleniaceae

Asplenium obtusatum var. *obtusatum*

A large, robust *Asplenium* with distinctive, pale green leathery leaves; it is the most common *Asplenium* at the islands, but is often confused with *A. platybasis*; differs in having a green (not blackish) leaf stalk and rachis; rhizome is short and prostrate to erect, bearing a tuft of closely set erect fronds up to 40 cm long. Occurs in small clonal clusters. Lamina one-pinnate, ovate, with up to 21 pinna pairs. Pinnae oblong, with an acute to obtuse apex; margins serrated. Up to 22 pairs of linear sori are formed on each pinna. **Distribution**: Tristan, Nightingale, Inaccessible and Gough, from near sea-level to 500 m, mostly in fern bush, but also on cliffs and exposed rocks. It has a circum-Antarctic distribution.

Asplenium platybasis var. *subnudum*

A large, fairly robust *Asplenium*, often confused with *A. obtusatum*; best told by the black, rather than green leaf stalk and rachis and tapering pinnae; long, creeping rhizome is up to 1 cm across, closely set with black scales; fronds more widely spaced. Leaf stalks up to 60 cm; lamina one-pinnate, up to 26 cm long, is oblong to ovate. Pinnae are up to 9 cm long; firmly herbaceous and lance-shaped to ovate; margins serrated. **Distribution**: Variety endemic to Tristan, Nightingale, Inaccessible and Gough from 90–500 m. At most islands it occurs in fern bush, but also among *Spartina* tussocks at Nightingale. A different variety occurs at St Helena.

▲ (1) *Eriosorus cheilanthoides*

▲ (2) *Adiantum poiretii* Maidenhair Fern

▲ (3) *Histiopteris incisa* Bracken fresh growth INSET (4) sori

▲ (5) *Hypolepis villoso-viscida*

▼ (6) *Asplenium obtusatum*

▼ (7) *Asplenium platybasis*

Asplenium insulare

A medium-sized *Asplenium* that superficially resembles *A. aequibasis*, but is smaller and often bears plantlets near the tips of the lamina. Lamina one-pinnate, with up to 45 pinna pairs; rachis narrowly green-winged. Pinnae are herbaceous, glabrous, ovate to oblong and auriculate, with up to seven sori pairs per pinna. Indusium linear, membranous and entire. **Distribution**: Endemic to Tristan, Nightingale, Inaccessible and Gough; relatively common at all islands up to 500 m (300 m at Gough). Habitat includes sheltered streambanks, cliffs and moss-grown rocks.

Asplenium aequibasis

A medium-sized *Asplenium*, similar to *A. insulare* but with an erect rhizome, numerous tufted fronds, and stipes that are narrowly green-winged distally. Lamina up to 28 cm long, narrowly linear; one-pinnate, with up to 33 pinna pairs; does not form plantlets at the lamina apex like *A. insulare*. Pinnae reduce in size towards the base; firmly herbaceous to leathery, glabrous and lance-shaped; base blunt to broadly wedge-shaped, and often somewhat enlarged on the upper side. Pinnae are up to 3 cm long, and proximally lobed. Each pinna may have up to seven linear sori pairs up to 2 mm long, borne proximally along the veins. Indusium membranous and entire. **Distribution**: Endemic to Gough and Nightingale, but probably also Tristan. At Nightingale it occurs from 55–275 m, growing in dense tussock grass stands; at Gough it is confined to fern bush.

Asplenium monanthes

A medium-sized *Asplenium*, superficially resembling a delicate form of *A. insulare*, but with only a single sorus (rarely two) on each pinna, always below the pinna midrib; forms plantlets at the leaf base, not near the apex. Rhizome short and prostrate, bearing several tufted fronds up to 35 cm long. Lamina one-pinnate, up to 25 cm long, with up to 55 pinna pairs. Pinnae oblong, 1–2 cm long, firmly herbaceous and serrated along the upper and outer margins. **Distribution**: Tristan and Gough, largely confined to shaded gullies and on rock overhangs from 200–800 m. Widespread in South America and Africa.

Aspenium alvarezense

The smallest *Asplenium* at the islands, often forming large, clonal stands, due to the ability to form plantlets from the roots. Leaves tufted, up to 75 mm long. Lamina 2–3 pinnate, with firmly herbaceous alternate pinnae divided into 4–6 wedge- or spoon-shaped pinnules. A single sorus is borne on each lobe; indusium entire. **Distribution**: Endemic to Tristan, Inaccessible and Gough, occurring from near sea-level at Gough to 1,000 m at Tristan; mainly above 300 m at Inaccessible. Grows on moist, shaded rocks and on Bog Fern stems; most abundant at Gough, where it forms large, dominant stands in fern bush.

Blechnaceae

Blechnum palmiforme Bog Fern

A large, distinctive, cycad-like fern, with stems up to 1.6 m tall and 30 cm in diameter, sometimes with short side branches. Stems mostly erect in sheltered sites; decumbent in more exposed areas, especially in older plants. Leaves one-pinnate, leathery, up to 1 m long, borne in an apical rosette. New leaves are produced in a single growth surge in early summer (September–December). Initially these young uncoiling leaves have a beautiful golden colour. Fertile leaves, when present, generally overtop the sterile leaves. **Distribution**: Endemic to Tristan, Nightingale, Inaccessible and Gough. Found from sea-level to 800 m at Tristan, 500 m at Gough; abundant in fern bush, often forming dominant stands. Its fibrous stems generally host a wide range of epiphytic plants. Closely related species occur in South America and South Africa.

Blechnum penna-marina

The smallest and perhaps most abundant *Blechnum* at the islands, found in a wide range of habitats. Size of fronds varies with exposure, but usually smaller than *B. australe*; pinnae more leathery, and with rounded (not pointed) tips. Leaves elongate, linear to lance-shaped 10–20 cm long; one-pinnate. Leaf stalks reddish to black. Pinnae up to 15 mm long, oblong to triangular, and blunt-tipped. Creeping rhizome is scaled. Fertile leaves reddish; overtop sterile fronds. Fertile pinnae are linear and more widely spaced than sterile pinnae, with sori in two lines, one on either side and parallel to the pinna midrib; indusium linear and finely torn. **Distribution**: Tristan, Nightingale, Inaccessible and Gough, from sea-level to at least 1,200 m; often forms large stands in exposed areas. It has a circum-Antarctic distribution.

▲ (1) *Asplenium insulare* INSET (2) sori   ▲ (3) *Asplenium aequibasis*

▼ (4) *Asplenium monanthes*   ▼ (5) *Asplenium alvarezense*

▼ (6) *Blechnum palmiforme* Bog Fern   ▼ (7) *Blechnum penna-marina*

Blechnum australe

A medium-sized *Blechnum*, superficially resembling a large, slender *B. penna-marina*, but fronds usually longer, with less robust pinnae that have pointed tips. Rhizome is short-decumbent; tends to grow in small clonal stands. Leaves are erect to arching, up to 40 cm long, especially in sheltered sites; one-pinnate; pinnae are firmly herbaceous and glabrous, up to 43 mm long. New leaves are reddish. Fertile leaves, when present, generally overtop the sterile leaves. Fertile pinnae are linear, up to 37 mm long, with long sori in two lines, one on either side and parallel to the pinna midrib; indusium linear. **Distribution**: Tristan, Nightingale, Inaccessible and Gough, extending from near sea-level to 500 m. It grows commonly in gullies, in rock crevices, on cliffs and in *Phylica* scrub. It also occurs in South Africa.

Thelypteridaceae

Amauropelta bergiana var. tristanensis

The only fern at the islands with small circular sori protected by a reniform hairy indusium; leaves bear short needle-like hairs. Rhizome is erect to suberect and closely set with persistent stipe bases, roots, and scales. Leaves suberect to arching, up to 45 cm long, borne in a tuft. Leaves deeply two-pinnate; narrowly oblong with veins of adjacent lobes not meeting below the sinuses. Hairs on the lower rachis and costule surfaces are needle-shaped or hooked. Sori form two rows on the lobes. **Distribution**: Endemic to Tristan, Nightingale, Inaccessible and Gough, in fern bush and along shaded stream banks, usually below 400 m. The typical variety occurs in South Africa.

Dryopteridaceae

Dryopteris wallichiana

A large fern characterised by a short erect rhizome, closely set with persistent stipe bases, roots and scales. Leaves one-pinnate, up to 60 cm long, borne in an apical rosette. Pinnae firmly herbaceous, up to 13 cm long; pinnatifid with rectangular lobes. Sori occur in two rows on the lobes; indusium is reniform. **Distribution**: Gough, where it occurs in fern bush and wet heath. Near sea-level it grows in sheltered conditions, mostly along stream banks, shaded by Island Trees. The fronds are considerably smaller when it grows in wet heath at up to 400 m. It is common in India, with isolated populations in Africa and Madagascar.

Rumohra adiantiforme Seven Weeks Fern

A medium-sized fern with rather stiff, distinctly erect fronds, easily recognised by its circular sori covered by an umbrella-like indusium. It has a central ridge formed in the groove on the upper side of the leaf stalk and rachis. Rhizome widely creeping; often forms large clonal stands. Lamina deltate, divided up to three times; lower pinnae longest. Pinnae leathery with the circular sori arranged in two rows on the underside; when young they are covered by an umbrella-shaped indusium with near-entire margins. **Distribution**: Gough, Inaccessible and Tristan, from near sea-level to 660 m, in fern bush and wet heath; also locally in open areas among tussock grassland. It is widespread throughout the temperate southern hemisphere.

Woodsiaceae

Ctenitis aquilina

A large fern, easily recognised by its brownish colour and broadly ovate lamina up to 50 cm long and nearly three-times divided. Rhizome short and erect to decumbent; fronds up to 80 cm long and arching. The pinnae are firmly herbaceous with oblong lobes and blunt tips; margins somewhat inrolled. The leaf and upper parts of the leaf stalk are closely set with short needle-shaped hairs. Sori small and circular, forming two rows on the lobes; indusium absent. **Distribution**: Endemic to Tristan, Nightingale, Inaccessible and Gough, mainly in fern bush, but also in open tussock grassland and sheltered sites up to 600 m. Forms dense stands more than 1 m deep under a canopy of Island Trees in parts of the eastern plateau of Inaccessible.

Athyrium medium

A fairly inconspicuous, medium-sized fern with rather pale green, shiny leaves that are somewhat brittle; sori J-shaped. Rhizome short and erect, closely set with persistent leaf stalk bases, roots and scales. Leaves ovate, two-pinnate, up to 30 cm long. Pinnules are shallowly to deeply lobed; margins dentate. Indusium minutely torn. Apparently deciduous, with new fronds formed each spring without any trace of old fronds. **Distribution**: Endemic to Tristan and Inaccessible, from 100–500 m in damp, shaded rock faces and along stream banks; most common in wet heath above 400 m.

▲ (1) *Blechnum australe*

▲ (2) *Amauropelta bergiana* var. *tristanensis* INSET (3) sori

▲ (4) *Dryopteris wallichiana* INSET (5) sori

▲ (6) *Rumohra adiantiforme* Seven Week Fern INSET (7) sori

▼ (8) *Ctenitis aquilina* INSET (9) sori

▼ (10) *Athyrium medium*

Vittariaceae

Vittaria vittarioides Bootlace Fern

An unusual fern with distinctive narrow, strap-shaped leaves. Rhizome is short-creeping, densely set with dull brown scales. Leaves up to 30 cm long; erect or arched and crowded together; narrowly linear and leathery with a shallow groove on the upper surface. Sori are in two sunken grooves on the underside of the leaves that extend almost the entire length of the lamina on either side of the midrib. **Distribution**: Endemic to Tristan, Nightingale, Inaccessible and Gough, from 50–500 m, growing in sheltered conditions along streams and under Island Tree canopies; also on shaded rocks and epiphytic on Bog Fern stems. Leaves more erect in exposed plants.

Grammitidaceae

Grammitis magellanica

A small fern with entire fronds 4–6 cm long, resembling a tiny *Elaphoglossum*, but with sori in discrete patches on the underside of the frond. Indusium absent. It is slightly larger than *G. poeppigiana*, with a short erect rhizome and usually more than five sori pairs per leaf. **Distribution**: Gough, Inaccessible and Tristan, from 200–760 m, mostly on damp shaded cliffs or as an epiphyte on the stems of Bog Ferns or Island Trees.

Grammitis poeppigiana

Similar to *G. magellanica*, but rhizome creeping (not erect), fronds generally <4 cm long, and usually <6 pairs of sori per leaf. Indusium absent. **Distribution**: Gough and Tristan, mostly above 400 m on the stems of Bog Ferns, damp cliffs, or exposed rock outcrops. Also found at other Southern Ocean islands, with isolated populations in the southern Cape mountains of South Africa.

Lomariopsidaceae

Ferns with simple leaves; sporangia cover the entire lower surface of fertile lamina, with no indusium. Species on the islands can be divided into three groups: those with glabrous or near-glabrous leaves (*Elaphoglossum laurifolium*, *E. gracilifolium*); with awl-shaped scales on the leaves (*E. hybridum*, *E. obtusatum*); with fimbriate scales (with hair-like outgrowths along the margins) on the leaves (*E. succisifolium*, *E. insulare*).

Elaphoglossum laurifolium

The commonest *Elaphoglossum*, with tough, dark green, slightly glossy leaves. Rhizome widely creeping and branched; up to 5 mm across. Leaves erect, with fertile fronds overtopping sterile leaves. Leaf blade lance-shaped, up to 30 cm long; fertile leaves narrowly lance-shaped or oblong, up to 20 cm long. Minute substellate scales occur on the upper leaf surfaces of both the sterile and fertile leaves. **Distribution**: Endemic to Tristan, Nightingale, Inaccessible and Gough, from near sea-level to 600 m. It often forms large stands in fern bush, incl. under Island Tree canopies; regularly grows on Bog Fern stems.

Elaphoglossum gracilifolium

Differs from *E. laurifolium* in having longer (up to 50 cm), more slender leaves with a more acute apex; it also differs in a few microscopic features. **Distribution**: Endemic to Inaccessible, but perhaps overlooked elsewhere. Locally common above 400 m in exposed conditions among Bog Fern heath, sometimes in large stands or as an epiphyte on Bog Fern stems. **Similar species**: *E. lasiolepium* (endemic to Gough) differs from *E. laurifolium* and *E. gracilifolium* by the upper leaf surface being sparsely set with straw-coloured scales; lower leaf surface more densely set with darker brown scales. Known from a single sterile collection at 65 m growing on a low cliff in fern bush.

Elaphoglossum hybridum

A distinctive, pale green *Elaphoglossum* with awl-shaped scales confined to the leaf margin and midrib. Rhizome short, densely covered in black scales; leaves tufted and firmly herbaceous. Sterile lamina is oblong and up to 30 cm long; fertile lamina is narrowly oblong and smaller, only up to 12 cm long. **Distribution**: Tristan, Inaccessible and Gough; usually found on sheltered cliffs, streambanks and Bog Fern stems, but occasionally at more exposed sites; 300–700 m at Tristan and Inaccessible; rare and local below 100 m at Gough. Also found in South and Central America and South Africa.

Elaphoglossum obtusatum

Differs from *E. hybridum* in the upper leaf surface being closely set with awl-shaped scales. Rhizome short, suberect. Leaves numerous and tufted; sterile fronds up to 26 cm long (lamina 14 cm); fertile fronds to 22 cm (lamina 5 cm). Sterile lamina ovate to oblong, fertile lamina broadly ovate to elliptic. **Distribution**: Endemic to Tristan and Inaccessible from 350–600 m; uncommon, found on moss-covered rocks in gullies and moist, sheltered cliffs.

▲ (1) *Vittaria vittarioides* Bootlace Fern

▲ (2) *Grammitis magellanica*

▲ (3) *Elaphoglossum laurifolium*

▲ (4) *Elaphoglossum gracilifolium*

▼ (5) *Elaphoglossum hybridum*

▼ (6) *Elaphoglossum obtusatum*

Elaphoglossum succisifolium

The most common and largest scaly *Elaphoglossum*. Rhizome widely creeping, up to 4 mm across; densely set with reddish-brown scales. Fronds arching or erect; closely spaced on the rhizome. Leaves firmly herbaceous to leathery; sterile lamina narrowly oblong and blunt-tipped, up to 17 cm long; fertile lamina narrowly lance-shaped up to 12 cm long. The upper surface of the blade is densely set with pale brown appressed scales with fimbriated margins. **Distribution**: Tristan, Nightingale, Inaccessible and Gough, from near sea-level to 600 m, in a wide range of habitats, including deeply shaded gullies, fern bush and exposed, moss-covered rocks at higher elevations; often grows as an epiphyte on Bog Fern stems. Also found at Amsterdam Island. **Similar species**: *E. campylolepium* (endemic to Tristan and Inaccessible at 450–700 m) is almost identical to *E. succisifolium*; differs in being slightly smaller, with conduplicate scales and in a number of microscopic features.

Elaphoglossum insulare

Similar to *E. succissifolium* but with a much thinner rhizome, <1.2 mm in diameter; fronds erect and widely spaced; leaf blades much smaller (<6 cm). Leaf-blades firmly herbaceous to leathery; upper surfaces sparsely to densely set with appressed fimbriated scales. Sterile leaves rotund to oblong; fertile leaves narrowly oblong, up to 5 cm long. **Distribution**: Endemic to Gough and Tristan where it is restricted to higher elevations above 400 m. On Gough, occurs in wet heath among a dense layer of grasses and mosses; usually only the laminae are exposed.

CLUBMOSSES, QUILLWORTS AND SPIKEMOSSES Lycophyta

Lycophytes are small plants with simple, needle-like leaves. They are thought to have separated from the other vascular plants approximately 400 million years ago, during the early–mid Devonian. Today they form less than 1% of vascular plants. Of the three main subgroups, only three clubmosses occur at Tristan and Gough. All have pale yellow spores released through a slit along the distal margin of the spore cases or sporangia.

Lycopodiaceae

Huperzia insularis

The only clubmoss on the islands with crowded, stiff, often forked, upright stems up to 25 cm tall. Stems closely set with firm pale to yellowish-green linear, overlapping leaves up to 6 mm long. Sporangia are mostly obscured; somewhat flattened, kidney-shaped structures up to 1.5 mm in diameter borne in leaf axils at stem apices. **Distribution**: Tristan, Nightingale, Inaccessible and Gough, ranging from upper parts of fern bush at 400 m to exposed moss-covered rock crevices around 800 m. Also found on Ascension, St Helena, Prince Edwards and South America.

Lycopodium diaphanum Devil's Fingers

A common clubmoss with a distinctive silvery sheen. Vegetative stems are creeping, with aerial stems up to 14 cm tall, often topped by short-lived cones up to 4 cm long. Stems closely set with firm, awl-shaped leaves up to 5 mm long ending in a hair-like tip. Cone leaves are up to 6 mm long and terminate in a long, hair-like apex. A large, somewhat flattened kidney-shaped sporangium is borne in the axil of each cone leaf. **Distribution**: Endemic to Tristan, Inaccessible and Gough. Mostly confined to fern bush, extending in some places to *Empetrum*/*Blechnum* heath where it often forms large stands. Occurs up to 650 m on Tristan, but only 450 m on Gough. Common pioneer of peat slips.

Lycopodium magellanicum

A small, compact clubmoss, with short, firm, awl-shaped leaves <5 mm long. The widely creeping stems, rooted at irregular intervals, are mostly concealed under mosses and other vegetation. The stems bear widely spaced scale-like leaves and closely branched upright aerial stems up to 15 cm tall. Some aerial branches bear short-lived, simple or branched cones up to 45 mm long, closely set with stalked, lance-shaped leaves. A large, somewhat flattened kidney-shaped sporangium is borne in the axil of each cone leaf. **Distribution**: Tristan and Gough. Plants often form small clonal stands in exposed wet heath and on mossy slopes from 300–750 m. Also in South America and at other Southern Ocean islands.

▲ (1) *Elaphoglossum succisifolium* (exposed form)

▲ (2) *Elaphoglossum succisifolium* (shaded form)

▲ (3) *Lycopodium diaphanum* Devil's Fingers
◄ (4) *Huperzia insularis*
▼ (5) *Lycopodium magellanicum*

TERRESTRIAL NON-VASCULAR PLANTS

Although vascular plants (flowering plants and ferns) dominate the terrestrial vegetation, the species richness of non-vascular plants is far greater. Many species have small, lightweight spores or other propagules that are readily dispersed by wind or stuck to the bodies of seabirds, allowing them to colonise oceanic islands. Because they disperse easily, few species are endemic to the islands. Mosses and lichens are the most conspicuous non-vascular terrestrial plants. Other groups include fungi and terrestrial algae, of which the diatoms are particularly diverse. In this account we do not treat the complete non-vascular flora of the islands, but illustrate some examples of each group.

MOSSES, LIVERWORTS AND HORNWORTS Bryophyta

Bryophytes differ from the vascular plants by the absence of a vascular system for the transport of water and nutrients through the plant. They do not produce flowers and seeds; most reproduce by single-celled spores. Within the Bryophyta three major groups are recognised: mosses, liverworts and hornworts. Most mosses have stems and leaves, but they do not possess roots, although some have hairlike rhizoids. Some liverworts as well as the hornworts do not have stems and leaves, but have a thin and more or less flat thallus, which is usually divided into lobes.

Bryophytes lack a mechanism to actively regulate the uptake or loss of moisture. They absorb water through the whole surface of the plant, and lose water in a similar way. Some species have growth forms which facilitate water uptake or reduce moisture loss. For example, mosses that grow in dense turfs may transport water upwards from the soil by capillary action. By growing in dense cushions, some species create their own microclimate to reduce the rate of water loss.

Liverworts Hepaticae

Most liverworts consist of a creeping stem with leaves that lack a midrib. The leaves are usually arranged in three rows, but the row on the underside of the stem is often much reduced or absent. Other liverworts are thallose, ie they consist of a more or less flat, lobed body, not differentiated into stems and leaves (eg *Marchantia*). The spore capsules in most liverworts are black globular structures that stand on thin, translucent stalks. When ripe, the capsules burst open, shedding the spores, after which the capsules shrivel and disappear within a few days (see picture of *Chiloscyphus*). Worldwide there are some 6,000–8,000 species, and some 165 have been reported from Tristan and Gough. They are most abundant in damp environments in the lowlands, but some species such as *Jamesoniella colorata* are important constituents of upland bog communities. Thallose liverworts of the genus *Marchantia* are characteristic of nutrient-rich habitats, and are often found in dense mats in areas with large numbers of seabirds or seals. Many small liverworts grow in loose tufts on damp soil (eg *Lethocolea*) or in moss turfs, mostly in shaded sites (eg *Chiloscyphus*), but some are epiphytic (eg *Frullaria*).

Hornworts Anthocerotae

Hornworts are similar in form to the thallose liverworts, but have very different spore capsules. Their spores are produced in long-lived, greenish, horn-like sporangia. Not all spores ripen at once; new spores are produced at the lower end of the sporangium as it grows. Thus spores at the top ripen and are released first. When the spores are ripe, the capsule slowly splits in two lengthwise from the top down. The spores are mostly dispersed by water. Some hornworts form a symbiosis with nitrogen-fixing cyanobacteria, which live in colonies in cavities within the hornwort thallus. Three species of hornwort occur at the Tristan islands, usually growing in large mats in wet, shaded environments, mostly in the lowlands. The two most common species are *Anthoceros plicatus* and *Phaeoceros chiloensis*.

▲ (1) *Lethocolea prostrata* growing in dense mats on soil

▼ (3) *Chiloscyphus coadunatus* forming dense tufts on dead fern material; note the round spore capsules on the translucent stalks

▲ (2) *Frullania stipatiloba* often grows on stems and branches of the Island Tree *Phylica arborea*

▼ (4) *Marchantia polymorpha* growing in large mats in areas influenced by animals

▼ (5) *Anthoceros plicatus* growing in large mats on wet vertical peatface, shaded by tussock grass. Several other bryophyte species grow between the *Anthoceros* lobes, eg the small liverwort *Clasmatocolea vermicularis*

▼ (6) *Phaeoceros chiloensis* forming dense mats in vertical peatface next to a stream, just above the water level

Mosses Musci

Mosses are small plants that usually consist of stems and leaves with a midrib. They are usually green, but some are silvery, yellow, reddish or brown. Most species reproduce by spores which are formed in long-lived spore capsules or sporangia, which are often green when young, but usually turn brown when ripe. The sporangia generally have a mechanism that opens when the spores are ripe, usually a lid at the top that falls off, although some have vertical slits that open when ripe, but close again in wet conditions.

Worldwide there are some 10,000 species of mosses, of which at least 150 occur at Tristan and Gough. Mosses are found in almost all habitat types on the islands. They are dominant in the early stages of vegetation development, and are among the first plants to colonise bare slopes exposed by peat-slips. Their diversity is low only in areas heavily influenced by salt spray or impacted by animals. They are more abundant in dense fern bush vegetation in the lowlands, but they reach their highest abundance at higher elevations, often forming the dominant plant cover. Together with lichens, mosses are the only large plants found on the upper reaches of the Peak on Tristan.

They are grouped into three classes:

Peat mosses Sphagnopsida

There are only two genera of peat mosses, and only *Sphagnum* occurs at Tristan. It has a characteristic growth form, with a vertical stem and bunches (fascicles) of 3–6 branches. At the top of the plants the stem is very compact, and the branches sit close together, forming a dense head. The sporangia are more or less spherical, with a small lid at the top. In contrast to the 'true' mosses, the spore capsules lack a peristome (a ring of tooth-like structures surrounding the opening). The leaves have two types of cells: narrow green cells containing chloroplasts for photosynthesis, and large dead cells, which allow the plant to absorb up to 20 times its weight in water. *Sphagnum* forms spongy cushions in pioneer communities on peat-slips, but is most abundant in bogs on the islands. Here it forms dense stands covering extensive areas, and is important in building up deep peat deposits. Walking through *Sphagnum* bogs is not to be recommended, because you tend to sink deeply into the bog, leaving long-lasting footprints. Several species occur at the islands.

Granite mosses Andreaeaopsida

The granite or lantern mosses usually form dense reddish or black cushions on rocks. They are characterised by a spore capsule that opens by four or eight vertical slits; a peristome is lacking. The slits only open in dry conditions, when spores are easily dispersed by wind; the slits close again in wet conditions. About five species of granite moss (*Andreaea*) are known from the islands.

'True' mosses Bryopsida

Most moss species belong to the Bryopsida, and this is true for the majority of species at Tristan and Gough. They exhibit a large variation in growth form and size, ranging from 1–2 mm to >20 cm high. Their sporangia have a peristome, a ring of tooth-like structures surrounding the opening, which play a role in the gradual release of spores during dry periods. Mosses with short, erect growth forms such as *Polytrichum*, *Tortula*, and *Racomitrium* are adapted to habitats where desiccation is a regular occurrence, such as on rocks, in open vegetation and in upland areas on relatively dry soils. Other mosses such as *Thuidiopsis* grow more or less horizontally, and are often profusely branched, forming dense or loose mats. This growth form is suited to more moist habitats such as under fern bush and other dense vegetation.

▲ (1) *Sphagnum* sp. forming large tufts in pioneer vegetation on recent peatslips

▼ (3) *Tortula muralis* forming small cushions on concrete

▲ (2) *Polytrichum piliferum* growing in loose groups on damp soil; pink structures contain the male reproductive organs

▼ (4) *Racomitrium lanuginosum* forming small or large colonies on lava rock and on mineral soil

▼ (5) *Rhizogonium spiniforme* growing in loose groups on the foot of trunks of Island Tree *Phylica arborea*

▼ (6) *Thuidiopsis furfurosa* growing in loose mats on rocks, in sheltered and shady spots

LICHENS AND FUNGI

Lichens are symbiotic organisms, combining a fungus with one or, in some cases, more species of algae or cyanobacteria. The fungus supplies water and nutrients, and forms the larger part of the lichen thallus, protecting the algae, which through photosynthesis provides carbohydrates to the fungal component. They obtain most of their nutrients from precipitation, rather than from the substratum they grow on. As a result they are sensitive to chemicals in the air, and are good indicators of air pollution. Many lichens are able to survive extreme environmental conditions, by becoming dormant when they become dry and very cold. They can survive immersion in liquid nitrogen (-196°C), and one species even survived 14 days exposure to the vacuum of outer space. Lichens frequently colonise rock surfaces and wood, while some species grow on soil or on other plants. Unlike mosses, many species are quite tolerant of salt spray, and often live on coastal rocks (eg *Ramalina siliquosa*).

Each combination of fungus and algae has a stable, and recognisable habit, but the form, size and colour of a lichen in many cases is not enough to identify it with certainty, and often chemical characteristics of the thallus are necessary for identification. Although in a strict taxonomic sense a lichen is not a plant species but a combination of two, or sometimes more plant species, because of the specific and distinct characteristics of each symbiotic combination, for convenience sake they are usually referred to as species. The fungus in each lichen 'species' is different, and the name formally applies to the fungus. There are only a limited number of algal species that make up the algal element in lichens.

Some 65 lichen species are known to occur in the islands, but not all collections have been studied yet. It is likely that other, especially smaller species have been overlooked. They range in size from <1 mm to 40 cm, and in colour from bright orange and yellow to white, green and black. They are widespread at the islands, but are especially common on rocks, especially at high elevations and along the coast, and growing epiphytically on the stems of Bogferns and Island Trees. Lichens show a wide range of growth forms, with three functional groups recognised. Crustose lichens such as *Caloplaca*, *Tephromela* and *Verrucaria* are attached with their whole underside to the substratum on which they grow. They are common on rocks, but some species also grow on wood and the bark of trees. Foliose lichens have a more or less flat thallus, usually divided into lobes, which is loosely attached to the substratum. Species of *Parmelia*, *Sticta* and *Pseudocyphellaria* are common epiphytes on Island Trees. Fruticose lichens are perhaps the most spectacular species, having a more three-dimensional structure. The thallus is usually round, or flattened in some species (eg *Ramalina*), but not leaf-like. They either grow upward (eg *Ramalina* and *Stereocaulon*), or hang down from the branches of trees (eg Old Man's Beard *Usnea*). The branches of many Island Trees are densely covered by lichens, both foliose (eg *Sticta*) and fruticose species (eg *Usnea*).

Fungi also occur at the islands, but they have not been studied systematically. Small creamy-white mushrooms about 1 cm across are common in wet heath, and larger mushrooms with caps up to 20 cm across grow on dead wood of Island Trees. However, perhaps the most abundant fungus is the orange-red *Scutellinia* that superficially resemble *Nertera* fruit. It is common at higher elevations, especially at Gough.

DIATOMS

Damp environments such as mosses and wet soils contain a complex world of microscopic organisms such as tardigrades, rotifers, unicellular algae and protozoans. Of these, diatoms are among the most interesting and beautiful. Diatoms are unicellular algae characterised by their finely decorated silica shells. Each diatom shell has two parts, fitting together like the top and bottom of a small box, and each species can be identified by the size, structure and decoration of their shells. Because their shells remain recognisable long after the diatoms have died, diatoms from peat cores or lake sediments can be used to reconstruct past environmental conditions. Most species are too small to see with the naked eye, but if you take scrapings from rocks in streams or ponds, or water pressed from plants growing in wet places and put it under a microscope, you are quite likely to find diatoms.

There are estimated to be at least 10,000 diatom species worldwide, most of which occur in the sea. However, they are also fairly common in damp terrestrial systems, such as those found at Tristan and Gough. Studies of diatoms at the islands are in their infancy, but almost 100 species have been found, and based on the diversity at other Southern Ocean islands, the actual number of diatom species is likely to be at least 200. The Tristan islands have a highly specific diatom flora, with several endemic species found in rivers, lakes, wet soils and among mosses. Most are pennate diatoms, which have an elongate shape, but a few are centric, ie round or triangular in outline.

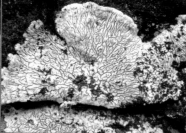

▲ (1) *Tephromela atra* growing on coastal rocks

▲ (2) *Verrucaria durietzii* growing on coastal rocks

▲ (3) *Caloplaca* sp. on coastal rocks

▼ (4) *Sticta* sp. growing on stems and branches of *Phylica* trees

▼ (5) *Pseudocyphellaria aurata*

▼ (6) *Teloschistes flavicans*, *Sticta* sp. and several *Parmelia* spp. on a branch of a *Phylica* tree

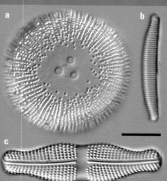

▲ (7) A beard lichen *Usnea* sp. growing on a *Phylica* tree trunk

▲ (8) *Hypothachyna gondylophora* (foliose species) and *Ramalina siliquosa* growing on coastal rocks

▲ (9) *Stereocaulon atlanticum* on young lava

▼ (10) *Scutellinia* sp.

▼ (11) *Agrocybe cylindracea*

▼ (12) Diatoms (scale bar 0.01 mm long):
(a) *Orthoseira gremmenii* (b) *Eunotia* sp.
(c) *Achnanthes coarctata*

Atlantic Yellow-nosed Albatrosses and a Sooty Albatross on the cliffs of Inaccessible Island

BIRDS

Birds are among the most mobile organisms, and several species have colonised the islands. Most are seabirds that only use the islands as a place to breed. They dominate the landscape and play a major ecological role by importing vast amounts of energy and nutrients, and creating openings in natural vegetation by their trampling and burrowing. Their populations are not constrained by the small size of the islands, because they forage hundreds or thousands of kilometres from the islands, even while breeding. As a result, they can attain very high densities, and were an important source of food for the island community. By 1900, the islanders, ably assisted by feral cats and rats, had greatly depleted seabird populations on Tristan, causing the extinction of several species. This forced the islanders to travel to Inaccessible and later Nightingale to collect seabirds and their eggs and chicks. Faced with evidence of population decreases at the outer islands, conservation measures were introduced in the 1950s, and currently exploitation is limited to Great Shearwaters on Nightingale and Rockhopper Penguin eggs on Nightingale and Alex Island. Unfortunately some species remain at risk due to pressures off the island (mainly mortality on fishing gear such as long-lines) as well as ongoing predation by rats and mice at Tristan and Gough.

The islands are home to 22 breeding seabirds, of which four breed nowhere else. Most species have affinities with the sub-Antarctic, but the Brown Noddy is mainly tropical, reaching its most southerly extent at Tristan and Gough. Other seabird species are non-breeding visitors, either from elsewhere in the Southern Ocean or from the North Atlantic. Two seabirds feed ashore. Giant petrels visit seal and penguin colonies, scavenging carcasses and killing unwary or sick animals. But the top predators are Tristan Skuas, which make a living in summer almost exclusively by killing other seabirds. Their predatory activities force most of the smaller seabirds to breed in burrows and only visit the islands at night, when they have a better chance of avoiding being eaten. Each pair of skuas defends a territory containing enough seabirds to support themselves and their chicks, but there are more skuas than available territories. Hundreds of non-breeding skuas wait around in 'clubs', testing for vacancies by flying over territories. If they fail to elicit an indignant response from the incumbents, the vacancy is filled instantly.

Vagrant land birds also reach the islands, mainly carried in the prevailing westerly winds from the Americas. Most are young birds that are unable to correct their course if they are blown sideways on their first north-south migration. Accordingly, birds breeding in South America such as egrets, herons and gallinules tend to arrive in autumn, when young birds disperse, whereas those from North America such as waders and Barn Swallows tend to arrive in spring. Most records are from the main island of Tristan, partly because of the larger number of observers, and partly because there are fewer skuas to eat vagrants at Tristan.

Only a few land birds have colonised the Tristan islands, and all have evolved into distinctive species, found nowhere else. Land birds often undergo rapid morphological evolution at oceanic islands. *Nesospiza* buntings have undergone an adaptive radiation similar to Darwin's finches at the Galapagos. Recent evidence suggests that large-billed forms adapted to open the woody fruits of the Island Tree *Phylica arborea* evolved independently at Inaccessible and Nightingale Island, requiring a revision to their taxonomy. The Tristan Thrush exploits many niches by being a supreme opportunist, attacking anything new in their environment, especially round or shiny objects which could conceivably be eggs. They have brush-tipped tongues for lapping up the egg contents, and even catch and kill adult White-faced Storm Petrels, holding them down with their strong feet and bludgeoning them to death with their bills.

Some species become flightless in the absence of terrestrial predators. Wings and their associated musculature are costly to develop and maintain, and are soon lost in species where flight develops late in their growth as chicks, such as rails. These flightless species are especially susceptible to extinction when islands are colonised by humans and their commensals, but all island birds are at risk, because they lose the ability to cope with terrestrial predators. More than 90% of bird extinctions since 1600 have been of birds on oceanic islands. The Inaccessible Rail holds the dubious distinction of being the smallest flightless bird in the world. There were other, smaller species, but they have all gone extinct. Doubtless the Inaccessible Rail will follow suit should rats or mice ever reach Inaccessible.

PENGUINS Spheniscidae

Flightless seabirds, supremely adapted for pursuit diving. Wings reduced to small, rigid flippers ideal for 'flying' underwater; largest species can dive to 520 m (maximum depth) and remain underwater for up to 22 minutes (maximum duration). They replace all their feathers in an annual moult, when they remain ashore, living off stored reserves. Eighteen species in six genera; confined to the Southern Hemisphere; one breeding species at Tristan; four vagrants.

Northern Rockhopper Penguin *Eudyptes moseleyi*   Pinnamin

55–65 cm; 1.6–2.2 kg, but up to 4 kg immediately before moulting. Females 2–5% smaller than males in body size, 10–15% smaller in bill length and depth. Formerly lumped with the Southern Rockhopper *E. chrysocome*, it differs genetically as well as having longer head plumes and a deeper voice. A fairly small penguin, black above and white below with pink feet and red eyes and bill. Adults easily identified by their luxuriant golden-yellow head plumes, although these often hard to see at sea, when slicked against the sides of the head. Juveniles lack head plumes and have greyish throats and duller red bills. Chicks downy, grey-brown above and whitish below. **Behaviour**: Occurs singly or in small flocks at sea; often in larger groups near colonies. Fairly agile ashore, hopping and clambering over rocks and boulders. Breeds in coastal colonies, under dense tussock grass on Inaccessible and Nightingale, but colonies more open on Tristan and Gough. Presence of hidden colonies betrayed by birds resting on nearby landing beaches. Strongly seasonal; adults return in late July–August, eggs laid September, hatch mid-October–early November, chicks fledge end December–January. Adults then depart to sea on brief, pre-moult fattening trip, returning February–March to moult. Juveniles moult earlier, from December, as do adults who did not breed or who lost their eggs or chicks. Timing of breeding and moult delayed 3–4 weeks on Gough. Often retains same mate in successive years. Adults display with loud, deep braying calls, given with raised flippers and head thrown back, shaking head plumes. Female forms the shallow nest scrape; male delivers a few sticks, bones and stones which female arranges around nest. Lays two whitish eggs; displaced eggs sometimes give impression of three-egg clutches. First laid a-egg invariably smaller (62 × 47 mm) than b-egg (69 × 53 mm). Incubation by both adults, 32–34 days. Chicks brooded for 20–26 days by male, fed by female, then gather in loose creches, where fed by female for one week while male recovers from long guarding fast, then by both adults. Seldom if ever raises two chicks; chick from b-egg hatches first and monopolises food, usually causing chick from a-egg to starve. Fifty-one percent (41–61%) of clutches fledge one chick on Tristan. Diet mainly crustaceans (euphausids, shrimps, amphipods, isopods), with some small squid and fish. Diving behaviour little known; closely related Southern Rockhopper travels at 7–8 km/h, dives during day to 70 m, but most dives <40 m. **Distribution**: Breeds at Tristan, Nightingale, Inaccessible, Gough up to 200 m above sea level. Location of colonies determined by suitable landing sites, but only along east coast of Tristan from Jew's Point to Stony Beach following exploitation; some moulters come ashore around Edinburgh. Seldom observed at sea other than small groups porpoising near colonies, so distribution poorly known; vagrants reach Africa and South America. Elsewhere breeds on Amsterdam and St Paul, Indian Ocean. **Population**: More than 90% of world population breed at Tristan: some 10,000 pairs at Tristan, numbers increasing following protection; 10,000 pairs in two colonies at Nightingale; up to 100,000 pairs at Alex Is, but decreasing due to displacement by fur seals; 30,000 pairs at Inaccessible in eight colonies, possibly decreasing; recently 30,000–80,000 at Gough, down from 144,000 pairs in 1984; reason for decrease unknown. **Conservation**: Vulnerable. Range greatly reduced on Tristan due to exploitation; formerly bred along most of coastline; killed for food, bait and decorative head plumes. Currently eggs collected on Nightingale and Alex Is; harvest sustainable provided   a-eggs collected and disturbance minimised, but evidence of population decrease. Harvest 25,000–40,000 eggs/year in 1970s; consumption has decreased in recent years. Guano collected from some colonies after the breeding season.

Vagrant penguins

King Penguin *Aptenodytes patagonicus*, **Gentoo Penguin** *Pygoscelis papua* and **Macaroni Penguin** *Eudyptes chrysolophus* are scarce visitors from sub-Antarctic islands and Antarctica. One record of a **Magellanic Penguin** *Spheniscus magellanicus* from South America. Only Macaroni Penguins are likely to be confused with Northern Rockhoppers, but they are larger with a heavier bill and fleshy pink gape. Adults have golden crest feathers extending across the front of the forehead.

▲ **(1) Northern Rockhopper Penguin**
Eudyptes moseleyi, **chick at nest**

◀ **(2) Adult**

▼ **(3) Juvenile**

Vagrant penguins ▶

LEFT TO RIGHT **(4) King Penguin**
Aptenodytes patagonicus,
(5) Gentoo Penguin
Pygoscelis papua,
(6) Macaroni Penguin
Eudyptes chrysolophus

ALBATROSSES Diomedeidae

Large, long-winged seabirds, adapted for dynamic soaring; able to cover vast distances with little energy expenditure. Nostrils in tubes on sides of bill, not joined on top as petrels. Three toes webbed for swimming; diving ability limited due to long wings. Raise at most one chick per year; breeding protracted; chicks fed by regurgitation. Take at least two years to replace primaries. Twenty-one species in four genera worldwide; three breeding species at Tristan; six non-breeding visitors, one vagrant.

Tristan Albatross *Diomedea dabbenena*   Gony

100–110 cm, wingspan 280–300 cm, 6–7 kg; male slightly larger and acquires whiter plumage than female. A large, hump-backed albatross; flight laboured and heavy in light to moderate winds, but graceful in strong winds. Easily distinguished from smaller *Thalassarche* mollymawks by its pink bill and white underwing with narrow black trailing edge; remainder of plumage changes with age. Juvenile chocolate brown with white face; body gradually whitens with each moult, going through mottled 'leopard' stage. Typical adult female retains some brown mottling on crown, back, breast, and flanks; most adult males have white body and some white in base of upperwing; some have mostly white upperwing and tail. Adults often have crescent-shaped pink stain on sides of neck; some adults have blackish tips to bill, similar to Amsterdam Albatross *D. amsterdamensis*, which is not known from Tristan waters. Easily confused with Wandering Albatross; probably not safely separable at sea. Chick covered in white down; bill pale pink. **Behaviour**: Usually occurs singly at sea, but flocks gather at food sources such as fishing boats and dead whales. Habitually follows ships. Spends most of day flying, travelling at up to 100 km/h, but often sits on water at night. Fairly clumsy ashore; requires large open areas to land and take off; breeds in loose colonies on windswept uplands. Adults return in November–December, males before females; eggs laid January, following short pre-laying exodus by females; chicks hatch in March; fledge end November–December; breeding season so long that successful adults take a year off after breeding to moult and recover body condition; failed breeders attempt to breed in following year, provided failure occurs early enough. Wailing sky-calls and dances with spread wings usually confined to courting birds; paired birds make various croaking calls and bill claps. Pairs usually remain together for successive breeding attempts. Immatures return to land at 4–5 years old; start breeding at 6–14 years old; longevity at least 35 years. Lays one large white egg (average 127 × 77 mm) in a mound of vegetation c1 m across. Incubation by both adults for 70–78 days with shifts lasting up to 10–12 days. Chick fed by both adults; brooded for first few weeks and then guarded for another week or so until it can defend itself against giant petrels and skuas by clappering its bill and spitting stomach oils. Old chicks wander away from nest site, and often build 'practice' nests; fledge after 8–9 months. Breeding success on Gough only 27% due to mice killing downy chicks, starting even before end of brood phase. Diet mainly squid and fish, with some crustaceans and offal, caught or scavenged at sea surface; dives <1 m; squid mainly <400 g (60 g–4.4 kg). **Distribution**: Endemic to Tristan group; ranges through oceanic waters of temperate South Atlantic; vagrant to Australia. Breeds at 400–700 m on Gough; locally on Gony Ridge at 500 m on Inaccessible. Formerly on Tristan Base; still occasionally visits Tristan. **Population**: 1,500–2,500 pairs breed annually on Gough; 0–2 pairs on Inaccessible. Gough numbers inflated by low breeding success; fledge only 300–1,100 chicks per year, so a high proportion of pairs breed each year. **Conservation**: Killed historically for food on Tristan and Inaccessible; extinct on Tristan by 1900. Chicks eaten by feral pigs on Inaccessible prior to 1930s; numbers have failed to recover at Inaccessible despite protection, possibly due to very small population size. Endangered by long-line fishing and mouse predation at Gough; population decrease estimated 3–5% per year. Breeding adults occasionally killed by peat-slips.

Wandering Albatross *Diomedea exulans*

110–135 cm, wingspan 270–350 cm, 7–11 kg. Probably a common non-breeding visitor; status uncertain due to confusion with Tristan Albatross; slightly larger and longer billed, but probably not safely separable at sea due to large age- and sex-related variation. Plumage whitens more rapidly. Old males all white apart from black trailing edge to wings; easily confused with adult Southern Royal Albatross, but has pinker bill with no black cutting edge, forehead appears steeper due to feathering extending less far down lower mandible; pink stains on neck diagnostic if present. Most adults told by some black in tail tip and more coarsely-patterned upperwing. Biology similar to Tristan Albatross. Around 9,000 pairs breed annually at sub-Antarctic islands: South Georgia, Prince Edwards, Crozets, Kerguelen, Macquarie and Heard; disperses widely throughout the Southern Ocean; non-breeding birds sometimes circumnavigate the world. Vulnerable due to drowning on long-lines; greater mortality of females results in male-biased populations.

▲ (1) Tristan Albatross *Diomedea dabbenena*, adult female

▲ (2) Tristan Albatross *Diomedea dabbenena*, adult male with chick

▼ (3) Tristan Albatross *Diomedea dabbenena*, juvenile

▼ (4) Wandering Albatross *Diomedea exulans*, adult male

Northern Royal Albatross *Diomedea sanfordi*

105–115 cm, wingspan 300–330 cm, 6–7 kg. Scarce non-breeding visitor. A very large, white-bodied albatross with crisp black upper wings at all ages; Tristan and Wandering Albatrosses with black upperwings have black tail tips. Bill pale yellowy-pink with a black cutting edge to the upper mandible. Underwing white with a narrow black trailing edge and broader black wrist patch. Immature has some black in outer tail feathers and mottling on back. Distinct from Southern Royal Albatross by solid black upperwing, including leading edge of wing, and black wrist patch. Biology similar to Tristan Albatross. Around 5,200 pairs breed annually at Chatham Islands and Taiaroa Head, New Zealand; non-breeders disperse widely, circumnavigating the Southern Ocean. Endangered; breeding success reduced due to storms removing soil from Chatham Islands and egg-shell thinning; occasionally caught on long-lines.

Southern Royal Albatross *Diomedea epomophora*

115–125 cm, wingspan 320–350 cm, 7–11 kg. Scarce non-breeding visitor. A very large, white-bodied albatross superficially similar to Tristan and Wandering Albatrosses but with more finely patterned upperwings and mostly white tail at all ages. Bill pale yellowy-pink with a black cutting edge to the upper mandible. Underwing white with a narrow black trailing edge. Immature has some black in outer tail feathers and mottling on back; distinct from Northern Royal Albatross by some white on upperwing, especially on leading edge of wing; lacks a broad black wrist patch. Biology similar to Tristan Albatross. Around 8,500 pairs breed annually at Campbell and Auckland Islands, New Zealand; non-breeders disperse widely, circumnavigating the Southern Ocean. Vulnerable due to long-line fishing and introduced rats, pigs and cats on breeding islands.

Atlantic Yellow-nosed Albatross *Thalassarche chlororhynchus*   Molly

75–80 cm, wingspan 200–210 cm, 1.8–2.8 kg; males slightly larger. A small albatross with a long, slender black bill. Adults have a golden stripe along top of bill; tip cherry-pink; at close range, has narrow golden line at base of lower mandible, and exposes golden gape stripe when displaying; head washed smoky grey, darker around eyes. In flight, has dark grey-brown upperwing, back and tail, white rump; underparts white. Underwing largely white with fairly narrow black leading and trailing edges at all ages. Immatures have a white head and all black bill. Smaller than other mollymawks; underwing pattern and long, slender bill diagnostic. Chick covered in white down; bill and gape stripe black. **Indian Yellow-nosed Albatross** *T. carteri* is a possible vagrant; adult differs in having a white head and pointed end to golden stripe at base of bill (rounded in Atlantic Yellow-nosed Albatross). **Behaviour**: Usually occurs singly or in small groups at sea; occasionally follows ships. Rafts of 10–50 birds roost on the water near colonies. Fairly agile ashore; clambers under trees and into steep-sided hollows to reach sheltered breeding sites; often walks >100 m to exposed ridges to take off. Breeds in loose colonies among fern bush, *Scirpus* bogs and meadows, and locally under *Spartina* tussocks. Occurs offshore year round; adults return ashore in August–September; eggs laid mid-September–early October; chicks hatch in late November–December; fledge March–April; breeding delayed one week at Gough. Non-breeding birds gather at exposed sites termed 'molly knobs' to court, mainly in fine weather, October–January. Display by bowing with fanned tail and exposed gape stripe, making loud reeling call; also calls in flight, arching neck back. Pairs repeatedly bill point at each other; frequently allopreen each other's heads. Most pairs breed annually, usually remaining together for successive breeding attempts, but may divorce or breed opportunistically with another bird if mate fails to arrive. Immatures return to island at 5–8 years old; start breeding at 6–13 years old; longevity at least 37 years. Lays one (rarely two, probably by two females) large white egg (average 95 × 63 mm) in a bowl-shaped pedestal of mud up to 40 cm high, built with bill. Often re-uses same nest in successive years, but refurbishes it with fresh mud; old nests often have large numbers of ticks. Incubation by both adults for 64–70 days with shifts lasting up to 10–12 days. Chick fed by both adults; brooded for first three weeks; fledges after four months; defends itself against skuas by clappering its bill and spitting stomach oils if threatened. Breeding success on Gough and Tristan averages 68%. Diet fish and squid with some crustaceans and offal; obtained by surface seizing, surface plunging and occasional plunge dives; squid mainly <200 g (10–570 g). Often forages in association with tunas and other marine predators. **Distribution**: Endemic to Tristan group; ranges through temperate South Atlantic; rarely to Australia and New Zealand. Widespread on all islands, up to 800 m on Tristan, 450 m on Gough; absent from lower slopes on Tristan and Inaccessible but almost to sea level on Nightingale and Gough. On Tristan, most abundant in south-east sector between Sandy Point and Stony Beach. **Population**: 20,000 pairs estimated on Tristan in 1970s, but probably fewer now; 5,000 on Gough; 2,000 on Nightingale and 2,000 on Inaccessible. **Conservation**: Killed historically for food on Tristan, Nightingale and Inaccessible; up to 2,000 eggs and 1,500 chicks killed per year in 1950s; now protected at all islands. Endangered by drowning on long-lines; adult survival on Gough only 92%, too low to maintain a stable population; study populations at Tristan and Gough decreasing by 1.2% per year; numbers breeding at The Ponds on Nightingale fell from 3,000 pairs in early 1970s to 1,000 in 1999.

▲ **(1) Northern Royal Albatross**
Diomedea sanfordi

▲ **(2) Northern Royal Albatross**
Diomedea sanfordi

▲ **(3) Southern Royal Albatross**
Diomedea epomophora

▼ **(4) Atlantic Yellow-nosed Albatross** *Thalassarche chlororhynchus*, adult

▲ **Atlantic Yellow-nosed Albatross**
Thalassarche chlororhynchus
TOP **(5) subadult**
CENTRE **(6) courtship display**
BOTTOM **(7) chick**

Black-browed Albatross *Thalassarche melanophrys* Cape Molly

80–95 cm, wingspan 210–250 cm, 3.0–4.4 kg. Fairly common non-breeding visitor. Adult has an orange bill with a pinkish tip and a dusky eyebrow; upperwings, back and tail blackish; underwing white with broad black leading and trailing edges. Juvenile has a slate grey bill with blackish tip, grey partial neck collar and dark grey underwings. Sub-adult has yellowish bill with dark tip. 700,000 pairs breed annually at islands off Cape Horn, Falklands and South Georgia, with small numbers at Crozets, Kerguelen, Heard, Macquarie and New Zealand islands; disperses throughout the Southern Ocean, but most forage in productive shelf waters. Often scavenges at fishing vessels; dives up to 5 m. Endangered, due to drowning on long-lines and trawl cables.

Grey-headed Albatross *Thalassarche chrysostoma*

75–85 cm, wingspan 180–205 cm, 2.8–4.2 kg. Scarce non-breeding visitor, mainly in winter; most are juveniles, which differ from juvenile Black-browed Albatross by having a darker grey head and neck, merging smoothly into mantle; appear more bull-necked; bill blackish, lacking pale streaks. Adult has a grey-washed head and a grey bill with narrow yellow stripes along top and bottom; larger and more chunky than Yellow-nosed Albatross, with broader black underwing margins. Few adults breed in the year after a successful attempt. 94,000 pairs breed annually at islands off Cape Horn, South Georgia, Prince Edwards, Crozets, Kerguelen, Macquarie and Campbell; non-breeders disperse widely. Vulnerable, mainly due to drowning on long-lines.

Shy Albatross *Thalassarche cauta*

90–100 cm, wingspan 210–256 cm, 3.2–5.2 kg. Scarce non-breeding visitor. A large mollymawk with a paler grey back than the upperwings; underwing largely white with narrow black leading and trailing edges and a diagnostic black spot at the base of the leading edge. At Tristan most are immatures, which have a pale grey wash on face and neck; bill grey with blackish tip. Adults have grey wash confined to the cheeks and blue-grey bills with a yellowish tip. 87,000 pairs breed annually, 12,000 off Tasmania and 75,000 on Auckland Island; disperse across the Indian and Pacific Oceans to shelf waters off southern Africa and the west coast of South America; scarce in South Atlantic. Near-Threatened, due to drowning on long-lines and trawl cables.

Sooty Albatross *Phoebetria fusca* Peeoo

85–90 cm, wingspan 200–210 cm, 2.1–3.2 kg; males slightly larger. A slender, sooty brown albatross with elongate wings and a long, wedge-shaped tail, narrow white eye-ring and whitish shafts to primaries and tail feathers. Bill black; adult has yellow stripe on side of lower mandible. Juvenile eye-ring and bill stripe dull buffy-grey; feather shafts brown. Immatures in worn plumage have pale collars. Downy chick grey with white face; bill and gape line black. **Behaviour**: Usually single at sea; seldom follows ships. Flight graceful; clumsy ashore. Breeds singly or in loose colonies of up to 15 pairs on cliff ledges or ridges. Occurs year round at sea; returns to land in early September; eggs laid early October; chicks hatch in mid-December; fledge mid-May. Display in air, calling and performing tandem glides. On ground, unmated birds call to flying birds, throwing head back and giving *peee-aaaarh* call. Male walks around female on nest; bows and fans tail; bill fence and preen each other's heads; both sexes call. Immatures return to island after 5–14 years; start breeding at 9–15 years. Nest is a bowl-shaped pedestal of mud built with bill; often refurbished and re-used. Lays one large white egg (average 102 × 65 mm). Incubation by both adults for 68–73 days; shifts up to 10–12 days. Chick fed by both adults; brooded for 2–3 weeks; fledges after five months; defends itself by clappering its bill and spitting oil. Breeding success 54–58%; few successful pairs breed again in following year. Diet mainly squid; also birds, carrion, fish and crustaceans; obtained by surface seizing and occasional plunge dives. Prions and small petrels possibly killed at sea. Capable of swallowing large prey; one ate two adult Great Shearwaters. **Distribution**: Widespread on all islands, up to 1,200 m on Tristan, 500 m on Gough. Also breeds at Prince Edwards, Crozets, Kerguelen, Amsterdam and St Paul; ranges through temperate South Atlantic and southern Indian Oceans. **Population**: Poorly known due to cliff nesting habits; crudely estimated 2,000 pairs on Tristan; 200 on Nightingale, 500 on Inaccessible, 5,000 on Gough; globally 15,000 pairs. **Conservation**: Killed historically for food at Tristan; early visitors reported colonies of 50–100 birds on the Base; now protected. Endangered, due to drowning on long-lines; at Gough has decreased 50% in last 30 years.

Light-mantled Sooty Albatross *Phoebetria palpebrata*

80–90 cm, wingspan 200–220 cm, 2.2–3.5 kg. Scarce non-breeding visitor, mainly in winter. Has paler, greyer back and rump than Sooty Albatross, contrasting with dark head; adult has violet bill stripe; white eye ring shorter but broader. Beware immature Sooty Albatross, which has variable pale mantle, but always has a dark lower back and rump. 22,000 pairs breed annually at sub-Antarctic islands: South Georgia, Prince Edwards, Crozets, Kerguelen, Heard, Macquarie and New Zealand islands; non-breeding birds disperse widely, mainly south of 40°S. Near-Threatened, due to drowning on long-lines. Dives up to 12 m.

▲ (1) Black-browed Albatross
Thalassarche melanophrys, adult

▲ (2) Grey-headed Albatross
Thalassarche chrysostoma, adult

▲ (3) Shy Albatross *Thalassarche cauta*,
immature

▲ ▼ (4 and 5) Sooty Albatross
Phoebetria fusca

▼ (6) Sooty Albatross
Phoebetria fusca, chick

▼ (7) Light-mantled Sooty Albatross
Phoebetria palpebrata

PETRELS Procellariidae

Small to large seabirds; most species fairly long-winged adapted for dynamic soaring; some have smaller wings adapted for diving. Nostrils tube-shaped, joined on top of bill. Three toes webbed for swimming. Raise at most one chick per year; breeding protracted; chicks fed by regurgitation. Moult all primaries each year. Eighty-five species in 15 genera worldwide; 12 breeding species at Tristan; nine non-breeding visitors.

Southern Giant Petrel *Macronectes giganteus*   Nellie, Stinker, Boneshaker

80–100 cm, wingspan 150–210 cm, males 4.2–5.5 kg, females 3.3–4.7 kg. A huge, lumbering grey-brown petrel; bill massive, pale-horn with a greenish tip. Juvenile uniform blackish-brown with pale bill only faintly tinged greenish at tip. Plumage gradually becomes paler with age; oldest birds mottled ash-grey. Scarce white morph is all white with scattered black feathers; comprises <10% globally, but none breed at Gough; rare visitor to Tristan waters mainly in winter. Dark morph easily confused with Northern Giant Petrel; reliably told only by greenish (not reddish) bill tip, but adults often show whitish head, lacking contrast between crown and face. Sooty Albatross is much more slender and elegant with a long, wedge-shaped tail and black bill. Chick covered in whitish down; bill pale horn. **Behaviour**: Usually occurs singly at sea, but 50–100 gather at food sources such as fishing boats and dead whales. Flight heavy and cumbersome except in strong winds; habitually follows ships, soaring in updrafts along windward side. Fairly agile ashore; better able to walk than most petrels; often feeds ashore in seal and penguin colonies. Breeds in loose colonies in open grassy areas or under shelter of bogferns and small *Phylica* trees. Present offshore year round; adults return to colonies in August, eggs laid September, chicks hatch in November; fledge in April. Display with whinney call, given with gaping bill, neck arched back, and head shaking from side to side; also calls in flight. Paired birds bill fence and allopreen. Pairs usually remain together for successive breeding attempts; most breed annually. Immatures return to land at 3–5 years old; start breeding at 4–12 years old; longevity at least 40 years. Lays one (rarely two) large white egg (average 102 × 64 mm) in a low mound of vegetation c0.6 m across. Incubation by both adults for 55–66 days with shifts lasting up to 8–10 days. Chick fed by both adults; brooded for first few weeks; fledges after 108–130 days, with male chicks remaining on the nest longer than females (average six days). Diet mainly carrion, squid, fish, crustaceans and other birds; almost certainly uses scent to locate prey. Males feed at seal and penguin colonies, using large size to compete for access to carcasses; smaller females spend more time at sea, taking prey by surface seizing and shallow plunges; dive up to 1–2 m. Kill penguin chicks, fledglings and adults on land and at sea; also diving petrels, prions and other small petrels caught in the air at sea; one killed a sleeping Black-browed Albatross off Australia. Often fierce physical contests over food; birds charge with wings spread, neck and chin feathers raised and tail cocked and fanned to look as intimidating as possible. Adults and chicks spit stomach oils when threatened. **Distribution**: Breeds at three sites in wet heath between Low Hump and Triple Peak on Gough; also a few pairs on Long Beach; extinct on Tristan. Elsewhere, breeds in ice-free areas of coastal Antarctica, Patagonia and at sub-Antarctic islands. Disperses widely throughout the Southern Ocean. **Population**: 250 pairs breed at Gough; globally some 31,000 pairs. **Conservation**: Extinct on Tristan by 1900, due to killing of chicks and local extinction of seals. Vulnerable due to drowning on long-lines and disturbance at breeding sites.

Northern Giant Petrel *Macronectes halli*

80–100 cm, wingspan 150–210 cm, males 4.2–5.8 kg, females 3.0–4.5 kg. Fairly common non-breeding visitor; only safely told from Southern Giant Petrel given good views of the dull reddish bill tip. Some old adults have scaly pale grey head and body, but usually shows a darker crown than face; lacks a white morph. Immatures all dark; bill tip colour poorly developed. Biology similar to Southern Giant Petrel, but nests singly; breeds six weeks earlier at sites where both species breed together. Some 12,000 pairs breed annually at South Georgia, Prince Edwards, Crozets, Kerguelen and islands off New Zealand; disperses widely throughout the Southern Ocean. Near-Threatened, due to drowning on long-lines.

Southern Fulmar *Fulmarus glacialoides*   Snow Gull

45–50 cm, wingspan 115–120 cm, 700–900 g. Uncommon non-breeding visitor, mainly in winter. A pale-silver-grey petrel with a distinctive white panel in the outer wing; bill pink with dark tip; nostrils blue-grey. Usually loosely associated with smaller Pintada Petrels; frequently follows ships. Diet mainly fish and crustaceans; also squid, fishery wastes and carrion; forages by surface seizing or shallow dives. Adults return to colonies October; brief pre-laying exodus in early November; lay early December; hatch January and chicks fledge March. At least 1 million pairs breed at ice-free coastal areas in Antarctica and adjacent islands, including South Shetlands, South Orkneys, South Sandwiches and Bouvet; disperses widely throughout the Southern Ocean, irrupting north of Subtropical Front in some winters. Not threatened.

▲ (1) Southern Giant Petrel *Macronectes giganteus* with chick
▼ (2) Southern Giant Petrel *Macronectes giganteus*

▼ (3) Southern Giant Petrel
Macronectes giganteus, white phase

▼ (4) Northern Giant Petrel *Macronectes halli*, adult

▼ (5) Southern Fulmar
Fulmarus glacialoides

Pintado Petrel *Daption capense*   Cape Pigeon, Cape Petrel

35–42 cm, wingspan 80–90 cm, 370–530 g. Common non-breeding visitor, mainly in winter. A distinctively patterned petrel; upperparts mottled black-and-white, head, bill and tail black; remainder of underparts white. Often in small flocks; frequently follows ships, soaring in updrafts. Diet mainly fish and crustaceans; also squid, fishery wastes and carrion; uses scent to locate prey. Forages by surface seizing, shallow plunging and filtering, using muscular tongue to pump water over serrated bill; occasionally dives using feet and wings; dives last up to 27 seconds. Sedentary in north of breeding range; adults from southern colonies return in September–October; brief pre-laying exodus in late October; lay November–early December; hatch January and chicks fledge late February–March. Several million pairs breed at ice-free coastal areas in Antarctica and sub-Antarctic islands mainly south of 50°S; disperses north throughout Southern Ocean into temperate waters in winter. Not threatened.

Blue Petrel *Halobaena caerulea*

26–30 cm, wingspan 62–70 cm, 150–250 g. Uncommon non-breeding visitor, mainly to southern waters in winter. A fairly small, blue-grey petrel with a dark M across the upperwings and mostly white underparts; superficially similar to prions, but has a diagnostic white tail tip and a blackish cap and collar; flight action more direct. Diet crustaceans, fish, small squid, salps, fishery wastes and carrion. Forages mainly by surface seizing, dipping and shallow dives to 3–5 m. Adults arrive at colonies August–September; lay end October after a brief pre-laying exodus; hatch early December, fledge end January–February. Adults again return to colonies April–June after moulting, then typically absent July–early August. Some 1 million pairs breed at sub-Antarctic islands off Cape Horn, South Georgia, Prince Edwards, Crozets, Kerguelen and Macquarie; disperses widely throughout the Southern Ocean, generally south of Subtropical Front. Not threatened.

Broad-billed Prion *Pachyptila vittata*   Nightbird, Whalebird

28–30 cm, wingspan 62–66 cm, 140–230 g. A fairly small, blue-grey petrel with a dark M across the upperwings, mostly white underparts and a fairly long, black-tipped tail. Bill large and broad-based, with correspondingly large head and steep, angular forehead. In the hand, bill width 18–24 mm; filtering lamellae exposed along basal half of bill. By far the most common prion in Tristan waters; see Antarctic Prion for differences. **Behaviour**: Usually occurs in flocks at sea, often in large numbers. Flight erratic, especially close to land and ships; sometimes follows ships, occasionally soaring in updrafts. Largely nocturnal at breeding islands, arriving after dark, but sometimes flies over coastal cliffs in daylight. Breeds in burrows 1–1.5 m long dug into peat; burrow entrances typically 15 cm across, 9 cm high; also in rocky crevices, caves, lava tunnels and stone walls of huts on Nightingale and Inaccessible. Present offshore year round; adults return to colonies in early July, eggs laid August, chicks hatch from late September; fledge in late November–early December. Adults disperse to moult after breeding, then return to colonies in March–May to display and clean-out burrows. Typical calls are a deep, dove-like cooing with some more guttural notes; paired birds allopreen. Presumably breeds annually; other prions start breeding at 5–6 (rarely three) years old. Lays one white egg (average 50 × 37 mm) on the burrow floor; seldom any nesting material. Incubation by both adults for 45–50 days. Chick fed by both adults; brooded for first week or so; fledges after about 50 days. Large numbers of adults, fledglings and some chicks killed by skuas; wings in middens 208–225 mm. Diet mainly copepods 2–4 mm long; also other crustaceans, small squid and fish; frequently ingests plastic litter at sea. Forages by surface seizing and hydroplaning: sits or patters on water with raised wings, using its muscular tongue and distensible gular pouch to filter water through the stiff lamellae fringing the upper mandible like a tiny baleen whale. **Distribution**: Widespread at Nightingale, Inaccessible and Gough, occurring in all habitats up to 500 m; rare on Tristan, apparently confined to rat-free refugia; disperses in South Atlantic, occasionally reaching southern Africa. Elsewhere, breeds at islands around New Zealand; populations disjunct. **Population**: Poorly known; perhaps 2 million pairs on Gough, at least 100,000 at Nightingale and Inaccessible; <5,000 on Tristan. New Zealand population 1 million pairs. **Conservation**: Not threatened; formerly killed for food by lighting fires to attract birds at night; population on Tristan severely impacted by rats; mice on Gough may kill some chicks.

Antarctic Prion *Pachyptila desolata*

25–27 cm, wingspan 58–64 cm, 120–180 g. Status uncertain due to confusion with Broad-billed Prion; probably fairly common away from the islands in winter. Best identified from Broad-billed Prion by its smaller, bluer bill; head more rounded and paler blue-grey with a more prominent white supercilium. Diet and behaviour at sea similar. In the hand, bill width 12–16 mm; few if any filtering lamellae visible when bill closed. Some 20 million pairs breed at sub-Antarctic islands; migrates north in winter, mainly found north of the Subtropical Front May–September. Not threatened. **Slender-billed Prion** *Pachyptila belcheri* is a rare non-breeding visitor, although it may have been overlooked; bill even narrower than Antarctic Prion; head paler and outer tail more extensively white. In the hand, bill width 8–11 mm; lacks filtering lamellae.

▲ (1) Pintado Petrel *Daption capense*

▲ (2) Pintado Petrel *Daption capense*

▲ (3) Blue Petrel *Halobaena caerulea*

▲ (4) Broad-billed Prion *Pachyptila vittata*

▼ (5) Broad-billed Prion *Pachyptila vittata*   ▼ (6) Broad-billed Prion *Pachyptila vittata*   ▼ (7) Antarctic Prion *Pachyptila desolata*

Spectacled Petrel *Procellaria conspicillata* Ringeye

50–58 cm, wingspan 134–144 cm, 1.0–1.3 kg. A large, dark brown petrel with a distinctive white spectacle extending from the back of the head under the eye and joining across the forehead. In most birds it is well-defined and often joined to a white chin patch; some have a narrow, broken spectacle, and a few only have a white forehead. Bill whitish with black skin between the bill plates; tip of bill dusky, appearing darker at a distance. **Behaviour**: Occurs singly or in small groups at sea; often follows ships. Largely nocturnal at colonies, but some active through the day. Breeds in burrows 1–3 m long dug into peat, usually sloping uphill with an entrance moat; often in colonies of 10–100 pairs, with multiple burrows sharing a common pool. Burrow entrances typically 25–35 cm across and 20–60 cm high; re-uses burrows in successive years. Most abundant in Tristan waters in summer; adults return to colonies in September, eggs laid late October, hatch in late December; fledge in March. Adults disperse to moult after breeding, then some return to colonies in May–June to display and clean-out burrows. Typical calls are deep, guttural rattles and melodic groans, given from inside burrow or open display areas nearby. Probably breeds annually, starting at 5–8 years old. Lays one white egg (average 81 × 55 mm) on sparse bed of green vegetation on mound of mud on burrow floor. Incubation by both adults for 56–60 days. Chick fed by both adults; brooded for first week or so; fledges after about 95 days. Adults and fledglings occasionally killed by skuas. Diet squid, fish, crustaceans, fishery discards and offal; forages by surface seizing, shallow plunging and diving with wings and feet to at least 12 m. Probably forages during day and night like closely-related White-chinned Petrel. **Distribution**: Breeds in Bog Fern and wet heath on higher parts of Inaccessible plateau. Endemic to Inaccessible, although may have occurred on Amsterdam (extirpated by introduced predators); disperses throughout temperate South Atlantic; rarely to Australia. **Population**: Some 10,000 pairs at Inaccessible, increasing at 7% per year since 1930s. **Conservation**: Critically Endangered, due to drowning on long-lines, but recent surveys indicate the population is still growing, following near-extinction caused by predation by feral pigs prior to 1930; mortality on long-lines perhaps less severe than initially estimated.

White-chinned Petrel *Procellaria aequinoctialis* Shoemaker, Cape Hen

50–58 cm, wingspan 134–146 cm, 1.1–1.5 kg. Common non-breeding visitor. Similar to Spectacled Petrel, but lacks white spectacle; bill has a whitish tip. White chin varies in size; usually small and hard to see, but occasionally larger, covering entire throat. Up to 14% of birds show some white on plumage other than white chin, usually on belly, but also on wings, tail or head; unlikely to have symmetrical spectacle marks. Biology similar to Spectacled Petrel. Some 2 million pairs breed at sub-Antarctic islands, with the vast majority at South Georgia; non-breeding birds disperse widely through the Southern Ocean. Vulnerable, due to drowning on long-lines and trawl cables.

Grey Petrel *Procellaria cinerea* Pediunker

50 cm, wingspan 115–130 cm, 950–1,200 g. A fairly large, silvery-grey petrel with a white belly and yellowish bill; underwings grey-brown. Easily told from Atlantic, White-headed and Soft-plumaged Petrels by its more languid flight, pale bill and distinctive plumage; from Cory's Shearwater by its dark underwings and heavier bill. **Behaviour**: Occurs singly at sea; sometimes follows ships. Largely nocturnal at colonies, but often arrive and depart in afternoon and early morning. Breeds in shallow burrows, often on stream banks or next to rock faces and boulders; burrow entrances sometimes flooded. Present offshore year round, but most abundant in winter; adults return to colonies in late February, eggs laid April–June, hatch June–August; fledge in September–December. Typical calls are a series of groaning moans lasting 1–2 seconds, followed by a long rattle. Probably breeds annually. Lays one white egg (average 81 × 56 mm); incubation by both adults for 55–65 days. Chick fed by both adults; brooded for 2–3 days; fledging period extremely variable, 87–165 days, possibly reflecting unpredictable food supply in winter. Diet mainly squid and fish, with some crustaceans and offal; forages by surface seizing, plunge diving from up to 8 m in air and diving with wings and feet for 'several minutes'. Often forages in association with whales. Adults and especially fledglings killed by skuas. **Distribution**: Breeds at 300–600 m on Gough, Tristan and probably Inaccessible; also at sub-Antarctic islands: Prince Edwards, Crozets, Kerguelen and islands off New Zealand; disperses widely in Southern Ocean, but scarce north of Subtropical Front. **Population**: Poorly known; at least 10,000 pairs on Gough and <100 on Tristan, where formerly abundant; globally some 70,000 pairs. **Conservation**: Near-Threatened, due to drowning on long-lines and predation by introduced mammals. Killed for food on Tristan historically; now protected, but still impacted by rats; chicks probably killed by mice on Gough.

▲◀ ▲ (1 and 2) Spectacled Petrel
Procellaria conspicillata

▼ (3) White-chinned Petrel
Procellaria aequinoctialis

▼ (4) Grey Petrel *Procellaria cinerea*

▼ (5) Grey Petrel *Procellaria cinerea*

Cory's Shearwater *Calonectris diomedea*

42–50 cm, wingspan 100–125 cm, 600–950 g. Uncommon summer non-breeding visitor. A large, broad-winged shearwater with a yellowish bill, rather uniform grey-brown upperparts and white underparts; underwing white with narrow brown leading edge and broader grey-brown trailing edge. Sometimes has whitish band across uppertail coverts. White underwing and languid flight action, low over water, separate it from Grey Petrel. Both smaller nominate and larger *C. d. borealis* found in Tristan waters. Occurs singly or in groups of 2–20 birds; frequently rests on water, especially in calm weather; seldom follows ships. Diet mainly epipelagic fish; also some squid and crustaceans. Forages by shallow plunging, sometimes taking garfish and flying fish in air; also pursuit dives up to 5–10 m. Often feeds in association with dolphins, tunas and other predators. Some 200,000 pairs breed in the boreal summer at islands in north-east Atlantic and Mediterranean; migrates south to South Atlantic and south-west Indian Oceans November–May, occasionally reaching Australia and New Zealand. Not threatened, although sometimes drowned on long-lines; impacted at colonies by introduced predators and human exploitation.

Great Shearwater *Puffinus gravis*   Petrel

43–51 cm, wingspan 100–118 cm, 720–1,100 g. A fairly large shearwater with a blackish-brown crown, scaly grey-brown upperparts, narrow white band across uppertail coverts and blackish tail; underparts mainly white with variable brown belly patch; underwings white with brown margins and brown-streaked underwing coverts. Bill rather long and slender. Darker above than Cory's Shearwater with black bill and distinctly capped appearance. **Behaviour**: Occurs singly or in small-large groups at sea; sometimes follows ships. Gathers in large rafts off breeding sites. Largely nocturnal at colonies, arriving at dusk, but active throughout the day once chicks hatch. Breeds in burrows 0.5–1.5 m long dug into peat, often under roots of *Spartina* tussock or *Phylica* trees, but up to 30% on ground under dense tussock grass. Burrow entrances typically 15–25 cm across, 12–15 cm high; re-uses burrows in successive years. Strongly seasonal; adults return to colonies from late August, although most arrive mid-September to court and prepare burrows; pre-laying exodus in late October; eggs laid early November, hatch early January; fledge in late April–May, after adults depart in mid-April. Typical calls are loud, raucous screams, given in air and on ground. Probably breeds annually. Lays one white egg (average 80 × 52 mm) on sparse bed of green vegetation or directly on ground. Incubation by both adults for 55 days. Chick fed by both adults; brooded for first week or so; fledges after 105–110 days. Adults and fledglings occasionally killed by skuas. Diet mainly fish; also some squid, crustaceans and fishery discards; forages by surface seizing, shallow plunging (rarely from 10 m in air) and diving with wings and feet, probably to at least 20 m. **Distribution**: Near-endemic to Tristan; elsewhere <100 pairs breed at Falklands; migrates to North Atlantic in winter, travelling to waters off Newfoundland and Greenland late May–early August for rapid moult, then returning south mainly along Brazil coast. Many visit Cape waters during October pre-laying exodus and again March–May; also ranges into south-west Indian Ocean; rarely to Australia and California. Breeds in virtually all habitats on Nightingale and Inaccessible; confined to coastal tussock on Gough. **Population**: 2–3 million pairs at Nightingale (saturated), 2 million at Inaccessible (possibly increasing), 1 million at Gough; status at Tristan unclear; possibly a few pairs remain. **Conservation**: Not threatened. Virtually extinct on Tristan due to collecting for food, habitat destruction and introduced predators. Impacted historically on Inaccessible by collecting and pigs. Currently protected at all islands except Nightingale, where adults, chicks and eggs harvested; up to 15,000 eggs and 50,000 chicks collected annually in 1970s, but fewer now. Chicks killed by mice on Gough. Most frequently killed bird on long-lines set in Tristan waters. Almost all birds contain plastic litter eaten at sea.

Sooty Shearwater *Puffinus griseus*

40–48 cm, wingspan 95–105 cm, 670–970 g. Uncommon; a fairly large, grey-brown shearwater with distinctive silvery underwing flashes. Smaller than White-chinned Petrel, with slender, dark grey bill; has straighter wings, stiffer flight action and longer, more slender head and bill than Great-winged and Kerguelen Petrels. Biology similar to Great Shearwater; calls a series of deep, guttural grunts, increasing in pitch and tempo. Diet fish, crustaceans, squid, salps and fishery wastes; dives up to 40 m (rarely 67 m). Some 5 million pairs breed mainly off New Zealand and Cape Horn, with smaller numbers at Falklands and south-east Australia; <10 pairs found breeding at Big Green Hill, Tristan in 1980s; may also breed in small numbers on other islands. Disperses throughout Southern Ocean; most migrate to North Pacific and North Atlantic in winter. Near-Threatened; population decreased by 37% over last 30 years at one key site; threats include drowning in fishing gear, introduced predators, collecting of chicks for food and perhaps changes in North Pacific circulation patterns.

Manx Shearwater *Puffinus puffinus*

30–36 cm, wingspan 76–88 cm, 300–490 g. Rare non-breeding visitor. A fairly small black-and-white shearwater, larger than Little Shearwater with a longer, heavier bill and more pointed wings with broader black trailing edges; flight action slower. Some 300,000 pairs breed at islands in North Atlantic March–September, migrating south into South Atlantic Ocean November–February, although some remain year round. Not threatened; longevity 47 years. Sometimes forages in association with whales and dolphins.

▲ **(1) Cory's Shearwater** *Calonectris diomedea*

▲ **(2) Great Shearwater** *Puffinus gravis*

▲ **(3) Great Shearwater** *Puffinus gravis*

▼ **(4) Great Shearwater** *Puffinus gravis*

▼ **(5) Sooty Shearwater** *Puffinus griseus*

▼ **(6) Manx Shearwater** *Puffinus puffinus*

Little Shearwater *Puffinus assimilis* Whistler, Nighthawk

25–30 cm, wingspan 58–67 cm, 180–300 g. A small black-and-white shearwater; upperparts often appear silvery-grey. Flight action distinctive: rapid bursts of flaps, barely raising wings above horizontal. Smaller than Manx Shearwater with a tiny bill and shorter, more rounded wings with narrower black trailing edges, especially on primaries. **Behaviour**: Occurs singly or in small groups at sea; often flies alongside ships. Arrives at colonies after dark; breeds in 0.5–1 m long burrows dug into peat under dense tussock grass. Present at sea year round; adults return to colonies intermittently February–July; eggs laid August–September after a pre-laying exodus of up to 1 month; hatch October–November; fledge in December–January. Flight call is a shrill, *preep preep*; ground call a laughing series of screeching whistles; female call deeper and harsher. Probably breeds annually. Lays one white egg (average 55 × 37 mm). Incubation by both adults for 52–58 days. Chick fed by both adults; brooded for first week or so; fledges after 70–76 days. Adults and fledglings killed by skuas; wings in middens 178–195 mm. Diet fish, squid and crustaceans; forages by surface seizing, shallow plunging and diving with wings and feet, probably to at least 20 m. **Distribution**: Breeds in coastal tussock and adjacent fern bush on Nightingale, Inaccessible and Gough; elsewhere breeds at Amsterdam, St Paul and islands off south-west Australia and New Zealand; disperses throughout the Southern Ocean. **Population**: Poorly known; perhaps 20,000 pairs, mainly at Inaccessible and Gough; globally 300,000 pairs. **Conservation**: Not threatened; probably extinct on Tristan due to introduced predators and collecting for food; chicks likely killed by mice on Gough.

Kerguelen Petrel *Lugensa brevirostris* Blue Nighthawk

33–36 cm, wingspan 80–85 cm, 200–420 g. A fairly small, dark grey petrel with silver highlights along leading edge of wing and bases of lower primaries; distinctly large headed and thick-necked; flight action stiffer than gadfly petrels. Smaller and more bull-necked than Great-winged Petrel, with shorter wings and distinctive flight action; distinct from rare dark morph of Soft-plumaged Petrel by its more bulky, compact shape, shorter tail, large eye and silver highlights on the wing. Legs usually dark grey; rarely pinkish. **Behaviour**: Occurs singly or in small groups at sea; seldom follows ships; often hovers high above sea. Gathers off breeding sites at dusk, coming ashore after dark. Breeds in burrows 1–2 m long dug into peat, often on steep slopes and gulleys; many nests have an entrance moat. Adults return to colonies August; pre-laying exodus in September; eggs laid October, hatch end November–December; fledge at end January–February. Burrow call is a series of loud, raucous squeals. Probably breeds annually. Lays one white egg (average 57 × 45 mm), rounder than other petrel eggs. Incubation by both adults for 46–51 days. Chick fed by both adults; brooded for only 1–2 days; fledges after 59–62 days, unusually short. Adults and fledglings killed by skuas; wings in middens 245–274 mm. Diet mainly squid; also some fish and crustaceans; forages mainly by surface seizing; rarely surface plunges and shallow dives. **Distribution**: Breeds in relatively short vegetation above 200 m on Gough and Tristan, possibly Inaccessible; elsewhere at sub-Antarctic Prince Edwards, Crozets and Kerguelen. Ranges widely in the Southern Ocean; adults disperse south to Antarctica after breeding; occasionally irrupts north of its usual range in winter. **Population**: At least 20,000 pairs at Gough, possibly many more; >100 at Inaccessible; may breed at Nightingale; globally c100,000 pairs. **Conservation**: Not threatened. Probably extinct on Tristan due to collecting for food and introduced predators. Some chicks on Gough probably killed by mice.

Soft-plumaged Petrel *Pterodroma mollis* Littlest Whitebreast, Whistler

32–37 cm, wingspan 85–95 cm, 280–350 g. A fairly small, slender, grey and white petrel with erratic, agile flight. Wings held well forward, bent at wrist; tail long, giving distinctive short-necked shape in flight. Typical pale morph has grey upperparts with darker M across upperwings and back; underparts white with variable grey collar; underwings dark grey with paler highlights. Legs and base of toes pink; tips black. Rare dark morph is easily confused with Kerguelen Petrel, but is more slender, longer tailed and retains a darker M across the upperwings. **Behaviour**: Occurs singly or in small groups at sea; seldom follows ships. Gathers off breeding sites at dusk, coming ashore after dark. Breeds in burrows 1–2 m long dug into peat; burrow entrances typically 15 cm across, 9 cm high; may occasionally breed on ground under dense tussock. Adults return to colonies August–September; pre-laying exodus lasts up to 4–5 weeks, but some birds present throughout; eggs laid November–December, hatch late January–February (rarely to April); fledge in April–May. Flight call is a distinctive, wailing moan *huuooo*; burrow call a loud, excited yelping. Probably breeds annually. Lays one white egg (average 60 × 43 mm) on a mat of vegetation. Incubation by both adults for 50 days. Chick fed by both adults; brooded for first week or so; fledges after 90 days. Adults and fledglings killed by skuas; wings in middens 233–263 mm. Diet mainly squid; also some fish and crustaceans; forages mainly by surface seizing; rarely surface plunges and shallow dives. **Distribution**: Breeds in fern bush and coastal tussock at Tristan, Nightingale, Inaccessible and Gough; elsewhere at sub-Antarctic islands: Prince Edwards, Crozets, Kerguelen, Amsterdam and islands off Tasmania and New Zealand; ranges widely in South Atlantic, Indian and south-west Pacific Oceans. **Population**: Some 400,000 pairs at Gough; at least 10,000 on Inaccessible and 1,000 on Nightingale; 100 at Tristan; globally <1 million pairs. **Conservation**: Not threatened. Almost extinct on Tristan due to collecting for food and introduced predators. Some chicks on Gough probably killed by mice.

▲ (1) Little Shearwater *Puffinus assimilis*　　　　　　　　▲ (2) Little Shearwater *Puffinus assimilis*

▲▼ (3 and 4) Kerguelen Petrel *Lugensa brevirostris*　　　▲▼ (5 and 6) Soft-plumaged Petrel *Pterodroma mollis*　　　▲ (7) Soft-plumaged Petrel *Pterodroma mollis,* ▼ (8) dark morph

Great-winged Petrel *Pterodroma macroptera*   Black Haglet (corruption of eaglet)

38–42 cm, wingspan 98–102 cm, 400–700 g. A fairly large dark brown petrel with long, slender wings and a stout black bill. Smaller than White-chinned Petrel with more dashing flight and short, dark bill. Larger than Kerguelen Petrel with relatively smaller head and longer wings; plumage browner and lacks silvery highlights along leading edge of wing. Chicks have grey down and blackish legs. **Behaviour**: Occurs singly or in small groups at sea; often rests on water in calm weather. Seldom follows ships. Gathers off breeding sites at dusk, coming ashore after dark. Breeds in burrows 0.6–3 m long dug into peat. Adults return to colonies from mid-March; pre-laying exodus from mid-May; eggs laid late May–mid-June, hatch late July–early August; fledge in November. Typical calls are sharp, liquid whistles given by pairs in flight; burrow call is a high-pitched *ki-ki-ki-ki*. Most pairs breed annually; starts breeding from six years old. Lays one white egg (average 67 × 48 mm). Incubation by both adults for 52–58 days. Chick fed by both adults; brooded for a few days; fledges after 100–120 days. Adults and fledglings killed by skuas; wings in middens 290–320 mm. Diet mainly squid; also some fish, crustaceans and fishery discards; forages mainly by surface seizing; rarely surface plunges and shallow dives. **Distribution**: Breeds in fern bush and wet heath up to 1,400 m at Tristan, 500 m at Gough, perhaps at Inaccessible; elsewhere at sub-Antarctic Prince Edwards, Crozets, Kerguelen and Amsterdam; *P. m. gouldi* off North Island, New Zealand. Disperses widely in South Atlantic, Indian and south-west Pacific Oceans, moving north into warm temperate waters in summer. **Population**: At least 10,000 pairs at Gough; 1,000 at Tristan in 1970s, but probably fewer now. Globally some 400,000 pairs. **Conservation**: Almost extinct on Tristan due to collecting for food and introduced predators; thousands of chicks collected each October in 1950s. Currently protected, but chicks killed by rats on Tristan and mice on Gough.

Atlantic Petrel *Pterodroma incerta*   White-breasted Black Haglet, Biggest Whitebreast

42–45 cm, wingspan 110–115 cm, 440–700 g. A large, chocolate brown gadfly petrel with a white lower breast and belly; black bill is short and heavy. Appreciably larger and more bulky than Soft-plumaged Petrel; flight less erratic, but still swift like all gadfly petrels. A rare dark morph has a grey-brown belly; told from Great-winged Petrel by pink (not blackish) legs. Chicks have grey down and bluish-pink legs. **Behaviour**: Occurs singly or in small groups at sea; seldom follows ships. Gathers off breeding sites at dusk; starts coming ashore just before complete darkness. Breeds in burrows 0.5–2.5 m long dug into peat in fern bush and coastal tussock; burrow entrances typically 16–25 cm across, 11–15 cm high; re-uses burrows in successive years. Adults return to colonies late March–April; pre-laying exodus from late April–mid-June; eggs laid mid-June–late July, hatch August–early September; fledge in December–January. Flight calls are high-pitched, rather raucous whistles; burrow call a donkey-like braying *kaaaaar-haaa*. Breeding frequency unknown; possibly largely biennial given protracted breeding cycle. Lays one white egg (average 69 × 50 mm). Incubation by both adults for 50–60 days; nesting chamber has distinctive white feathers. Chick fed by both adults; brooded for a few days; fledges after 135–140 days, exceptionally long for a bird of this size. Breeding success on Gough only 20%, mainly due to high chick mortality. Adults and fledglings killed by skuas; wings in middens 308–342 mm. Diet mainly squid; also some fish, crustaceans and fishery discards; mainly forages by surface seizing. **Distribution**: Endemic to Tristan; breeds up to 400 m on Gough; 600 m at Tristan, where rare and confined mainly to south-east quadrant; may breed on Inaccessible plateau. Disperses widely in South Atlantic; rare in south-west Indian Ocean. **Population**: Some 1.8 million pairs at Gough; <100 at Tristan. **Conservation**: Endangered; almost extinct on Tristan due to collecting for food and introduced predators; thousands of chicks collected each October in 1950s. Currently protected, but most chicks killed by rats. High chick mortality on Gough mainly due to mouse predation.

White-headed Petrel *Pterodroma lessonii*

40–45 cm, wingspan 105–110 cm, 500–800 g. Uncommon non-breeding visitor. A fairly large, heavily-built petrel with a distinctive whitish head and tail and black eye patch. Upperwing dark grey, linking across lower back in dark M. Underparts white, with pale grey collar; underwings dark grey. Larger and heavier than Soft-plumaged Petrel with paler head and tail; flight more direct. Distinct from Grey Petrel by its paler head and uppertail, distinctive gadfly petrel shape and short, stout black bill. Food mainly squid and crustaceans; forages by surface-seizing. Successful breeders seldom breed in successive years; some 250,000 pairs breed each year at sub-Antarctic islands: Crozets, Kerguelen and New Zealand islands; disperses throughout Southern Ocean. Not threatened.

(1 and 2) Atlantic Petrel
Pterodroma incerta

(3) Atlantic Petrel
Pterodroma incerta

(4) Great-winged Petrel
Pterodroma macroptera

(5) White-headed Petrel
Pterodroma lessonii

Common Diving Petrel *Pelecanoides urinatrix* — Flying Pinnamin

20–25 cm, wingspan 33–38 cm, 80–140 g. A small, compact petrel dark grey above merging into whitish underparts. Wings small and rounded, adapted for propulsion underwater; very high wing-loading results in fast, fluttering flight low over water; often crashes into wave-crests. **Behaviour**: Occurs singly or in small groups at sea; does not follow ships. Often feeds in large, loose flocks close to islands. Usually observed on water or flushed by ship. Breeds in shallow burrows 0.2–1.5 m long, often in banks or under rocks. Adults return to colonies mid-July; eggs laid August–September, hatch October–November; fledge December– January; cycle 3–4 weeks later at Gough. Adults remain inshore until May, then disperse offshore in mid-winter. Typical call is a fairly loud note, rising in pitch, sometimes followed by a series of sharp notes: *kooo-ah* or *kerrraaaaa-ek ek ek*; given in air and on ground. Probably breeds annually; returns to colonies from one year old and starts breeding at 2–3 years; annual survival only 75%, much lower than other petrels and albatrosses. Lays one white egg (average 38 × 30 mm). Incubation by both adults for about 55 days. Chick fed by both adults; fledges after 49–59 days. Adults and fledglings killed by skuas. Diet mainly small crustaceans; forages by pursuit diving using small wings for propulsion; legs used for tight turns; dives up to 60 m. **Distribution**: Breeds in fern bush and coastal tussock at Nightingale, Inaccessible and Gough; elsewhere at Falklands, sub-Antarctic islands and islands off South Australia and New Zealand; ranges locally up to 1,000 km from colonies, mainly in winter. **Population**: Crudely estimated at least 10,000 pairs at Nightingale, 5,000 at Inaccessible and 20,000 at Gough; extinct at Tristan. Globally perhaps 7 million pairs. **Conservation**: Not threatened. Extinct on Tristan due to habitat loss and introduced predators; chicks possibly killed by mice on Gough.

STORM PETRELS Hydrobatidae

Small pelagic seabirds with relatively large, broad wings, giving low wing loadings (mass per unit of wing area); feed by surface seizing or pattering; rarely dive. Nostrils tube-shaped, joined on top of bill. Three toes webbed for swimming and pattering on water. Twenty-two species in eight genera worldwide; three breeding species at Tristan; two non-breeding visitors, two vagrants.

Wilson's Storm Petrel *Oceanites oceanicus*

15–19 cm, wingspan 38–42 cm, 30–40 g. Fairly common non-breeding visitor. A small black storm petrel with a broad white rump and rather long, square tail; legs long; toes extend beyond tail tip in flight. Often shows paler brown bars across upperwing coverts. Lacks white underparts of all breeding storm petrels; smaller than Leach's Storm Petrel with shorter, straighter wings and more erratic, flappy flight action. In hand, has yellow webs between toes. Strongly attracted to ships; feeds on small crustaceans, fish and squid by surface pattering. At least 5 million pairs breed March–May at ice-free areas in Antarctica, Cape Horn, Falklands and sub-Antarctic Islands: South Orkneys, South Georgia, South Sandwiches, Bouvet Islands, Crozets, Kerguelen and Heard; disperses widely through almost all oceans, although rare in north Pacific. Vagrant **European Storm Petrel** *Hydrobates pelagicus* is smaller and more compact, with faster flight action and short legs not extending beyond tail tip; white flash on underwing diagnostic; breeds in North Atlantic, winters in coastal waters off South Africa.

Grey-backed Storm Petrel *Garrodia nereis*

15–18 cm, wingspan 38–40 cm, 26–34 g. A tiny storm petrel with black head and breast, merging into a pale blue-grey back, upperwing coverts, rump and upper tail. Belly and underwings white. Smaller than White-bellied Storm Petrel; lacks distinct white rump. **Behaviour**: Occurs singly at sea; easily overlooked as it merges into grey sea; seldom follows ships. Comes ashore after dark; silent in air; a repeated, wheezy croak on ground. Breeds in shallow burrows up to 0.5 m long in dense vegetation. Present at sea year round; breeding phenology poorly known; adults ashore August–April. Lays one egg (average 31 × 23 mm), white with fine reddish speckles. Incubation by both adults for about 45 days; egg often abandoned for 1–5 days. Chick fed by both adults; fledging period unknown. Adults killed by skuas. Diet mainly barnacle larvae; also other small crustaceans and fish; forages by surface pattering. **Distribution**: Breeds in coastal tussock, fern bush and wet heath at Gough; elsewhere at Falklands and sub-Antarctic islands: South Georgia, Prince Edward, Crozets, Kerguelen and New Zealand Islands. Disperses in sub-Antarctic waters around breeding islands; scarce at sea off Tristan, Nightingale and Inaccessible. **Population**: Crudely estimated at least 10,000 pairs at Gough; perhaps 100,000 pairs worldwide. **Conservation**: Not threatened; chicks probably killed by mice on Gough.

▲ (1) Common Diving Petrel *Pelecanoides urinatrix* trailing a trematode anklet

▲ (2) Common Diving Petrel *Pelecanoides urinatrix*

▲ (3) Wilson's Storm Petrel *Oceanites oceanicus*

▲ (4) Wilson's Storm Petrel *Oceanites oceanicus*

▼ (5) Grey-backed Storm Petrel *Garrodia nereis*

▼ (6 and 7) Grey-backed Storm Petrel *Garrodia nereis*

White-faced Storm Petrel *Pelagodroma marina* — Skipjack

20–21 cm, wingspan 41–44 cm, 40–60 g. A pale grey-brown storm petrel with white underparts, paler rump, extremely long legs and blackish tail and flight feathers; toes long with slender, pointed nails; toe webs yellow. Distinguished from all other storm petrels by its white throat and patterned face. **Behaviour**: Occurs singly or in small groups at sea; seldom follows ships. Dances and jumps low over the water with legs trailing. Comes ashore after dark; remains offshore until chicks hatch, then often feeds in kelp beds around islands. Silent in air; gives low, moaning calls *oooo oooo* or *ooo-aaa-ooo* from ground. Breeds in shallow burrows 0.3–0.8 m long, often little more than a runway through dense vegetation. Adults return to colonies July–August; eggs laid August–September, hatch mid-October–November; fledge late December–January. Lays one egg (average 36 × 26 mm), white, sometimes with fine reddish speckles at large end. Incubation by both adults for about 50 days; egg frequently abandoned for 1–3 days. Chick fed by both adults; fledges after 55–65 days. Adults often killed by skuas; wings in middens 149–173 mm. Some have 'anklets' formed by gelatinous larvae of a parasitic trematode that get entangled around their legs when they feed on euphausids. Feeds on small crustaceans, fish and squid by surface pattering. **Distribution**: Breeds in coastal tussock and fern bush at Nightingale, Inaccessible and Gough; extinct at Tristan; elsewhere at temperate islands in north-east Atlantic and off Australia and New Zealand. Disperses widely around breeding islands. **Population**: Crudely estimated at least 10,000 pairs on Gough, 5,000 on Inaccessible and 1,000 on Nightingale; global population some 2 million pairs. **Conservation**: Not threatened; most contain ingested plastic; chicks probably killed by mice on Gough.

White-bellied Storm Petrel *Fregetta grallaria* — Storm Pigeon

20–22 cm, wingspan 46–48 cm, 45–63 g. A fairly large, grey-brown storm-petrel with a white rump, broad wings and rounded tail; toes short with broad, blunt nails; toe webs black. At close range, mantle feathers fringed whitish. Easily distinguished from Wilson's and Leach's Storm Petrels by its white belly and central underwing; from White-faced Storm Petrel by its black head and breast. Grey-backed Storm Petrel is smaller and more slender with a blue-grey rump and upper tail. **Black-bellied Storm Petrel** *F. tropica* is a rare vagrant; has a black stripe down the central belly, but this can be hard to confirm in the field as the bird rapidly rocks from side-to-side; mantle darker brown. **Behaviour**: Usually occurs singly at sea; seldom follows ships. Flies low over the water, rocking from side-to-side and often dragging its feet or belly. Comes ashore after dark, but occasionally flies around during day at Inaccessible, possibly after being chased out of burrows by Tristan Thrushes. Breeds in shallow burrows up to 1 m long in dense vegetation and in rock crevices. Present at sea year round; adults return to colonies from late September, but only lays January; chicks hatch mid-February; fledge in April–May. Flight and ground call is a long, high-pitched, ventriloqual whistle *peeeeeeeee*. Probably breeds annually. Lays one egg (average 36 × 26 mm), pinkish-white with fine reddish speckles concentrated at broad end. Incubation by both adults for about 35–40 days. Chick fed by both adults; fledges after about 70 days. Adults killed by skuas and Tristan Thrushes; main prey of non-breeding skuas at Inaccessible; wings in middens 145–182 mm. Diet small crustaceans, fish and squid; forages by surface seizing. **Distribution**: Breeds in coastal tussock and fern bush at Nightingale, Inaccessible and Gough; elsewhere at temperate islands in southern Indian Ocean (St Paul) and south Pacific (Lord Howe, Kermadec, Rapa and Juan Fernandez). Disperses widely in South Atlantic, Indian and Pacific Oceans, moving north into subtropical waters. **Population**: At least 50,000 pairs at Inaccessible, 1,000 at Nightingale; estimated 10,000 pairs at Gough, but probably decreasing. Global population only 100,000 pairs. **Conservation**: Extinct on Tristan due to introduced predators; chicks probably killed by mice on Gough.

Leach's Storm Petrel *Oceanodroma leucorhoa*

19–22 cm, wingspan 45–48 cm, 40–52 g. Rare non-breeding visitor. A fairly large, blackish-brown storm petrel with long wings, forked tail and narrow white rump, sometimes divided centrally; paler bar across upperwing coverts. Flight action distinctive; glides more than other storm petrels with wings held angled and bowed at wrist. Often sits on water in calm weather, frequently with Great-winged Petrels. Seldom follows ships. Diet small fish, crustaceans and squid; forages by surface seizing. Some 8 million pairs breed mainly at islands in North Atlantic and North Pacific; migrates into South Atlantic November–April. Not threatened.

◀ ▲ **(1 and 2) White-faced Storm Petrel**
Pelagodroma marina

▼ **(3) White-bellied Storm Petrel**
Fregetta grallaria

▼ **(4) White-bellied Storm Petrel**
Fregetta grallaria

▼ **(5) White-bellied Storm Petrel**
Fregetta grallaria

▼ **(6) Leach's Storm Petrel**
Oceanodroma leucorhoa

SKUAS, GULLS AND TERNS Laridae

Small to fairly large seabirds; lack tube-like nostrils of petrels and albatrosses. Three toes webbed for swimming. Skuas are pugnacious with strong claws and plated bills; attack other birds and steal their food. Gulls are familiar generalist omnivores. Terns are elegant birds with long slender wings, pointed bills and often forked tails; feed by plunge-diving or surface picking. Occur mainly in coastal waters, but a few species are truly pelagic. One hundred and seven species in 20 genera worldwide; three breeding species at Tristan; two non-breeding visitors, five vagrants.

Tristan Skua *Catharacta antarctica hamiltoni*   Seahen

52–64 cm, wingspan 130–160 cm, 1.2–1.8 kg; females slightly larger. A large, brown gull-like bird with broad rounded wings and large white flashes in primary bases. Bill dark grey; legs blackish. Plumage rather variable, often streaked and mottled golden in adults; cap blackish. Juvenile has rather plain rufous-brown plumage and reduced white patches in wings. Downy chicks tan brown with dark grey bill and blue-grey legs. **South Polar Skua** *C. maccormicki* is a rare vagrant; slightly smaller and more slender; plumage unstreaked, often colder grey-brown with paler feathering at the base of the bill and hind-neck. **Behaviour**: Usually occurs singly at sea, but up to 50 gather at fishing boats. Flight direct and powerful, accelerating with deep strokes. Pairs breed singly or in loose groups in open grassy areas. Strongly territorial, chasing intruding skuas. Non-breeders forced into large 'clubs', often along the coast or near bathing pools. Present year round, but scarce on islands in winter; breeding protracted, with eggs laid September–early January, chicks fledge December–March. Display is a series of 8–10 loud, raucous notes (two per second) uttered with wings raised and neck arched; both sexes call. Pairs usually remain together for successive breeding attempts; breed annually. One record of a trio of two males and one female breeding at Gough. Probably start breeding at 5–6 years old, but shortage of territories may delay breeding. Nest is a shallow scrape. Lays 1–2 eggs (70 × 51 mm), pale brown with dark brown spots and mottling. Incubating bird can only brood two eggs, resting them on their feet; occasional records of three-egg clutches probably laid by two females. Incubation by both adults for 28–32 days. Chicks fed by both adults; brooded for first week, but guarded closely throughout; adults give plaintive alarm call and dive at intruders; small chicks crouch motionless; larger chicks run away and hide. Chicks fledge after 55–60 days; remain on territory for 3–4 weeks then gather in clubs. Diet mainly seabirds; also carrion, fish, offal, rats, goose barnacles and land birds. Seabird prey varies between territories; main prey of most breeding birds are Broad-billed Prions, Soft-plumaged Petrels and Great Shearwaters; penguin eggs and chicks in some territories; non-breeding birds at Inaccessible mainly eat storm petrels. Non-breeders move between islands; rats caught on Tristan found in pellets at Inaccessible. Mainly kill seabirds at night on ground, walking around listening for movement; attack with bill only. Also catch birds in flight during day and dig up burrows to reach adults and chicks. Breeding pairs store carcasses in larders, sometimes returning to feed on scraps from past kills. **Distribution**: Endemic to Tristan, Nightingale, Inaccessible and Gough, breeding in all habitats up to 1,200 m; disperses at sea in winter; range unknown. Usually regarded as a subspecies of Subantarctic Skua *C. a. lonnbergi* (breeds Antarctic Peninsula and sub-Antarctic islands) and Falkland Skua *C. a. antarctica* (Falklands and southern Argentina). **Population**: Some 1,000 pairs at Gough, 100 at Inaccessible, 100 at Nightingale and <10 at Tristan; also large numbers of non-breeding birds in addition to breeding pairs; at least 200 at Inaccessible, 500 at Gough and 100 at Nightingale. Globally some 12,000 pairs. **Conservation**: Not threatened; population at Tristan greatly reduced by persecution.

Long-tailed Jaeger (Skua) *Stercorarius longicaudus*

35–40 cm plus 15–25 cm tail streamers in breeding plumage; wingspan 100–110 cm, 220–400 g. Uncommon non-breeding visitor from Holarctic tundra. A small, tern-like jaeger. Plumage varies seasonally and with age, but always rather cold grey-brown above with white in upperwing confined to white shafts of outer two primaries. Adult has dark cap, yellow wash on neck and smoky grey body; long, slender tail streamers in breeding plumage. Young birds have barred underwing, rumps and vents. Flight buoyant; flaps continuously, usually 5–20 m above sea; frequently rests on water. Occurs singly or in small groups November–April. Two other Holarctic-breeding jaegers are vagrants: **Arctic Jaeger** *S. parasiticus* is larger and heavier, with shorter, broader wings, darker brown upperparts and more extensive white in outerwing; adult tail streamers shorter. **Pomarine Jaeger** *S. pomarinus* is even larger, with a distinctly deep chest, pale base to bill and even more white in outer wing; adults have heavier breast band and diagnostic twisted, spoon-shaped tail streamers in breeding plumage.

▲▼ (1 and 2) Tristan Skua *Catharacta antarctica hamiltoni*

▼ (3) Tristan Skua, chicks

▼ (4) Long-tailed Jaeger
Stercorarius longicaudus

Kelp Gull *Larus dominicanus*

55–65 cm, wingspan 128–142 cm, 900–1,340 g. Vagrant from South America, South Africa or sub-Antarctic islands, mainly in winter. A large gull; adult has black back and upperwings with white trailing edge; head, body and tail white; bill yellow with red spot on gonys. Most records of immature birds; brown above streaked whitish; tail white with dark tip; neck and underparts white, variably streaked and mottled brown; bill blackish. Franklin's Gull *L. pipixcan* is a vagrant from North America that winters in South America; smaller with a grey back, white tail (tipped blackish in immature), blackish head with white crescents around eye and dull reddish bill. Upperwing grey with broad white trailing edge and black subterminal band to outer primaries.

Antarctic Tern *Sterna vittata tristanensis*   Kingbird

38–43 cm, wingspan 76–80 cm, 110–170 g. A fairly small, grey and white tern with a full black cap, long outer-tail streamers and striking red bill and legs in breeding plumage; underparts grey, contrasting with white cheek. Non-breeding birds lose streamers and have a white forehead; appear heavy-bodied. Juveniles washed brown on head, back and sides of breast; mantle and wing coverts barred blackish; moults into grey backed immature plumage 1–6 months after fledging, but retains some barred wing coverts; bill and legs blackish-red. Downy chick is pale brown with darker bars above. **Behaviour**: Occurs singly, in pairs or small groups, usually within sight of islands, but at sea on migration. Roosts communally when not breeding; sometimes rests on water. A few remain year round, but most present September–May. Breeding protracted, possibly due to repeat clutches after breeding failures: lays November–February, chicks fledge mid-January–April. Breeds singly or in loose colonies on ledges at coastal cliffs and stacks; rarely at back of boulder beaches. Males courtship feed females; pairs display with harsh *chit-chit krrrr* calls while raising head and tail, or in tandem display flights. Lays 1–2 eggs (45 × 32 mm), pale olive blotched dark brown. Incubation by both adults for 23–25 days. Chicks fed by both adults; fledge after 28–32 days; fed by adults for several weeks after fledging. Pugnacious; adults give harsh alarm call and dive at intruders near nest or chicks; chicks crouch motionless. Adults occasionally killed by skuas. Diet small fish and crustaceans (amphipods, isopods) caught by plunge-diving or surface picking. **Distribution**: *S. v. tristanensis* endemic to Tristan, Nightingale, Inaccessible and Gough; winters on south coast of South Africa. Other subspecies breed at Antarctic Peninsula and sub-Antarctic islands, dispersing north in winter. **Population**: Some 50 pairs at Tristan, 200 at Nightingale, 100 at Inaccessible, 500 at Gough; globally some 50,000 pairs. **Conservation**: Not threatened; formerly more common on Tristan, breeding along beaches; probably displaced by rats and cats.

Arctic Tern *Sterna paradiseus*

33–35 cm, wingspan 75–85 cm, 80–110 g. Uncommon non-breeding visitor. Easily confused with Antarctic Tern, but has a shorter, more slender bill and much shorter legs; underparts paler grey; lacks heavy belly. Underwing has more translucent primaries with contrasting trailing edge and blackish outer web of outer primary; edges of tail feathers grey (not white). Breeds in Holarctic, migrating throughout Southern Ocean October–May.

Brown Noddy *Anous stolidus*   Woodpigeon

40–45 cm, wingspan 80–86 cm, 160–230 g. A sleek grey-brown tern with blackish flight feathers, a distinctive pale crown, white eye crescents and a slender black bill; tail long and broad with a notched end. Downy chick sooty brown with paler crown. **Behaviour**: Occurs singly or in small groups, usually close inshore. Present at islands September–March (rarely May), arriving end September at Gough; some depart Tristan by mid-February. Eggs laid mid-October–early January, chicks fledge January–March. Breeds singly or in loose colonies on ledges on coastal cliffs and in *Phylica* and other trees, up to 1 km inland on plateau of Inaccessible. Utters harsh *gaarrrr* in flight; also displays orange tongue by gaping and raising tongue. Builds a flimsy nest of *Spartina* and other vegetation on cliff sites, but tree nests are substantial, made of twigs; re-used in successive years. Lays one egg (52 × 35 mm), cream blotched reddish-brown and pale grey. Incubation by both adults for 32–36 days. Chicks fed by both adults; fledge after 55–60 days; fed by adults for several weeks after fledging. Much less aggressive to intruders than Antarctic Tern. Diet mainly epipelagic fish (saury) caught by surface picking or shallow surface dives. Longevity 25 years. **Distribution**: Breeds at Tristan, Nightingale, Inaccessible and Gough; winter range unknown. Elsewhere breeds at islands throughout the tropics. **Population**: Some 40 pairs at Tristan, 300 at Nightingale, 50 at Inaccessible, 200 at Gough; globally some 300,000 pairs. **Conservation**: Not threatened.

▲ Kelp Gull *Larus dominicanus*, LEFT (1) adult, RIGHT (2) juvenile

▲ Antarctic Tern *Sterna vittata tristanensis*, LEFT (3) adult, RIGHT (4) juvenile

▼ Brown Noddy *Anous stolidus* LEFT (5) adult, RIGHT (6) chick

LAND BIRDS

The islands support seven endemic land birds; two rails (Rallidae), one thrush (Turdidae) and four 'buntings' derived from South American finches (Thraupini). One rail and a bunting went extinct at Tristan before 1900. Numerous vagrant land birds also arrive sporadically, indicating the amazing numbers of birds that stray off course during their migrations or post-fledging dispersal.

Inaccessible Rail *Atlantisia rogersi*   Little Island Cock

13–15 cm, 34–52 g. A tiny rail with soft, fluffy-looking plumage, slender bill and bright red eye. Head and underparts dark sooty-grey; remainder of upperparts rich brown with fine white spots on wing coverts and vent; bill and legs grey. Female paler and slightly smaller; immature like female with dull brown eyes. Chick has blackish down, bill and legs. **Behaviour**: Creeps through dense cover, dashing across openings like a mouse. Uses favoured runways, which resemble mouse runs; also climbs up sloping *Phylica* branches and dense sheaves of *Spartina*. Occurs singly, in pairs or family groups. Pairs defend territories, advertising with a trilling song, recalling a Little Grebe; contact call is a soft *chik* or *chik-ik*; also a sharp *chip* alarm call when skuas fly over and a seldom heard *weet-rrrrr*, possibly only when herding chicks. Raises its wings and makes loud squealing calls when confronting an intruder. Male courtship feeds female. Breeds October–January; nest is a woven ball of *Spartina* leaves and other grasses and sedges with an entrance at the narrow end, reached through a short entrance tunnel. Nest built by both sexes on the ground among dense vegetation. Lays two eggs (33 × 23 mm), creamy white with fine reddish-brown spots. Eggs incubated by both adults; bird off nest often delivers food to its mate. Chicks precocial; leave nest within one day of hatching but return to the nest to be brooded at night for a few days; remain under close supervision and fed by adults for several weeks. Adults defend eggs and chicks vigorously against Tristan Thrushes; occasionally eaten by skuas. Diet mainly invertebrates, including earthworms, centipedes, caterpillars, moths, amphipods and weevils; also seeds and berries. Mainly diurnal, but also calls at night. **Distribution**: Endemic to Inaccessible; occurs in all habitats from edges of boulder beaches and vegetated cliffs to highest peaks; most abundant in marshy areas. **Population**: Some 5,000 pairs. **Conservation**: Vulnerable, given its small range and susceptibility to accidental introduction of predators such as rats and mice.

Gough Moorhen *Gallinula comeri*   Island Cock

32–36 cm, 400–530 g. A fairly large, robust rail with a yellow-tipped red bill and red frontal shield; resembles a Common Moorhen, but with reduced wings and more robust, largely red legs. Adult is mainly sooty grey with a warm brown mantle and wings; undertail coverts and flanks striped white; eye dark red. Juvenile is dull grey-brown with olive-yellow bill and legs. **Behaviour**: Remains in dense cover; sometimes climbs larger branches of *Phylica* trees and enters seabird burrows. Occurs singly, in pairs or family groups. Pairs defend territories, advertising with a loud *chuk-chik-chuk*; also a softer contact call *kek-ek-kek*. Breeds September–February (mainly October–December); nest is an open cup built by both sexes low down in dense vegetation, usually a dense tussock; nest often reached through a tunnel up to 1 m long. Lays 2–5 (rarely 6) eggs (51 × 34 mm); pale buff with brown and purplish spots and blotches. Eggs incubated by both adults for 20–22 days; partner may feed incubating bird on nest. Chicks precocial; leave nest shortly after hatching but remain under close supervision for several weeks. Pairs may raise two broods per season, with chicks from first brood assisting with rearing second brood. Diet mainly invertebrates, seeds and other plant material; also scavenges from skua kills and takes abandoned seabird eggs. **Distribution**: Endemic to Gough; introduced to Tristan. Occurs in coastal tussock and fern bush where there is sufficient cover to avoid skuas. At Tristan, range is still expanding, but is now almost all around the Base; occurs almost to sea level at Sandy Point, but not found on Settlement Plain. **Population**: Poorly known; perhaps 3,500 pairs at Gough and 2,000 at Tristan. **Conservation**: Vulnerable, given its small range and susceptibility to accidental introduction of predators. **Tristan Moorhen** *G. nesiotis* occurred on Tristan; apparently went extinct before 1900, killed off by feral cats, hunting and perhaps rats. Current population at Tristan likely derived from eight Gough Moorhens released at Sandy Point in Gough Expedition in 1956, although there is a chance that some Tristan Moorhens persisted. It is unknown why Tristan Moorhen disappeared when the very similar Gough Moorhen is thriving at Tristan.

Purple Gallinule *Porphyrula martinica*   Guttersnake

30–36 cm, 170–195 g, vagrants as little as 120 g. Surprisingly frequent vagrant, mainly in autumn; some remain through winter, especially at Tristan. A fairly large, slender rail. Adult has purple-blue head and body, greeny-blue mantle and wings, and white undertail coverts; bill red with yellow tip; frontal shield powder blue; legs yellow. Almost all records of juveniles; duller with buffy-brown head and body; bill and frontal shield olive-yellow; moults into adult plumage in late winter. Up to 47 in one year at Tristan, mainly around Edinburgh, taking shelter in gardens and among flax. Other vagrant rails include **Common Moorhen** *Gallinula chloropus*, **Red-gartered Coot** *Fulica armillata* and **Paint-billed Crake** *Neocrex erythrops*. .

▲ **(1) Inaccessible Rail** *Atlantisia rogersi*, chick

◀ **(2) Inaccessible Rail, adult**

▼ **(3) Gough Moorhen** *Gallinula comeri*

▲ **(4) Gough Moorhen** *Gallinula comeri*

Tristan Thrush *Nesocichla eremita*   Starchy

23–26 cm, 80–120 g. A compact thrush with a long, stout bill, short, rounded wings and long, robust legs and feet; apparently evolved from a *Turdus* thrush vagrant from South America. Warm brown above with narrow buffy tips to wing coverts; face buffy; underparts buffy, with large brown spots. Bill dark grey; legs pinkish-grey. Juvenile has peachy-buff stripes on back feathers, broad buff primary bases and edges to wing coverts, and underparts more finely spotted blackish-brown. Different sub-species found on each island; nominate birds at Tristan are distinctly smaller and duller; *procax* at Nightingale is slightly larger and more richly-coloured than *gordoni* at Inaccessible. **Behaviour**: Opportunistic; investigates any novel event from elephant seals to people; pecks at bags, boots and anything else left lying around. Social structure poorly understood; occurs singly or in pairs, but often gathers in groups of 10–20 birds, squabbling noisily over food items. Typical calls are shrill, high-pitched whistles, used to maintain contact between mates; louder whistles attract a posse of other thrushes; alarm call is a series of harsh shrieks. Song is an attractive series of musical warbles and trills, but is uttered very softly, and barely audible from >10 m. Breeds September–December; probably 1–2 weeks later at high elevations. Nest is a deep cup of *Spartina* leaves and other dry vegetation built by female up to 1 m up in dense vegetation or on a bank or cliff. Lays 2–3 eggs (3-egg clutches only known from Nightingale); greenish-blue with a few reddish-brown spots. Incubating birds sit tight; period and role of sexes unknown. Chicks initially brooded closely, mainly by female; both sexes feed chicks, which fledge after 20 days. Fledglings remain with parents for 3–4 weeks, begging vociferously for food. Diet catholic; invertebrates, seeds, berries and carrion from skua kills; breaks open eggs with its bill and even catches and kills adult White-bellied Storm Petrels on plateau of Inaccessible. Tongue has fringed edge adapted for lapping up egg contents. Chicks fed mainly earthworms; *Empetrum* berries important for juveniles. Forages down bird burrows and regularly along beaches; scratches with feet to expose invertebrates such as earthworms. Longevity at least 11 years. Occasionally eaten by skuas. **Distribution**: Endemic to Tristan, Nightingale and Inaccessible; occurs in all habitats at Nightingale and Inaccessible; confined to gulches and the Base on Tristan, up to 1,200 m. **Population**: Scarce at Tristan; <50 pairs. Common at other islands, but abundance not as great as it might appear due to aggregation around visitors; some 400 pairs at Nightingale and 850 at Inaccessible. **Conservation**: Near-Threatened, given its small range and susceptibility to introduced predators; population at Tristan greatly reduced due to predation by cats and rats.

Gough Bunting *Rowettia goughensis*

23–26 cm, 50–56 g. A large bunting with a rather long, slender bill. Adults are dull olive-green with a grey wash on neck and blackish face and bib, darker in males. Bill and legs dark grey. Juveniles and immatures are buffy, streaked dark brown; immature plumage retained for at least two years, but some birds breed in transitional or immature plumage. **Behaviour**: Occurs singly or in pairs. Fairly obvious on open highland vegetation, but easily overlooked in coastal tussock and fern bush if not calling or seen in flight. Breeds September–December (mainly October–November). Males advertise territories with high-pitched whistled song *tsweeeep*; female gives a slightly deeper chattering call, often duetting with male. Nest is a cup made from *Spartina* and sedge leaves; built by female in dense vegetation, on or close to the ground, often on a steep slope; sometimes in a bogfern head. Lays two (rarely 1–3) eggs (28 × 19 mm); light blue finely speckled dark brown. Incubation by female only, fed near nest by male. Chicks initially brooded by female; later both male and female provision chicks. Nestling period 20–26 days; chicks remain in dense cover near nest for another week or so, then accompany adults while foraging. Only raise at most one brood per season, but may re-lay following breeding failures; <48% of eggs result in fledged chicks. Diet includes various insects, spiders, seeds and berries (especially *Nertera* fruit); also occasionally scavenges from skua kills. Forages by gleaning from vegetation; often pulls up moss and other loose vegetation with bill or feet to expose prey. **Distribution**: Endemic to Gough, occurs in all habitats from boulder beaches to highest peaks. **Population**: Some 1,000 pairs. **Conservation**: Vulnerable; population reduced due to predation of eggs and chicks by mice; nests below 400 m confined to steep cliffs.

▲ **(1) Tristan Thrush** *Nesocichla eremita*, adult

▼ **(2) Tristan Thrush**, juvenile

▲ **(3) Tristan Thrush** *Nesocichla eremita*, adult feeding on White-bellied Storm Petrel *Fregetta grallaria*

▼ **(4) Gough Bunting** *Rowettia goughensis*, adult female

▼ **(5) Gough Bunting** *Rowettia goughensis*, adult male

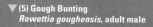

▼ **(6) Gough Bunting**, juvenile

Nesospiza buntings

These closely-related species confined to the northern islands provide a fascinating example of evolution in action, especially at Inaccessible, where three forms have evolved to exploit different habitats. Large- and small-billed forms were lumped together, but genetic evidence shows independent evolution at Inaccessible and Nightingale. A small-billed bunting at Tristan went extinct before 1900, probably due to predation by introduced mice and feral cats.

Nightingale Bunting *Nesospiza questi*   Nightingale Canary

16–18 cm, 24–29 g. A medium-sized bunting with a grey face mask, yellow-olive upperparts, finely streaked dark brown, and paler yellow-buff underparts, brightest on throat. Male brighter and plainer with grey wash on neck. Juvenile is duller with heavier streaking above; immature similar to adult but duller and more heavily streaked; plumage retained for up to two years. **Behaviour**: Occurs singly or in pairs. Breeds October–January; adults territorial at least September–March. Both sexes chase intruders. Male advertises territory with a high-pitched, sharp song, repeating *whit-wheu whit-wheu* monotonously; female has a subdued, querulous whistle. Also has chipping contact calls and a skua alarm call. Breeding biology little known; lays 1–2 light blue eggs, finely speckled dark brown, in an open cup nest. Chicks hatch naked and blind. Diet mainly seeds and berries; chicks fed invertebrates. Forages by gleaning vegetation and hopping on ground. **Distribution**: Endemic to Nightingale, Alex and Stoltenhoff. **Population**: Roughly 4,000 pairs. **Conservation**: Vulnerable, given its small range and susceptibility to accidental introduction of predators such as rats and mice.

Wilkins' Bunting *Nesospiza wilkinsi*   Big Canary

20–22 cm, 46–53 g. A massive, heavy-billed bunting, specialised to crack open fruits of *Phylica* trees. Bill almost twice as deep as Nightingale Bunting. Male song distinctly deeper and slower *whut-prreu whut prreu*. **Behaviour**: Occurs singly or in pairs. Adults territorial at least September–March. Breeds November–January. Breeding biology little known; lays 1–2 eggs in open cup nest. Diet mainly *Phylica* fruit. Clambers around canopy of *Phylica* trees, crushing woody fruits to obtain large seeds; also gleans invertebrates from surrounding vegetation. **Distribution**: Endemic to Nightingale, confined to areas with *Phylica* trees. **Population**: 50 pairs. **Conservation**: Critically Endangered, given its very small population and range; susceptible to habitat loss and accidental introduction of predators.

Inaccessible Bunting *Nesospiza acunhae*   Inaccessible Canary

17–21 cm, 24–49 g. A remarkably variable bunting, with three distinctive subspecies: large-billed Dunn's Bunting *N. a. dunnei* mainly in *Phylica* woodland and two small-billed birds: bright yellow Upland Bunting *N. a. fraseri* on the plateau averages larger with a smaller bill than drab Lowland Bunting *N. a. acunhae* of *Spartina* tussock. Some immature Upland Buntings feed along the coast in winter and spring. All three subspecies hybridise on the eastern plateau; hybrids are intermediate in size. **Behaviour**: Occurs singly or in pairs. Breeds November–January. Male song more varied than birds on Nightingale, with 3–4 notes repeated; Dunn's Bunting song deeper and slower than small-billed buntings; hybrids have distinct song. Usually monogamous, but one male had two females on adjacent territories. Lays 1–2 (1.8) eggs; Lowland average 24 × 17 mm, Upland 25 × 17 mm, Dunn's 26 × 18 mm. Nest is a cup made from *Spartina* and sedge leaves; built by female in dense vegetation, usually close to the ground, but sometimes up to 1.2 m up in dense *Spartina* tussocks. Incubation by female only for 17–18 days; fed near nest by male. Chicks brooded by female for first 5–7 days, then both male and female feed chicks. Nestling period 18–21 days; chicks remain in dense cover for another 10 days, then accompany adults foraging on natal territory. Only raise one brood per season, but may re-lay following breeding failures; main causes of failure are predation by thrushes and bad weather. Pairs remain together for successive attempts. Diet seeds, fruits and invertebrates. Small-billed birds mainly eat seeds of sedges, *Spartina* and other grasses, *Nertera* fruit and insects; often forage in intertidal and among stranded seaweeds. Dunn's Bunting and large-billed hybrids feed on *Phylica* fruit; hybrids also glean insects from epiphytes on *Phylica* trees. Chicks fed on caterpillars and other invertebrates, but Dunn's Bunting chicks fed *Phylica* fruit from an early age; take longer to fledge and have lower breeding success (only 13% of eggs result in fledglings) than small-billed birds and hybrids (52%). Occasionally killed by skuas; longevity at least 12 years. **Distribution**: Endemic to Inaccessible. **Population**: 10,000 pairs. **Conservation**: Vulnerable, given its small range and susceptibility to accidental introduction of predators.

▲ (1) Nightingale Bunting *Nesospiza questi*, male

▲ (2) Wilkins' Bunting *Nesospiza wilkinsi*, male

▲ (3) Inaccessible Bunting *Nesospiza acunhae dunnei*
(Dunn's Bunting), male
▼ (5) Inaccessible Bunting *Nesospiza acunhae*,
hybrid male

▲ (4) Inaccessible Bunting *Nesospiza acunhae fraseri*
(Upland Bunting), male
▼ (6) Inaccessible Bunting *Nesospiza acunhae acunhae*
(Lowland Bunting), male

Cattle Egret *Bubulcus ibis*
48–52 cm, wingspan 90–96 cm, 300–400 g. Fairly common vagrant from South America and perhaps Africa. A small, compact white egret with yellow bill and yellow-brown legs. Breeding adult has buff plumes on crown, back and breast. Flocks of up to 10 arrive March–May; sometimes survive winter at Tristan, foraging on lowland pastures. Several other vagrant herons and egrets also arrive from South America, mainly in autumn: **Snowy Egret** *Egretta thula* is a slender white egret with black bill and legs; toes and face yellow; has longer bill, neck and legs than Cattle Egret; **Great Egret** *E. alba* is a very large white egret with a powerful, heron-like bill and gape extending behind eye; **Little Blue Heron** *E. caerulea* is a blue-grey egret; juvenile white with dusky wing tips; bill pale blue-grey with blackish tip; **Cocoi Heron** *Ardea cocoi* is a large grey heron with a black cap and mostly plain white neck; **Striated Heron** *Butoroides striatus* is a small, compact heron with a dark cap, scaly olive-grey back and rather short yellow legs.

Speckled Teal *Anas flavirostris*
38–44 cm, wingspan 62–72 cm, 600–820 g. A fairly small, grey-brown duck with a yellow bill, dusky head and plain grey-brown flanks; speculum iridescent dark green, narrowly bordered buff above and white below. Breeds in southern South America; southern populations migrate north to pampas in winter; one recorded at Tristan in October. Other records of unidentified ducks may refer to this species or perhaps **Yellow-billed Pintail** *A. georgicus* which has a similar range and movements with a resident subspecies on South Georgia; slightly larger with a pointed tail, white-bordered speculum and heavily mottled flanks.

Red (Grey) Phalarope *Phalaropus fulicarius*
20–22 cm, wingspan 40–44 cm, 40–70 g. Uncommon non-breeding visitor to Tristan waters from Holarctic breeding grounds. A small, grey and white shorebird that feeds and roosts on the sea. Usually seen flying low over waves; rapid flight action unlike any other seabird. Non-breeding bird superficially similar to Sanderling, with fairly boldly patterned upperwing in flight, but has plainer grey back and a darker patch around eye; foraging behaviour differs. Breeding adult has distinctive brick-red underparts. In the hand, lobed toes and broad, sword-like bill diagnostic. Forages by picking small crustaceans from the sea surface; in calm weather may spin to create a vortex, concentrating prey and pulling them to the surface.

Sanderling *Calidris alba*
20–21 cm, wingspan 40–44 cm, 40–70 g. Vagrant from Holartic breeding grounds; recorded occasionally along shoreline at Tristan, sometimes in small flocks. A fairly small, grey and white shorebird with a medium-length, rather heavy black bill. Runs rapidly along beaches, following waves, or searches for invertebrate prey on rocky shores, probing crevices and gleaning among seaweed. Other small vagrant waders recorded from the islands include **White-rumped** *C. fuscicollis*, **Pectoral** *C. melanotos* and **Sharp-tailed Sandpipers** *C. acuminata*, all from North America.

Ruddy Turnstone *Arenaria interpres*
22–24 cm, wingspan 50–57 cm, 80–130 g. Vagrant from Holarctic breeding grounds; recorded occasionally along shoreline at Tristan. A compact, boldly-patterned shorebird with striking black and white wings. Bill short, wedge-shaped; legs orange. Mainly forages on rocky shores. Other larger vagrant waders recorded from the islands include **Rufous-chested Dotterel** *Charadrius modestus*, **Upland Sandpiper** *Bartramia longicauda*, **Whimbrel** *Numenius phaeopus*, **Solitary Sandpiper** *Tringa solitaria* and **Spotted Sandpiper** *Actitis macularia* from the Nearctic and **Greenshank** *Tringa nebularia* from the Palearctic.

Barn Swallow *Hirundo rustica*
18–20 cm, wingspan 32–35 cm, 16–24 g. Vagrant from North America; migrates south to South America. A small, aerial-feeding insectivore with long, slender wings and a forked tail. Adult is glossy blue above and white below with a dull red forehead and throat. Most records of juveniles; duller brown above with buffy forehead and throat. Catches insect prey in air; often perches on wires or under eaves of buildings.

Other vagrant landbirds
Common Nighthawk *Chordeiles minor* and **Eastern Kingbird** *Tyrannus tyrannus* are Nearctic migrants wintering in South America; both recorded in spring. **Willow Warbler** *Phylloscopus trochilus* is a Palearctic migrant also recorded in spring. There have also been numerous unidentified vagrants at Tristan, including several small passerines.

▲ (1) Cattle Egret *Bubulcus ibis*

▲ (2) Speckled Teal *Anas flavirostris*

▼ (3) Red Phalarope *Phalaropus fulicarius*

▼ (4) Sanderling *Calidris alba*

▼ (5) Ruddy Turnstone *Arenaria interpres*

▼ (6) Barn Swallow *Hirundo rustica*

MAMMALS

Mammals are dominant predators and herbivores in continental ecosystems, but there are no native terrestrial mammals on the islands. Most mammals are poor dispersers across oceans, and the extreme isolation of the Tristan islands has prevented their arrival. One possible exception are bats. Although no bats have been recorded at Tristan or Gough, they have colonised other, even more remote islands such as Hawaii. The failure of bats to colonise Tristan may be a result of the small size of the islands and the low abundance of flying insect prey, rather than the physical barrier presented by the islands' isolation.

The absence of terrestrial mammals from the islands has had far-reaching implications for the terrestrial ecosystems. Native birds and invertebrates have evolved in the absence of mammals, and many species have lost the ability to cope with predators. When humans arrived, they brought with them several other mammals, often with dire consequences for the native biota. Compared to other oceanic islands, Tristan has got off fairly lightly, but rats and mice have contributed to the degradation of the main island of Tristan, and mice pose significant threats to the breeding birds, invertebrates and plants at Gough Island. Inaccessible and Nightingale are fortunate to be among the few islands free of introduced mammals, and strict quarantine measures are necessary to prevent accidental introductions. Should rodents or other predators reach Inaccessible Island, it would almost certainly result in the extinction of the Inaccessible Rail.

The only mammals native to the islands are marine species that feed at sea. Two seals, the Subantarctic Fur Seal and Southern Elephant Seal, come ashore at the islands to breed, moult and rest. Like seabirds, they are vulnerable when they are ashore, and historically they were subjected to severe exploitation. Both species were hunted to the brink of extinction at the northern islands during the late 1700s and early 1800s, and their numbers remained very small throughout the 19th and early 20th centuries, due in part to ongoing exploitation. The Stoltenhoff brothers' ill-fated attempt to earn their fortunes by sealing at Inaccessible Island in the 1870s failed miserably, because they killed fewer than 100 fur seals in almost two years on the island.

Since the cessation of sealing, fur seal numbers have slowly recovered at the northern islands, but elephant seals have all but disappeared, with just the odd animal hauling out. Sealing also took place at Gough Island, but the exposed western beaches provided a refuge for the fur seals, with Gough being one of the few sites world-wide where substantial numbers survived the period of intense sealing. Gough still supports the largest population of Subantarctic Fur Seals globally. The elephant seals were less fortunate. Being confined to the sheltered eastern coast of Gough, they provided easy pickings for sealers. Despite protection for more than 50 years, the population continued to decrease steadily until recently, and has perhaps stabilised at its current, perilously small size.

Unlike seals, whales and dolphins have completely severed their ties with land, giving birth to their young at sea. Several whales and dolphins occur in the waters around the islands, but they are less well known than the seals. Some species, notably the beaked whales, are notoriously difficult to identify at sea, and much of what we know about these species comes from examination of stranded animals. Whales also were exploited historically, and experienced dramatic population decreases. Most species are now protected, and recently Tristan declared a whale sanctuary throughout its 200 nautical mile Exclusive Economic Zone.

FUR SEALS AND SEA LIONS Otariidae

Fur seals and sea lions are carnivorous marine mammals with external ear pinnae and a dense pelage with underfur. They forage almost exclusively at sea, but haul out on land to breed, rest and moult. Limbs modified into flippers for swimming; front flippers provide propulsion, hindlimbs steer. Agile on land compared to phocid seals, using all four flippers to walk. Numbers ashore peak twice for breeding and moulting in some species, although they can moult gradually at sea. Pups remain ashore for several months, fed by females. Nine fur seals and seven sea lions worldwide; one breeds at Tristan; one vagrant.

Subantarctic Fur Seal *Arctocephalus tropicalis*

Sexually dimorphic, adult males 1.5–1.8 m, 74–158 kg; females 1.0–1.3 m, 21–46 kg. Adult males have an enlarged chest and shoulders, long white whiskers (mystacial vibrissae) and a prominent crest or tuft on top of the head, almost always absent in the more slender females. In both sexes, the creamy-buff face, throat and chest is diagnostic, contrasting with the darker greyish-brown crown and back. There is often a dark band between the flippers, with the rest of the belly paler brown. Vibrissae in adult females wholly white, and dark in immatures of both sexes. Immatures lack a clear demarcation between the dark upperparts and the pale face, throat and chest. Pups 30–40 cm, 3–6 kg at birth with a black coat; grow rapidly and moult to silver-grey coat by four months; remain at islands until almost one year old. **Behaviour**: Occurs singly or in small groups at sea; often rests at surface holding flippers out of water. Fairly agile ashore, clambering over rocks and boulders. Breeds in congested coastal colonies, favouring jumbled boulder beaches, but also among dense tussock and other coastal vegetation. Juveniles and females present year round, but males strongly seasonal; return October–December to compete for territories (average 20 m^2) on breeding beaches. Defeated males and larger subadults congregate away from breeding beaches. Females arrive soon after males and are gathered in harems (average seven females per territorial male); give birth to one black pup (one record of twins at Marion Island) late November–early January (median birthdate 10 December); males guard and impregnate females during a brief perinatal period. Adult males display with loud, high-pitched territorial wails; bark repetitively when interacting with females; intruders threatened with deep, guttural challenges, oblique or horizontal neck displays, charges and ultimately aggressive fights if intruder fails to withdraw. Adult males depart to sea when harems start breaking up in late December–early January; at least some return February–March to moult, although some moult from late December. Pups remain at the island for 10–11 months, fed by females; feeding trips to sea (average seven days) followed by visits to shore (average two days) to suckle pups; feeding trips longer in winter. Females locate their pups by a high-pitched pup attraction call; identification confirmed by sniffing the pup. Diet mainly myctophid fish and squid, mainly caught during shallow (<16 m), short (<1 minute) dives at night. Unlikely to compete with local fisheries. **Distribution**: Breeds at Tristan, Nightingale, Inaccessible and Gough on the narrow strip of beaches at the foot of coastal cliffs; some venture up through the huts on Nightingale and wander on the coastal plain at The Caves on Tristan. Abundant at Gough where all beaches are used during summer. Less abundant on northern islands, although numbers increasing. Rare on settlement plain on Tristan, but increasingly common on less disturbed beaches. Widespread at Nightingale and Inaccessible. At Gough, distribution of breeding colonies determined by accessibility of higher ground on windswept westerly beaches, and protection from high temperatures on leeward coasts where boulders or tussock grass are essential for shade. Distribution at sea poorly known; fairly often observed en route to Cape Town; vagrants reach Africa and South America. Also breeds at islands in southern Indian Ocean: Amsterdam, St Paul, Prince Edwards, Crozets and Macquarie. **Population**: The total population at Gough numbers some 300,000 animals and 60,000 pups are born, about 80% of world population; numbers probably still increasing, although westerly beaches at carrying capacity, others approaching capacity. Small numbers breed at Tristan (The Caves), Nightingale and Inaccessible. **Conservation**: Range greatly reduced on all islands due to hunting, mainly in late 18th and 19th centuries for pelts, meat and oil; more recently for rock-lobster bait. Extinct at northern islands in early 20th century. Currently protected at Gough and Inaccessible; disturbance minimised at Tristan.

Antarctic Fur Seal *Arctocephalus gazella* closely resembles Subantarctic Fur Seal, but adult males larger with grey, grizzled heads and necks; occasional vagrant to Gough from sub-Antarctic islands; mainly immatures in October–November.

▲ **(1) Subantarctic Fur Seal** *Arctocephalus tropicalis,* typical pose at sea

◄ **(2) bull** ▼ **(3) pup**

▼ **(4) Subantarctic Fur Seal** *Arctocephalus tropicalis,* cow with large pup

TRUE SEALS Phocidae

Carnivorous marine mammals with no external ear pinnae and a sparse coat lacking underfur. Forage at sea; haul out on land to breed, moult and sometimes to rest. Limbs modified into flippers for swimming; hind flippers provide propulsion, front limbs steer. Clumsy on land, using front flippers to hump along, with hind flippers trailing behind, unable to be folded underneath the body. Moult annually, replacing entire epidermis, during an obligate haulout; numbers of different age and sex classes ashore peak at different times. Nineteen species occur worldwide; one breeds at Tristan; one vagrant.

Southern Elephant Seal *Mirounga leonina*

Extreme sexual dimorphism; adult males 3.8–5.8 m, 1.6–4.5 tonnes; females 3–4 m, 400–800 kg. Males massive with large, erectile proboscis and barrel chest; thin pelage silver-grey tending to brown before moulting; shoulders and chest heavily scarred in older males. Females and immatures have fleshy, blunt noses. Pups 130 cm, 40–50 kg at birth with black woolly coat; moult into silver-grey coat after 3–4 weeks. **Behaviour**: Seldom seen at sea; lies low in water, resembling a small whale; only nose protrudes from water to breathe. Clumsy ashore; prefers gently-sloping sand or pebble beaches. Breeds regularly only at Gough on pebble beaches on leeward east coast; moults primarily on flat vegetated areas behind landing beaches. Strongly seasonal; adults return September–October; males set up territories with loud, bubbling roars, raising forequarters off the ground before lunging at an opponent; subordinate males hang around the fringes of harems, sometimes challenging resident males for access to females. Females arrive soon after males (peak numbers mid-October) and are gathered in harems (maximum 16 females per 'beachmaster' at Gough, elsewhere usually up to 50, rarely 300). Females give birth to one black pup by end October; emit a high-pitched moan after giving birth; pups yap. Females impregnated shortly before weaning pups at three weeks; depart on a two-month foraging trip before returning to moult December–February. Moult lasts about one month. Adult males depart to sea when most females have left; return to moult February–April; immatures moult from early November, progressively later with age. Pups depart in December, sometimes first dispersing to adjacent beaches; some return for winter haulout from March–April. Diet fish and squid; caught during deep (c500 m), relatively long (20–40 min) foraging dives both during the day (deeper) and at night (shallower). **Distribution**: Breeds at east coast of Gough on narrow sandy and pebbly beaches between Wild Glen and Deep Glen. Immatures regularly haul out at Tristan and Inaccessible; occasionally pups at Tristan. Distribution at sea poorly known, but can travel vast distances. Also breeds at Patagonia, Scotia Arc islands, South Georgia, Falklands, Bouvet, Prince Edwards, Crozets, Kerguelen, Heard and Macquarie. **Population**: Gough 15–20 pups per year. **Conservation**: Killed for blubber (oil) from 18th century; numbers and range greatly reduced at all islands; southern populations recovering, but numbers slowly decreasing at Gough over last 25 years. Currently protected at all islands.

Leopard Seal *Hydrurga leptonyx*

A long (up to 4 m), slender seal, with a defined neck, angular head and an extraordinarily wide mouth; rare vagrant from the Antarctic; two records at Gough.

▲ (1) Southern Elephant Seal *Mirounga leonina*, bull ▼ (2) cows ▼ (3) pup

▼ (4) Leopard Seal *Hygrurga leptonyx* ▼ (5) Leopard Seal *Hygrurga leptonyx*

WHALES AND DOLPHINS Cetacea

Whales and dolphins are carnivorous marine mammals completely adapted for a life at sea. Their forelimbs are adapted into flippers; hindlimbs vestigial; propulsion by a powerful tail with lateral flukes; most species also have a dorsal fin. Traditionally divided into toothed and baleen whales, but recent genetic evidence suggests that large toothed whales are more closely related to baleen whales than to dolphins. Distributions of many species poorly known, in part because of difficulty of identification at sea; some large whales undertake regular migrations. Occur singly or in small-large groups; females give birth to a single calf which remains with its mother for a protracted period. Baleen whales filter small prey with mesh-like baleen plates, pushing water through the plates; toothed whales and dolphins have teeth for grasping fish and squid prey, but some beaked whales lack teeth, or have them only in males, where they are used in conflicts. Some 80 species are found worldwide; nine occur regularly in Tristan waters and 12 more probably occur at least occasionally.

Southern Right Whale *Eubalaena australis*

11–18 m, 30–60 tonnes. A large, broad-bodied baleen whale easily recognised by its lack of a dorsal fin, white callosities on the head and a rather short, V-shaped blow. Body mainly black, with variable white belly patch; rarely entire animal whitish. Males slightly smaller, often with more callosities than females. Mainly feeds in sub-Antarctic waters in summer on small crustaceans, migrating north to calve and mate in temperate waters off South Africa, Australia, New Zealand and Patagonia in June–November. Dives usually shallow and fairly short, but occasionally deep (maximum 180 m), lasting up to 50 minutes. Often breaches, slaps its tail or flippers, or 'sails' by standing on its head with its tail out of the water for several minutes. Females calve every 2–4 years after 11–12 month gestation. Calf 5 m and 10 tonnes at birth; weaned after 12 months, when 8–10 m. Receptive females often surrounded by 3–4 males. Numbers severely reduced by hunting until 1937, when protected; population recovery at Tristan set back when hunted illegally by Russian whalers in 1961–62 following evacuation of Tristan; now scarce; could include some animals from African or Patagonian waters, because individuals move between these populations. **Pygmy Right Whale** *Caperea marginata* is much smaller; grey with a dorsal fin; most likely confused with minke whales (see below).

Fin Whale *Balaenoptera physalus*

16–26 m, 30–80 tonnes. A very large, slender baleen whale with a long head, pronounced blow-hole ridges and a very tall, narrow blow. Body grey above with whitish underparts; diagnostic white lower jaw on right side only. Dorsal fin rather long and slender with a gently-sloping leading edge; located far back on body; only visible after blow. Swims rapidly, up to 30 km/h; sometimes follows ships. Feeds on crustaceans, fish and squid, diving for 3–15 minutes (rarely 30) to 100–200 m (rarely 470 m). Females calve every 2–3 years in warm waters June–August after 11 month gestation. Move south in summer to feed around Antarctic pack ice, but fairly common around Tristan October–December, often in loose groups of up to 5–10 animals. Other rorquals likely to occur in Tristan waters include: **Blue Whale** *B. musculus* is massive with a smaller dorsal fin situated even further back on body and a distinctive bluish colour; **Sei Whale** *B. borealis* is darker with a steep leading edge to dorsal fin, which is usually visible while blowing. **Antarctic Minke** *B. bonaerensis* and **Dwarf Minke Whales** *B. acutorostrata* are smaller with more pointed snouts that typically emerge when surfacing; blows much shorter and more diffuse; much faster and with longer snouts than Pygmy Right Whale.

Humpback Whale *Megaptera novaeangliae*

10–18 m, 25–35 tonnes. A large baleen whale with tubercles on the head, exceptionally long flippers with a knobbly leading edge, a distinctive hump in front of the small, rounded dorsal fin and a ridged tail stock. Blow fairly short and bushy; could be confused with Southern Right Whale blow, but usually larger and less V-shaped. Body blackish with white flippers and varying amounts of white on the underside of the flukes. Often dives steeply, raising flukes before sounding, showing unique serrated trailing edge. Feeds on fish and crustaceans, lunging onto prey or circling below them and releasing bubble curtains to trap and concentrate prey before swimming up with its mouth open. Females calve every 2–3 years in tropical waters May–August following 11–12 month gestation; calves suckled for 6–12 months. Move south in summer to feed around Antarctic pack ice. Occasional in Tristan waters, mainly on migration.

▲ (1) Southern Right Whale *Eubalaena australis*   ▲ (2) Southern Right Whale *Eubalaena australis*

▼ (3) Fin Whale *Balaenoptera physalus*, showing white jaw   ▼ (4) Fin Whale *Balaenoptera physalus*

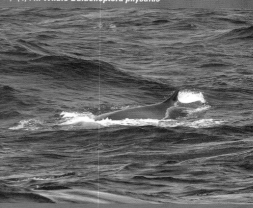

▼ (5) Humpback Whale *Megaptera novaeangliae*   ▼ (6) Humpback Whale *Megaptera novaeangliae*

Sperm Whale *Physeter macrocephalus*

Male 15–18 m, 40–55 tonnes; female 8–16 m, 15–20 tonnes. A large, square-headed whale with teeth on the lower jaw slotting into holes on the upper jaw. Body dark grey or grey-brown. Easily identified by its rounded dorsal fin, followed by a row of humps down the tail stock, and short, bushy blow, projected forward and to the left. Often in small groups of 2–20 animals; lies at the surface, blowing regularly, then dives steeply, often showing flukes. Foraging dives last 30–60 minutes (rarely >2 hours); usually dives to 400–500 m, exceptionally >3,000 m. Females calve every 3–5 years after 14–16 month gestation; calf suckled for up to 3 years. Large males range farther south than females. Fairly common in Tristan waters.

Shepherd's Beaked Whale *Tasmacetus shepherdi*

6–7 m, 2–3.5 tonnes. A very poorly known beaked whale, with scattered records from New Zealand, Australia, Argentina and Tristan, where it may be fairly common. Pods of 10–30 beaked whales regularly observed around the islands, but identification problematic; most stranded beaked whales have been this species. Has a pointed snout and small, melon-shaped head, but head seldom out of water; usually only the dark back and fairly small, falcate dorsal fin seen. Body dark grey-brown with paler stripes on flanks; larger males often scarred, presumably from fighting. Stranded animals easily identified by a full set of teeth (34–56) on both jaws; male has larger tooth protruding from tip of lower jaw. Beaked whales are notoriously difficult to identify at sea; other species probably found in Tristan waters include **Southern Bottlenose Whale** *Hyperoodon planifrons*, **Arnoux's Beaked Whale** *Berardius arnuxii*, **Gray's Beaked Whale** *Mesoplodon grayi*, **True's Beaked Whale** *M. mirus*, **Andrew's Beaked Whale** *M. bowdoini*, **Strap-toothed Beaked Whale** *M. layardii* and **Cuvier's Beaked Whale** *Ziphius cavirostris*.

Long-finned Pilot Whale *Globicephala melas*

4–7 m, 2–3 tonnes. A large, black dolphin with a distinctively broad-based dorsal fin; some animals show a paler blaze behind the dorsal fin and a narrow whitish stripe behind the eye. Males larger; outnumbered by females. Gregarious; occurs in pods of 10–100 animals. Diet mainly squid and fish, often taken in deep water and at night. Dives for 10–15 minutes; up to 600 m, although usually <200 m. Females calve every 3–6 years following 12–18 month gestation; calves suckled for 18–36 months. Uncommon in Tristan waters.

Orca, Killer Whale *Orcinus orca*

Male 6–9 m, 3–5 tonnes; female 5–7 m, 2–4 tonnes. Largest dolphin; striking black and white with a distinctive white patch behind its eye and pale saddle behind dorsal fin. Male larger with a very tall, triangular fin (sometimes bent over to one side); female smaller with a falcate fin. Occurs in small pods 2–20 (rarely 50) animals. Swims rapidly, up to 50 km/h; eats fish, squid, penguins, other seabirds, seals, dolphins and even whales. Females calve every 4–5 years after 12–18 month gestation; suckle calves for one year. Scarce in Tristan waters, despite large fur seal population at Gough. **Southern Right Whale Dolphin** *Lissodelphis peronii* is smaller and much more slender; black above and white below with white beak and flippers; easily recognised by its lack of a dorsal fin. Occurs in small to large pods; possible visitor to Tristan waters mainly in the south.

Dusky Dolphin *Lagenorhynchus obscurus*

1.5–2.2 m, 70–90 kg. A fairly small, compact dolphin with a short, blunt beak. Strikingly patterned; back dark grey, flanks pale grey, underparts whitish, with transverse stripes. Dorsal fin tall and falcate with slightly paler trailing edge. Gregarious, in pods of 10–200 (rarely 1,000) animals; often acrobatic, jumping and cartwheeling; sometimes attracted to ships. Feeds on pelagic schooling fish, crustaceans and squid; diet at Tristan unknown. Usually dives shallowly for 20–30 seconds, but up to 150 m. Females calve in winter after 13 month gestation; calf suckled for up to 18 months. Probably resident in waters around Tristan and Gough. **Hourglass Dolphin** *L. cruciger* is slightly smaller; black with distinctive white hour-glass marks on sides; largely sub-Antarctic, but may occur south of Gough.

Long-beaked Common Dolphin *Delphinus capensis*

1.8–2.4 m, 150–220 kg. A medium-sized dolphin with a long, slender beak. Easily identified by its creamy-yellow flanks, extending to below the fairly small dorsal fin; upperparts browner than Dusky Dolphin. Gregarious, in pods of 50–500 (rarely 2,000) animals. Feeds on fish, crustaceans and squid; usually dives shallowly for 20–60 seconds, but up to 280 m. Females calve every 2–3 years after 10–11 month gestation. Rare at Tristan, but more common in oceanic waters.

▲ (1) Sperm Whale *Physeter macrocephalus*

▲ (2) Sperm Whale *Physeter macrocephalus*

▼ (3) Long-finned Pilot Whale *Globicephala melas*

▼ (4) Killer Whale *Orcinus orca*, male

▼ (5) Dusky Dolphin *Lagenorhynchus obscurus*

▼ (6) Long-beaked Common Dolphin *Delphinus capensis*

▼ (7) Long-beaked Common Dolphin *Delphinus capensis*

INTRODUCED MAMMALS

Humans have introduced a variety of mammals to the islands, either deliberately for food and transport, or inadvertently through shipwrecks and stow-aways in cargo. Two species of rodents are serious pests and there are plans to attempt to eradicate them from Tristan and Gough using aerial drops of poisoned bait; Nightingale and Inaccessible remain rodent free. Domestic animals are now confined to Tristan, although they have been introduced to all the other islands in the past.

Black Rat (Ship Rat or House Rat) *Rattus rattus*

16–24 cm plus 18–26 cm tail; 100–200 g. A large, grey-brown rodent, much larger and more elongate than House Mouse; droppings 8–10 mm. Introduced to Tristan from a ship wreck in 1882. Territorial; has favoured runs to and from its nest, often revealed by greasy tracks. Agile, able to climb into ceilings of houses. Largely nocturnal; feeds on a wide range of plant and animal matter, including seabird chicks. Breeds mainly in summer; gestation 21 days (23–29 if lactating) with 5–8 pups/litter and 3–5 litters per year. Occurs all over Tristan, but most abundant on the Settlement Plain, where it causes significant damage to crops and stored goods; density up to 50/ha. Possibly responsible for extinction of Tristan Moorhen, and a major predator of burrowing petrel chicks, probably causing local extinction of several smaller seabirds. Also eats penguin and probably thrush eggs.

House Mouse *Mus musculus*

8–10 cm plus 7–8 cm tail; 10–25 g (up to 50 g on Gough). A fairly small, brown rodent, much smaller and more compact than Black Rat; droppings 6–7 mm, smaller than rat droppings. Not known when introduced; probably arrived in stores brought ashore by sealers; present on Tristan by 1830s, Gough by 1880s. Adults territorial, although some nests communal; often distinct runways leading to and from nests. Sound and scent important for communication. Largely nocturnal; diet mainly seeds, other plant matter and invertebrates; has a major impact on invertebrate populations. Breeds throughout summer; gestation 19 days (longer if lactating); average one litter per month, with average six pups per litter. Pups weaned at 14 days; breed at 35–40 days, allowing rapid population growth. Occurs mainly on the Seetlement Plain and in *Phylica* woodland on the Base at Tristan. Occurs throughout at Gough, attaining high densities of up to 300/ha in lowlands in late summer; numbers decrease in winter, when seeds and insects are scarce. Scavenges from dead seabirds (eg skua kills) and recently discovered to attack and kill chicks of Tristan Albatross, Atlantic Petrel and Great Shearwater. Most attacks occur in autumn and winter, when other food is scarce. Up to 10 mice attack a single albatross chick, eating through body wall. Probably kills chicks of other winter-breeding seabirds (Grey and Great-winged Petrels) and Gough Buntings; may have contributed to the extinction of buntings at Tristan.

Domestic animals

Sheep roam freely on the Base of Tristan and are kept on the Settlement Plain and coastal pastures towards Sandy Point; also formerly on Nightingale, Inaccessible and Gough. Cattle occur on the Settlement Plain, Sandy Point and between Stony Beach and the Caves on Tristan; formerly on the east coast of Inaccessible. Pigs are now confined to pens on the Settlement Plain on Tristan, but used to roam freely on Tristan and Inaccessible, where they ate large numbers of seabirds, almost wiping out Tristan Albatrosses and Spectacled Petrels. A few donkeys remain on the Settlement Plain; formerly used for transport. Goats are now extinct, but used to occur on Tristan, Inaccessible and Gough. Dogs are kept in the village and used to herd sheep on the mountain; formerly a few feral dogs roamed on Inaccessible, killing many birds, including penguins; feral dogs also roamed Tristan following the 1961 evacuation. Cats used to occur on Tristan, including a feral population, which apparently impacted breeding birds severely in the 19th century, but now extinct. Horses were introduced briefly to Tristan in the 19th century. Rabbits were reported by several early visitors to Tristan, but there is no firm evidence they occurred on the islands. There are also some domesticated birds confined to the Settlement Plain on Tristan: chickens, ducks and geese. Shortly after settlement there were some feral chickens, but these were killed by feral cats. Carrier pigeons were used briefly to send messages back to Tristan from the outer islands, but soon died out, and a few Budgerigars were kept as pets in the 1970s, but are no longer allowed for fear of introducing diseases to native birds.

▲ (1) Black Rat *Rattus rattus*

▲ (2) House Mouse *Mus musculus*

▼ (3) Mountain sheep being herded down Burntwood, Tristan

Gough Flightless Moth

TERRESTRIAL INVERTEBRATES

The invertebrate fauna is much less well known than the vascular plants and vertebrates. Few species groups have been studied, making it difficult to assess the total diversity, or the proportions of species endemic to the islands. However, it is clear that the invertebrate fauna is relatively depauperate, with only some 430 species recorded from all islands. Of these, some 20% are parasitic, including ticks, fleas, lice and louse flies, many of which are found only on birds. Among the better-known insect groups, more than 80% of native species are found nowhere else. The native species tend to be small and inconspicuous, but a few are relatively large, such as the flightless moths (14 mm) and the land nemertean (up to 30 mm). Although they are easily overlooked, invertebrates play important roles in the islands' ecosystems. In addition to providing food for the land birds, they are crucial for soil formation, breaking down plant material and releasing stored nutrients. They help to process the large amounts of seaweed stranded on the islands' shores and the carcases of dead animals. They also pollinate some plants, including the Island Tree *Phylica arborea*.

Most native invertebrates probably colonised the islands from South America, aided by the prevailing westerly winds and currents. Some groups are better suited to long distance dispersal, resulting in a rather different community to that found on continents. Species that can fly (eg moths and flies) or sail on silken threads (spiders) are well represented, whereas many other groups (eg ants, earthworms and millipedes) failed to reach the islands until introduced by humans. The many bird parasites presumably arrived with their hosts, but some other species also may have hitched a ride on birds (eg snail eggs stuck onto birds' feet or feathers) or drifted on logs and other debris. Vagrant insects are sometimes recorded, including occasional large Black Witch Moths *Ascalapha odorata* that travel at least 3,500 km from South America.

The new colonists found few competitors and no mammalian predators, but they faced new challenges in the windy island environment. Some species responded by evolving into new, often bizarre forms. Several flies and moths lost the ability to fly, often reducing their wings to small stumps. Other species, such as the *Scaptomyza* vinegar flies, *Tristanodes* weevils and *Balea* land snails, responded to the species-poor islands by evolving into many different species, providing examples of adaptive radiations. Others adopted unusual habits, such as the *Dimecoenia tristanensis* flies, whose larvae scrape algae off rocks on the bottom of ponds and streams. The adults squeeze under the surface meniscus and walk under water to deposit their eggs, retaining a film of air over their body that allows them to remain submerged for up to half an hour. They are quite buoyant, and once they let go of the bottom, they bob to the surface, taking flight as soon as they break the water surface.

Since humans discovered the islands 500 years ago, ships have brought a steady stream of new invertebrates to the islands. Some have inhabited the islands for so long, and are now so widespread, it is hard to decide whether they are native species or not. This confusion is compounded by a lack of knowledge about the basic diversity in some groups. Among the 'larger' animals, little is known about the islands' spiders and mites, collembolans and worms, and even less is known about microscopic groups such as tardigrades and rotifers, which inhabit damp vegetation and soil. However, many species are common European 'tramp' species that have been transported around the world during the last few centuries, and were almost certainly introduced by humans.

At Gough, where a detailed study has been made, a staggering 72% of winged insects probably have been introduced, with more than three-quarters arriving in the last 50 years, since the establishment of the weather station. Not surprisingly, there are even more alien species at the main island of Tristan, where several are agricultural pests. The 'cutworms', brown caterpillars of the night-light attracted *Agrotis* moths, and the smaller green caterpillars of the Diamond-back Moth *Plutella xylostella*, cause much damage to crops. Other pests include hemipteran bugs like the Glasshouse Whitefly *Trialeuroides vaporarium* that is prevalent on tomato leaves, and the Woolly Aphid *Eriosoma lanigerum* that attacks fruit trees. Some introduced snails and slugs also cause problems, with the Black-keeled Slug *Milax gagates* boring into potatoes.

Introduced species may out-compete native invertebrates. At Gough, some flies have become very rare, apparently replaced by introduced species. Some introduced species prey on other invertebrates (eg Brown Ground Beetle *Harpalus agilis* and centipedes), and mice at Tristan and Gough also eat large numbers of moths and beetles. An increasing number of introduced wasps parasitise native insects, which have evolved in the absence of such pressures. Introduced invertebrates also may alter the way the island ecosystems function. Alien earthworms, woodlice and millipedes are now found throughout all the islands, and doubtless affect the rate of decomposition. Given their impacts on native systems and significant damage to crops at Tristan, every effort should be taken to prevent new species from reaching the islands.

INSECTS

The best known terrestrial invertebrates are the insects, an enormously diverse group that includes all the winged invertebrates as well as many unwinged forms. All have three pairs of legs, a body divided into three regions (head, thorax and abdomen), one pair of antennae and external mouthparts. Insects make up over 60% of all the terrestrial invertebrates at the islands, with at least 270 species from 11 orders. Almost half of the insects are thought to be native to the islands, of which half are found nowhere else. In addition to the orders listed below, there are small numbers of species of silverfish (Thysanura), cockroaches (Blattodea), earwigs (Dermaptera), booklice (Psocoptera), and thrips (Thysanoptera). Almost all of these species are introduced, confined to human-modified areas, but the tube-tailed thrip *Bolothrips inaccessiblensis* is endemic to tussock grassland on the uninhabited islands.

Moths and butterflies Lepidoptera

Adults have two pairs of wings covered with overlapping scales. Nocturnal moths often vibrate wings to warm up muscles sufficiently for flight. Mouthparts are modified into a sucking tube, coiled at rest. They feed on nectar, honeydew, and other liquids, but some short-lived adults do not feed. Eggs are laid individually or in clusters, often on or near the food source (usually a specific plant). Caterpillars have chewing mouthparts; eat voraciously then pupate before emerging as adults.

Only one species of butterfly is known from the islands: the Southern Painted Lady Butterfly *Vanessa brasiliensis* (Tristan) has orange mottled wings 4 cm across. Like the Pink-spotted Hawk Moth *Agrius cingulata* (wingspan 10 cm), it may have colonised Tristan naturally or been introduced. Moths are more diverse, with 22 species: nine native (seven endemic), two naturally occurring vagrants and 11 introduced. Among the native species, the largest is *Dimorphinoctua pilifera* (up to 20 mm long), endemic to the three northern islands. Adults are drab grey-brown, with males quite large and fully winged, whereas females are smaller with reduced wings that only allow flight with difficulty. Males are often seen at night when they are attracted to lights, especially in summer in *Spartina* tussock at Inaccessible and Nightingale. Males can be confused with the introduced *Agrotis* moths that are common on the Settlement Plain. Perhaps the most interesting moths are the flightless ones. They resemble crickets more than moths: brown, 12–15 mm long with wings reduced to mere vestiges 3–4 mm long. The Tristan Flightless Moth *Dimorphinoctua cunhaensis* is found at the three northern islands, whereas the almost identical *D. goughensis* is restricted to Gough Island, mainly above 300 m (possibly because mice are less abundant at high elevations). A second species at Gough, *Peridroma goughi*, is slightly smaller and darker. Their caterpillars are leathery and pimpled on each segment, coloured brown or green with a yellow line running down either side. Pupal capsules are orange-brown. Flightless moths are fairly common at Nightingale and Inaccessible, but have become rare on islands with mice. Adults are mainly seen in summer.

Flies Diptera

Flies are a well-known insect order, characterised by membranous forewings used for flight and hindwings reduced to club-shaped stumps called halteres. They are abundant in most habitats at the islands, especially near water and along the coast. At least 66 species have been recorded, of which 31 are native (25 endemic). Among the introduced species are familiar tramp species such as the houseflies *Musca domestica* and *Fannia canicularis* and the larger blowflies often seen on animal wounds and carcasses, including the Greenbottle Sheep Maggot Fly *Lucilia sericata* and the less common Southern Bluebottle *Calliphora croceipalpis*. Several smaller flies also have been introduced, including gnats (eg the gall gnat *Mycophila fungicola* and other fungus and dark-winged gnats), midges (eg the chironomid *Limnophyes minimus* and the owl-midge or moth-fly *Psychoda albipennis*), the Scuttle Fly *Megaselia rufipes*, the Cheese Skipper *Piophila casei* (Tristan) and several lesser dung flies (Sphaeroceridae).

Along the coast, the most common and abundant flies are two introduced species that live on the kelp wrack, the slender Root-maggot Fly *Fucellia tergina*, and the large Kelp Fly *Coelopa* sp. Both are prone to being wind-blown, and are often encountered inland, particularly when high tides or large seas force them to vacate their seaweed homes. Further inland, eight species of shore flies, all endemic to the islands, occur associated with fresh or brackish water. They are commonly found on river rocks, floating vegetation or even underwater, in the case of *Dimecoenia tristanensis*. Less conspicuous are the *Scaptomyza* vinegar flies, which are only 2–3 mm long. They superficially resemble fruit flies (Tephritidae), and like fruit flies, they are attracted to fermenting substances. They have undergone an adaptive radiation at the islands, with nine species, all endemic. Three species are confined to Nightingale and two to Inaccessible. Perhaps the most interesting are the two species of strap-winged flies, *Scaptomyza frustulifera* and *S. brevilamellata*. Their thin wings extend beyond the body as narrow strips, but are useless for flight. They scurry among vegetation, dropping out of sight if disturbed. Even more bizarre is the endemic Crane Fly *Symplecta holdgatei*, which has virtually no vestige of wings left. With long, spindly legs, this tiny insect (5 mm) looks more like a daddy-long-legs spider than a fly. It is common on Gough in open coastal and mountain moorland areas. The louse fly *Ornithomyia parva* (Hippoboscidae) with its distinctive flat, leathery body is usually only encountered when handling land birds. It has well developed claws, enabling it to grip its hosts, and feeds on their blood. They can fly, albeit not strongly, and sometimes desert their hosts. If they land on people, they cling tightly to your skin, or scuttle up your sleeve! Fortunately they do not have a taste for human blood. Unlike most other insects, they do not lay eggs, instead nurturing a single young in their abdomen, only releasing the larva when it is about to pupate.

Beetles Coleoptera

Beetles are the most species-rich insect order. Most have a tough, horny exoskeleton and hardened forewings that protect the membranous hind wings. Like flies and wasps, they undergo a complete metamorphosis, with maggot-like grubs that pupate before emerging as adults. Although not often seen, beetles are the second most abundant insects at the islands after flies. Some 58 species have been recorded of which 21 are endemic.

Most beetles found at the islands are weevils (Curculionidae). The endemic *Tristanodes* weevils (4–6 mm long) evolved into 11 different species, ranging in colour from light brown to black. All have a long, elephant-like snout extending down from the head, with chewing mouthparts at the tip. The females use this snout to bore holes into stems and rhizomes where they lay their eggs. The maggot-like larvae remain inside the plant tissue, tunnelling along as they feed. Weevils are plant feeders and utilise a variety vegetation types, including tussock grasses, sedges and branches of the Island Tree. The native weevils look quite similar to a number of notorious pests, such as the Rice Weevil *Sitophilus oryzae* that is found from time to time in food stores at Tristan and Gough.

Another fairly abundant and diverse group are the rove beetles (Staphylinidae), with some 10 species. They look more like earwigs than beetles, having long, fairly slender abdomens and shortened forewings, but they lack the terminal pincers of earwigs. Their taxonomy is complex, and it is unclear if any species are native to the islands. One of the more peculiar beetles that is endemic to the islands is the tiny Featherwing Beetle *Ptinella natvigi* (1.5 mm long). With no hind wings or eyes, it is blind and flightless. Given its physical handicaps, it is hard to imagine how it came to be confined to Inaccessible and Gough. It occurs in wet heath and feldmark where it probably scavenges on fungal spores or other plant matter.

Water beetles (Dytiscidae) are represented by three species, all endemic. They live in streams and ponds, and have smooth, streamlined oval bodies adapted for swimming. They breathe from an air bubble trapped beneath their wing covers, which they refresh periodically by surfacing. This makes them quite buoyant, and they either cling to the bottom or kick strongly with their flattened, bristled hind legs to remain underwater. Two species are large (8–12 mm long) and look similar at rest, but differ in the size of their hind wings. *Lancetes dacunhae* (Tristan, Inaccessible and Gough) has well-developed hind wings, whereas *Senilites tristanicola* (Inaccessible and Nightingale) has very small wings and is unable to fly. The third species, *Liodessus involucer*, found at all four islands, is much smaller (2 mm), and it too is flightless. Wing reduction is rare in water beetles, because they cannot walk well, and rely on flight to colonise new habitats. All three species are predatory, feeding on other small aquatic invertebrates. Eggs are laid singly on aquatic plants or under stones. The larvae also are aquatic, growing to almost twice the size of their parents, but pupation occurs in wet soil next to the water.

The largest beetle on the islands is an introduced species, the Old House Borer *Hylotrupes bajulus* (15 mm). It is found associated with timber in houses at Tristan and Gough. Originally a forest dweller, this European species has become a cosmopolitan pest, seriously damaging roofs and rafters. Other introduced beetles closely associated with humans are the little Australian Spider Beetle *Ptinus tectus* and the Drugstore Beetle *Stegobium paniceum* (both 2–4 mm) that are pests of dried food products, including grain, biscuits, dried fruit, chocolate and spices. The larvae bore holes as they eat their way through the foodstuffs, contaminating them with droppings and then spinning cocoons in which to mature, leaving telltale silk webbing behind.

Some introduced beetles have invaded native habitats. The Brown Ground Beetle *Harpalus agilis* (10 mm) is a carabid that is often found under stones or in soil on Tristan. It is a predator of other insects, and could have serious impacts on native species if it were introduced to the other islands. The little yellow and black ladybird *Lioadalia flavomaculata* (4 mm) also is an introduced species that remains confined to Tristan, mainly in agricultural areas. When disturbed, adults exude drops of yellow blood from their leg-joints, which is strong-smelling and toxic to vertebrates. Their bright colour has evolved as a warning to would-be predators.

Bugs Hemiptera

True bugs are one of the largest groups of insects, and many are serious crop pests. Superficially beetle-like, they lack a pupal stage, instead having nymphs that resemble small, wingless adults. The long, slender mouthparts are adapted for sucking, and are held folded beneath the head when not feeding. There are two types of bugs: homopterans all feed on plants and have wings held like an A-frame tent over their bodies. Heteropterans may have more diverse diets, and have wings folded flat onto their bodies, with membranous wingtips creating an X-pattern on their backs. The only native homopteran is the plant hopper *Nothodelphax atlanticus*, found at all four islands. It feeds on grasses and sedges, but is small (2–4 mm) and well camouflaged, and is easily overlooked unless it jumps away. Introduced species recorded from the islands include at least

10 species of aphid, the Glasshouse Whitefly *Trialeuroides vaporarium* (Tristan), and the Armoured Scale Insect *Hemiberlesia rapax* (Tristan and Inaccessible), many of which are pests on crops and garden plants at Tristan. Among the heteroptera, the predatory damsel bug *Nabis hageni* (Nabidae) is the only native species, endemic to the three northern islands. Pale and slender, up to 9 mm long, it occurs in a wide range of habitats from the upper shore to the highest peaks. Introduced species include the debris bug *Lyctocoris campestris*, the potato bug *Calocoris norvegicus* and a stink- or shieldbug (Pentatomidae), all confined to Tristan.

Wasps and ants Hymenoptera
Wasps are a diverse group, many of which are difficult to identify. They have two pairs of membranous wings and a narrow constriction between the thorax and abdomen. Females of some species have modified their ovipositors into a sting. There are no native species, but at least one ant and 16 wasps have been introduced to the islands. The ant *Hypoponera* sp. is confined to the main island of Tristan, where it occurs at the dump site, among vegetation and under stones at the top of the shore. It is seldom seen, but the winged alates sometimes bite people and are called 'stingy flies' locally. Most wasps are tiny (<6 mm), but there are two large, distinctively marked species: a yellow-and-black striped species closely resembling *Ichneumon unicinctus* (14 mm, Tristan, Nightingale and Inaccessible) and another brown ichneumonid (12 mm) with a yellow dot behind its head, known only from the huts at Nightingale. Most are parasitoids, laying their eggs on other insects. The two large species belong to the Ichneumoninae that are known to parasitise noctuid moths, and may pose a threat to the islands' flightless moths. Other species target flies (eg *Aspilota* sp. [Nightingale], *Kleidotoma* sp. [Gough], *Spanglia* sp. [Tristan], *Stilpnus* sp. [Tristan, Nightingale, Inaccessible and Gough]) or aphids (eg *Aphidius colemani* [Gough]), and some even parasitise the developing larvae of other wasps (eg *Phaenoglyphis villosa* attacks *A. colemani* at Gough). Other species lay their eggs on plants, where their larvae form galls, with at least one species of gall-forming Cynipinae at Tristan.

Crickets Orthoptera
Generally rather large insects with long hind-limbs adapted for jumping. Only one species, among the smallest, has reached the islands, a pygmy mole cricket *Tridactylus subantarcticus*. Its shiny blackish body is only 5 mm long, with rudimentary wings and large, slightly protruding eyes. It is endemic to Tristan, where it uses its stout front legs to dig shallow holes in low cliffs at the back of the beach. It could easily be confused with the amphipods (sand hoppers) that share this habitat. Little is known about this species, but it is probably nocturnal, feeding on fungi, algae and bacteria found in damp soil.

Fleas Siphonaptera
In addition to free-living insects, there are numerous parasitic species. Fleas are small (1–3 mm), wingless, blood-sucking ectoparasites of warm-blooded animals. Their polished bodies are laterally compressed, allowing them to slip through fur or feathers with ease. Most are mobile and are renowned for their ability to jump considerable distances (up to 40 cm) using their long, well-developed hind legs. Their mouthparts are adapted to pierce skin and suck up blood, injecting an anti-coagulant into the wound that causes irritation and swelling. Most fleas are not confined to a single host species, biting any animal that is available. Body fleas spend most of their time on the host, whereas nest fleas spend most of their time in the burrows or nests of their host, only climbing onto the host to feed. They are remarkably tough, and can survive long periods between feeds (eg adult *Pulex irritans* can live for more than a year without feeding). After hatching, flea nymphs lie quiescent for weeks until a stimulus associated with a host arouses them, such as vibrations from footsteps. Apart from the irritation caused by their bites, fleas are intermediate hosts of cat and dog tapeworm, and rodent fleas are notorious for transmitting plague, a bacterial disease caused by *Yersinia pestis*. Three flea species occur at the islands: two native species, typically associated with birds, *Parapsyllus longicornis* and *Parapsyllus dacunhae* (Rhopalopsyllidae), whereas the third is the Human Flea *Pulex irritans* (Pulicidae), that was introduced to Tristan early in its history of human occupation.

Lice Phthiraptera
Lice also are small (2–10 mm), wingless ectoparasites found on mammals and birds, but unlike fleas their bodies are flattened dorso-ventrally and are less mobile, using their strong claws to cling to the hair or feathers of their hosts. Dispersal to other hosts requires close contact, and as a result lice species are often limited to only one or a few host species. For example, *Naubates prioni* only occurs on Broad-billed Prions and *Halipeurus gravis* on Great Shearwaters. They spend their entire life on a host, gluing their eggs or 'nits' onto the host's feathers or hairs. Not surprisingly, most lice found at the islands are bird lice (Philopleridae), which are all chewing lice that feed on feathers and skin debris. Some are adapted to specific areas on their host, with short, squat species generally confined to the head and neck, and more slender, active species occurring on the longer body feathers. A total of 53 bird lice have been recorded, including three endemics associated with the islands' endemic landbirds: two on the Inaccessible Rail (*Pseudomenopon rowani* and *Rallicola zumpti*) and one on the Tristan Thrush (*Brueelia* sp.).

▲ **(1)** *Vanessa brasiliensis* Southern Painted Lady Butterfly (alien)

▲ **(2)** *Agrius cingulata* Pink-spotted Hawk Moth (alien)

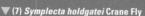

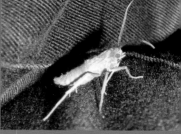

▲ **(3)** *Peridroma goughi* or *Dimorphinoctua goughensis* Gough Flightless Moth

▲ **(4)** *Peridroma goughi* or *Dimorphinoctua goughensis* Gough Flightless Moth, caterpillar

▲ **(5)** *Dimorphinoctua cunhaensis* Tristan Flightless Moth

▼ **(6)** *Scaptomyza frustulifera* Strap-winged Fly

▼ **(7)** *Symplecta holdgatei* Crane Fly

▼ **(8)** *Dicranomyia distans* Crane Fly (alien)

▼ **(9)** *Senilites tristanicola* Diving Beetle

▼ **(10)** *Stenoscelis hylastoides* Cossonid Woodborer (alien)

▼ **(11)** *Ichneumon* cf. *unicinctus* Wasp (alien)

OTHER INVERTEBRATES

Other invertebrate groups are generally less well known than the insects, but at least 160 species occur at the islands, of which almost half are arachnids (mites 28%, spiders 15%, ticks 5% and a pseudoscorpion). Various types of worms (annelids, nemerteans and platyhelminths) make up the next largest component (15%), followed by molluscs (snails and slugs, 13 %); collembolans (springtails 12%); crustaceans (ostracods, copepods, amphipods and isopods, 6%); myriapods (millipedes and centipedes, 4%) and tardigrades (waterbears 2%).

Springtails Collembola

Collembolans are tiny (<5 mm), wingless, six-legged invertebrates that superficially resemble insects but have internal mouthparts. They can 'jump' up to 30 cm with their springing organ, a forked tail-like appendage held folded under the abdomen. Also on the underside of the body they have a tube which enables adhesion to smooth surfaces. Collembola are principally soil and litter dwellers, preferring moist surroundings. Some species live on or near water, sometimes aggregating in rafts on the surface, making the water body appear as if covered by a slate-coloured powder. Most species consume microorganisms associated with decomposing organic matter. Nineteen species have been recorded from the islands, of which two are endemic: *Bourletiella guevarai* (Tristan) and *Metakatianna oceanica* (Nightingale).

Spiders Araneae

Arachnids are wingless invertebrates with eight legs and no antennae, including spiders, scorpions, mites and ticks. Spiders are abundant at the islands, but have been little studied, with most information from the main island of Tristan. At least 23 species from eight families occur. Most are dwarf- or hammock web spiders (Linyphiidae) which are adapted to disperse by 'ballooning', whereby spiders release a thread into the wind. This long tail of silk provides lift, carrying them high in the air, and allowing them to travel vast distances. Five endemic species occur; *Lepthyphantes tristani*, which co-occurs at Tristan with the introduced *L. leprosus*, and four species of *Laminacauda*: *L. maxima* (Tristan, Nightingale), *L. tristani* (Tristan, Inaccessible), *L. luscinia* (Nightingale) and *L. insulanus* (Inaccessible).

Button and widow spiders (Theridiidae) are also well represented, with several native species of cobweb spiders (*Theridion*) and cupboard or brown house spiders (*Steatoda*), as well as three introduced species: *Achaearanea tepidariorum*, *Teutana grossa* and the venomous Australian Red-backed Spider *Lactrodectus hasseltii*. The red-backed spider was first found at Tristan in 1968. The females have a neurotoxic venom, but they rarely leave their web, so people are only likely to be bitten if they prod the spider or its webbing. Females are the size of a large pea, with slender legs. Their black bodies have two orange-red markings, a broken stripe along the back and an hour-glass shaped mark on the belly. Juveniles have additional white markings. Red-backs can easily be mistaken for the native cupboard spiders (sometimes called 'black red-backs') that also have a painful bite, but lack the dangerous neurotoxic effects.

Another common spider around human dwellings is the introduced, harmless European House Spider *Tegenaria domestica* (Agelenidae), which spends most of its time on its web. Other species include the small huntsman spiders (Philodromidae) that are usually well camouflaged and run sideways when they flee; sac spiders (Clubionidae); daddy long legs spiders (Pholcidae) and jumping spiders (Salticidae) which make leaps at their prey. All spiders are predatory, normally taking prey that is no bigger than their own size. They typically have spinnerets with which they produce silk to construct webs, shelters and sacks for their eggs. The males are usually tiny and seldom seen; they are often eaten by the female after mating.

Mites and ticks Acarina

Mites occur in all habitats, from the highest mountains to deep-sea trenches and from the hottest deserts to Antarctica. They are very diverse, but are usually too small to notice or recognise. There are many free-living mites at the islands, with at least 40 species from more than 20 families, and more awaiting description. Most are thought to be native to the islands. Some species feed on detritus and fungal micro-organisms, whereas others prey on other small invertebrates. A few are aquatic, including an endemic subspecies of the cosmopolitan halacarid freshwater mite *Lobohalacarus weberi tristanensis*, found in coastal water bodies, and the seawater-tolerant hyadesid mites that occur on rocky beaches. Some mites are parasitic on vertebrates, invertebrates and plants. These are usually <1 mm and live externally on their hosts or burrow under the skin or in other tissues. Some cause allergies, such as the house dust mites, *Dermatophagoides pteronyssinus* and *D. farinae* that are the most common allergenic causes for asthma on Tristan. Others transmit diseases to poultry and livestock, including mange and scabies caused by sarcoptiform mites. Yet others damage crops, such as the two spider mites (Phytoseiidae) and one species of false spider mite (Tenuipalpidae) introduced to Tristan. Another introduced species confined to Tristan is the Acarid Grain

Mite *Acarus siro* that is common in hay, grain and foods. Infestations can make food unpalatable, and if the mites get onto human skin their bites cause itchiness known as 'grocer's itch'.

Ticks are larger than mites, with tough, leathery bodies. All are external parasites, feeding on blood of terrestrial vertebrates. Most species at the islands are associated with birds, especially seabirds, and include the soft tick *Carios capensis* (Argasidae) and the russet hard ticks *Ixodes uriae*, *I. percavatus*, *I. zumpti* and *I. diomedeae*. The females usually occur on birds' heads, often around the eye, where the bird's beak can't reach to preen them off, whereas the males probably live where the birds nest, but have not been found for some species. The blue tick *Rhipicephalus (Boophilus) decoloratus* has been introduced to Tristan, where it is associated mainly with livestock.

Pseudoscorpions Pseudoscorpiones

The pseudoscorpion *Chelanops atlanticus* is endemic to the islands (Tristan, Inaccessible and Gough). It is a small, tick-like creature 2–4 mm across, easily recognised by a pair of pincers at the end of its arm-like pedipalps, which are used for sensing, grasping and spinning. Unlike true scorpions, it has no tail or sting and is harmless. It is widespread from coastal tussock to montane habitats, typically in soil litter beneath stones. The outer claws have spinnerets that are used to build silken nests in which to rest, moult and catch small invertebrate prey. Females carry their eggs and developing embryos in a brood sac attached at their genital opening. The young suck nourishment from their mother through a long beak.

Crustaceans Isopoda, Amphipoda, Ostracoda, Copepoda

Crustaceans are largely aquatic, but some have colonised terrestrial habitats, especially in damp areas. They are classified based in part on the number and shape of their legs. Isopods ('similar legged') have seven pairs of legs. They are abundant in marine habitats, but the introduced woodlouse *Porcellio scaber* (Porcellionidae) is common at all the islands in leaf litter and peaty soils. It is up to 15 mm long, varying in colour from purple-grey to light brown, with a 10-segmented body. At Gough it has largely displaced the native isopod *Styloniscus australis* from lower elevations. Woodlice are omnivorous, using symbiotic bacteria to digest cellulose, and have developed rudimentary lungs, but the larvae are reared in a water-filled pouch or marsupium. The only other terrestrial crustaceans are three species of *Orchestia* amphipods (sand hoppers); laterally flattened, shrimp-like animals up to 12 mm long. They may have colonised the islands naturally, with *O. platensis* (Tristan, Inaccessible and Gough) widespread, *O. scutigerula* (Nightingale, Inaccessible and Gough) from Patagonia and South Georgia, and *O. gammarellus* (Tristan) also found in the North Atlantic and Mediterranean. Most occur in the coastal lowlands, but some occur among damp vegetation up to 500 m above sea level.

The freshwater fauna includes two species of *Iais* isopods: *I. elongata* (endemic to Tristan, Inaccessible and Gough) and *I. pubescens* (native to Gough). These slender, shrimp-like creatures <2 mm long live under rocks in coastal streams, feeding on diatoms and other plant matter. They lay at most four eggs, which are carried by the males under their body, where the young develop. Males also carry immature females to ensure they can copulate during the females' brief receptive period. Other freshwater crustaceans include ostracods ('seed shrimps'), tiny animals (<2 mm) with bodies enclosed within a hinged, greenish shell, which is unusual among crustaceans in being impregnated with calcium carbonate. Three species are known from the islands: *Cypridopsis* sp. (Tristan), *Potamocypris* sp. (Inaccessible) and *Sarscypridopsis elizabethae* (Inaccessible). They are found in the sediment at the bottom of ponds, and can be seen swimming smoothly through the water. Copepods are equally small, but move in a series of sudden darts. Two species are known: *Paracyclops poppei* (Cyclopidae) (Tristan and Inaccessible) and what is thought to be *Alona affinis* (Chydoridae) (Tristan).

Centipedes and millipedes Chilopoda and Diplopoda

These many-legged animals have elongate bodies comprising numerous segments. Centipedes have soft, flattened bodies of up to 20 segments, each bearing one pair of legs. Four species have been introduced to the islands, with three confined to Tristan, but *Lithobius melanops* (Lithobiidae) has also reached Inaccessible and Gough. It is rust red and grows up to 18 mm long. Centipedes prey on other invertebrates, injecting immobilising venom with their fangs, but their impact on native species is unknown.

Millipedes have cylindrical bodies with rigid plates strengthened by calcium and two pairs of legs on each body segment. They are slower moving than centipedes, and often curl into a defensive coil when disturbed. Four species have been introduced to Tristan, with *Cylindroiulus latestriatus* (Iulidae) also found on the other islands, and *Brachyiulus pusillus* (Iulidae) also on Inaccessible. They are generally rather drab, but the spotted snake millipede *Blaniulus guttulatus* (Tristan) is mustard yellow and red. Most feed on decaying vegetation, but they also scavenge carrion, with large numbers of *C. latestriatus* gathering to feed on bird carcasses.

Snails and slugs Gastropoda

Snails and slugs are molluscs with a soft, unsegmented body, protected by a shell in snails, that move using a large muscular 'foot'. They secrete mucus to aid their movement, leaving behind distinctive silvery trails.

Some species have sensory tentacles that they can extend or retract. They feed using a rasp-like radula that is covered in small teeth that scrape off small bits of food. Most are herbivores, grazing plant material, and can cause considerable damage to crops and garden plants.

Some 21 gastropods have been found at Tristan, with 11 endemic species of snails. The *Balea* snails (Clausiliidae), formerly put in their own genus *Tristania*, have evolved into nine species in yet another example of an adaptive radiation. All are small with turban-shaped shells 5–10 mm high and 2–4 mm wide, with 5–11 whorls that range from smooth and shiny to strongly ribbed. *B. tristensis* and *B. ventricosa* occur on all the islands, whereas the others are more restricted, with *B. swalesi* confined to Inaccessible and *B. levior* to Nightingale. *B. costellata* is found at Tristan, Inaccessible and Gough, with *B. holdgatei* at Inaccessible and Nightingale, and *B. costigera*, *B. flavida* and *B. goughensis* at Inaccessible and Gough. They are widespread up to 800 m, with *B. tristensis* the most common species, even occurring in dry kelp holdfasts on beaches. Little is known about their biology, but offspring probably can be produced without a mate that, together with their exceptionally sticky mucus, has aided their passive dispersal (perhaps by birds). Related species are found at other Atlantic islands, including St Helena, Ascension and the Canaries.

Two other small, turban-shelled snails occur at Tristan, both introduced: the Chrysalis Snail *Lauria cylindracea* and Slippery Little Pillar Snail *Cochlicopa lubrica* are both common in the settlement gardens. Unfortunately, the most commonly encountered snail at all islands is the coil-shaped Garlic Snail *Oxychilus alliarius*, introduced from Europe. Its shell has a light-brown translucent appearance, 5–7 mm across, and smells of garlic when crushed. Also spiral shaped but smaller and less obvious is the Milky Crystal Snail *Vitrea contracta*, an alien that is common, but confined to Tristan. Among the native snails, there are at least two species of succineid snails, readily distinguished by their smooth amber-coloured, flattened shells with only a small terminal whorl that resembles a stumpy tail. At least two different species are found, but only one has been described, *Succinea flexilis*, which is endemic to Gough. Its shell is 5–7 mm high and 4–5 mm wide, and is quite flexible when wet. Its body is dark grey with square spots on the tail.

At least five species of slugs occur at the islands, all introduced by man. The most common is the smallish Gray Field Slug *Deroceras reticulatum*, also called the Reticulated Slug, which has spread widely from Europe, and is found on all islands. It thrives on crops such as lettuce and cabbages at Tristan, but also occurs in natural vegetation. Two closely related species, the Brown Field Slug *D. panormitanum* and Meadow Slug *D. leave* are confined to Tristan and Inaccessible. The largest species is the Valencia Slug *Lehmannia valentiana* that reaches up to 10 cm long and is found on Tristan and Gough. The smaller Black-keeled Slug *Milax gagates* is confined to Tristan, where it is a pest boring into potatoes.

Segmented worms Annelida

These soft-bodied, moisture-loving invertebrates have been little studied, although they are common at the islands. At least seven earthworms (Lumbricidae) have been recorded from Tristan and four from Gough, all introduced from Europe. *Allolobophoridella eiseni* is the most abundant species, found at all four islands, with *Allolobophora chlorotica* known only from Tristan. Enchytraeiids are small, slender white worms found in soils that are easily mistaken for fine root hairs. At least 11 species are known, with eight at Tristan and five at Gough, but to date only one has been positively identified, *Cognettia sphagnetorum* (Tristan). Naidids are very small, translucent worms, mainly found in fresh water, often amongst algal filaments. Five species are known from the islands (two *Nais* sp. and three *Pristina* sp.), all probably introduced.

Other worms Nemertea, Nematoda, Platyhelminthes

The most impressive native worm is the land nemertean *Katechonemertes nightingaleensis* (Tristan, Nightingale and Inaccessible) that grows up to 30 mm long and 4 mm wide. It is olive grey with two broad dark brown stripes running along its back, and has a proboscis which can extend almost as long as its body. It lives at the back of the shore, among tussock bases, out of reach of the sea. Virtually nothing is known about the island's nematodes, but *Heterocephalobus goughiensis* (Cephalobidae) has been described from a female collected at Gough. A small flatworm *Obrimoposthia ohlini* occurs in streams at Gough and Inaccessible. It occurs in marine habitats elsewhere, but at Gough it is replaced along the coast by *O. variabilis*.

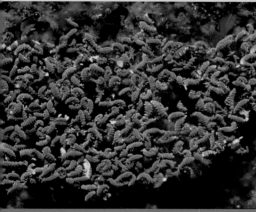

▲ **(1)** cf. *Hypogastrura* sp. springtails

▲ **(2)** *Ixodes uriae* seabird tick on Tristan Albatross host
INSET **(3)** Engorged seabird tick

▼ **(4)** *Chelanops atlanticus* pseudoscorpion

▼ **(5)** *Porcellio scaber* woodlouse (alien)

▼ **(6)** *Lithobius melanops* centipede (alien)

▼ **(7)** *Oxychilus alliarius* Garlic Snail (alien)

▼ **(8)** *Succinea* sp. snail

▼ **(9)** *Katechonemertes nightingaleensis* proboscis worm

▼ **(10)** *Lehmannia valentiana* Valencia Slug (alien)

Tristan Rock
Lobsters and large
kelps dominate
subtidal habitats

MARINE LIFE

The islands are specks in the vast South Atlantic Ocean. The surrounding seas support a wealth of biodiversity, which is of great economic importance. Marine systems impact the terrestrial biota through salt-spray and the actions of seabirds and seals that gather on the islands to breed and moult. These marine visitors import nutrients and energy and open the vegetation by trampling and digging. In general, marine ecosystems are less well studied, and only a brief overview of the larger, more conspicuous species is provided here.

Bathymetry and oceanography

The Tristan islands rise steeply from deep water close to the Mid-Atlantic Ridge. The seabed between Tristan and the two outer islands is more than 2,000 m deep, but is only 500 m deep between Nightingale and Inaccessible. Shallow, shelf waters are generally less than 2 km wide, but extend up to 10 km on the western side of Inaccessible Island, reflecting the extent of the original volcano. In addition to the islands, there are several seamounts around the islands that are important for fishing.

The inshore seabed is generally rugged, with subtidal reefs, boulders and coarse sand. Most coastlines are highly eroded, with narrow boulder beaches or cliffs, often with caves and arches, both above and below water. The few sandy beaches are on the main island of Tristan. In a few locations there are more extensive intertidal flats with rock pools and channels. The tidal range is small, with spring tides around 1 m. The usually strong wave action results in the whole intertidal zone being covered by breaking waves, even at low tide.

The waters around the islands are oceanic, little affected by silt deposition and freshwater run-off. The water is usually clear and blue, and Giant Kelp *Macrocystis pyrifera* grows from the seabed in waters up to 40 m deep. The islands lie in the west-wind drift of the Antarctic Circumpolar Current, augmented by the southern edge of the South Atlantic gyre which cycles water counter-clockwise around the South Atlantic Ocean. The Subtropical Front, the boundary between subtropical waters and cooler sub-Antarctic waters, lies north of Gough. Mean sea surface temperatures at the northern islands vary between 12–16°C in winter to 15–20°C in summer. At Gough, comparable temperatures are 10–13°C in winter and 12–15°C in summer. Water temperature falls rapidly with depth, and is only 2–3°C below 1,000 m, effectively isolating shallow marine ecosystems.

Colonisation and endemism

Just as terrestrial species have struggled to colonise the islands across thousands of kilometres of open ocean, so have many shallow-water marine species. Visitors to a Tristan beach might be surprised to find only one common seashell, that of the local whelk. A cursory inspection of the rock-pools reveals few large intertidal animals. Many groups are depauperate, with decapod crustaceans, gastropod molluscs, soft corals, starfish and urchins each represented by only 1–2 common species. Many species exhibit small body size or 'dwarfism', including polychaetes, bivalves and anemones. However, some of these species are present in great numbers; grazing by the urchin *Arbacia crassispina* dominates the subtidal ecosystem, while jewel anemones are abundant, and tiny bivalves, crustaceans and worms teem amongst the rich undergrowth of seaweeds.

Despite the low overall diversity, many marine species are endemic to the islands. Bottom-dwelling species confined to shallow water such as seaweeds are more likely to be endemic, because they are unable to spread via the deep sea floor. Up to 40% of seaweeds are found nowhere else. The proportion of endemic animals varies between groups: eight of 10 bivalves are thought to be endemic, whereas none of the 13 bryozoans are. Most fish are widely distributed with an extended pelagic or open ocean stage (eggs, larvae or pelagic juveniles), which may explain how they initially colonised the islands. Only the intertidal Klipfish *Bovichthus diacanthus* is endemic. The fauna is similar at Tristan and Gough, with the closest affinity to the Magellanic region of southern South America and the Falklands, although there are species from South Africa, New Zealand and adjacent sub-Antarctic islands, Antarctica, and temperate islands in the Indian Ocean. The seaweed floras are rather more divergent between the northern islands and Gough, with mainly sub-Antarctic species at Gough, and stronger South African affinities at Tristan.

Ocean currents are slow. It takes 4–10 months to drift from the Falklands to Tristan, and 1–2 years around the South Atlantic gyre from South Africa. These periods are much longer than most larvae survive in the plankton. Most animals probably were transported on drifting seaweeds or other floating debris, which often carry sessile animals including hydroids, bryozoans and serpulid worms. Buoyed by its many gas-filled bladders, Giant Kelp can drift for months. The life-styles of intertidal bivalves at Tristan support this colonisation route; all live on algae and most brood their young, avoiding the risk of planktonic larvae being swept away from the islands. A large proportion of the marine invertebrates is viviparous, retaining their eggs and giving 'birth' to live young.

Humans may have played a role in some marine organisms reaching the islands, either as fouling on ships' hulls or as spores or larvae in ballast water, which could easily survive the 5–7 day trip from Cape Town or South America. Such artificial introductions have the potential to cause havoc in the species-poor ecosystems of the islands, especially if they alter important predator-prey relationships, about which little is known. Given the importance of the Tristan Rock Lobster *Jasus tristani* fishery for the islands' economy, it is important that such introductions be limited as much as possible.

Intertidal zone

The rocky intertidal is small because of the small tidal range, steep shores and the exposed nature of the coastline. However, in places flat reefs with deep rock pools extend the area that can be explored, and the constant surf ensures a healthy cover of seaweeds that harbours numerous small animals. On Gough, the siphonariid limpet *Kerguelenella lateralis* and the herbivorous gastropod *Marinula tristanensis* are abundant on the upper shore, but limpets and snails are rare on Tristan shores, which perhaps contributes to Tristan's rich seaweed flora. Chitons are common midshore grazers at all islands, whereas barnacles, commonly found in dense bands on most temperate and coldwater seashores, are present only as scattered individuals, and mytilid mussels are entirely absent.

Mid-shore seaweeds are quite different on Tristan and Gough. Bands of the red seaweeds *Iridaea laminarioides* and *Polysiphonia* sp. are common on Gough but not reported for Tristan, although another species of *Iridaea* is common in the lower intertidal and upper subtidal on Tristan. On Tristan, a number of seaweeds are locally abundant that are not found on Gough, including the red seaweeds *Gigartina stiriata* and *Gymnogongrus gregarius*, and the brown *Halopteris funicularis* and *Splachnidium rugosum*. A band of Bull Kelp *Durvillaea antarctica*, a big brown seaweed, grows around the low water mark on Gough but is absent from Tristan.

More species occur in rock pools, often extending into the subtidal. Deeper pools on Tristan are heavily grazed by urchins *Arbacia crassispina*, and numerous small rock lobsters hide amongst the seaweeds and under overhangs. The endemic Klipfish is common in shallow, wave-washed pools, and the beautiful Tristan Wrasse *Nelabrichthys ornatus* occurs in deeper pools. Large octopus are numerous, presumably preying on the rock lobsters. Smaller creatures inhabiting rock pools include anemones, whelks, sea-slugs, polychaete worms, small crustaceans, bivalves, sponges and occasional brittlestars. Pale Kelp *Laminaria pallida* and Giant Kelp also grow in the deeper pools.

Sand and cobble shores are generally too mobile in such exposed conditions to support any but the most ephemeral intertidal marine life. However, the boulders often support a film of microscopic algae, making them extremely treacherous to walk on when wet. Stranded kelp attracts large numbers of sand-hoppers (Amphipoda) as well as kelp flies. A feature of the upper parts of some Tristan shores is numerous small insect larvae in mucus tubes attached to rocks in the uppermost part of the shore. These are thought to be the larvae of kelp flies.

Subtidal zone

The subtidal zone is characterised by forests of kelps and other seaweeds. At the northern islands, dense red seaweed turfs cover rocks down to around 10 m, together with Pale Kelp from a few metres down, and Giant Kelp from 10–30 m. Grazing urchins are abundant below 10 m, clearing the rocks of smaller seaweeds and animals, leaving only a hard pink coating of coralline seaweeds. On vertical rock, where urchins find it harder to reach without being knocked off by the waves, there is much more life and the rocks are a colourful patchwork of sponges, trumpet and jewel anemones and soft corals, with bryozoans and hydroids on reef crests. Large shoals of Five-finger *Acantholatris monodactylus*, together with Tristan Wrasse, forage in the kelp. Crevices in vertical rock faces are inhabited by False Jacopever *Sebastes capensis*, with occasional Soldier *Helicolenus mouchezi* in deeper waters. Sea fans and larger hydroids and bryozoans, teeming with tanaids, form a different community on bedrock below 40 m. A few hardy bivalves and the Swimming Crab *Ovalipes trimaculatus* inhabit the coarse, shifting sands, and interesting seaweeds grow on cobbles in sand in deeper water.

Open ocean and seabed

Much less is known about the communities of the open ocean and the deep-water benthos. The fish fauna includes numerous widespread species, which may be more or less transient in Tristan waters, including predators such as the Great White Shark *Carcharadon carcharias*. Oceanic drifters including the Portuguese Man-of-War or Blue-bottle *Physalia physalis* and the bubble-snails *Janthina* spp. are often stranded on these open shores. There have been few attempts to sample the deep water bottom fauna since the visit of HMS *Challenger* in 1873.

▲ (1) Red, green and brown seaweeds in lava channels

▲ (2) Pale Kelp *Laminaria pallida*

▼ (3) Giant Kelp *Macrocystis pyrifera*

▼ (4) Intertidal rocky reefs at Runaway Beach, Tristan

▼ (5) Breakers hitting the new volcano, Tristan

▼ (6) Steep rocky shores at low tide on Nightingale

BONY FISHES Osteichthyes

More than 50 species of fish have been recorded from the inshore waters around Tristan and Gough, mainly bony fish. Only the more common species likely to be encountered within 200 m of the surface are listed here; many more widespread oceanic species are known to occur in the pelagic zone while the fauna of deeper waters is poorly known (see Andrew *et al.* 1995 for a review).

Congridae

Hairy Conger *Bassanago nielseni*   Eel

A conger eel up to 1 m long with the tail longer than head and trunk combined; brownish above, pale below; median fins dark with pale margin; skin covered with minute, slender, darkly-pigmented villi (scattered and difficult to see in juveniles, but profuse in adults, giving a distinctive 'hairy' appearance). The most common eel at Tristan; two other species of conger eel have been recorded from the islands, but these appear to be rare. Most Hairy Congers have been collected in rock lobster traps set deeper than 70 m, and often in traps set overnight, suggesting they are nocturnal feeders. An adult male captured off Tristan in June was in breeding condition, suggesting a winter spawning season. **Distribution**: known only from Tristan, Nightingale, Inaccessible and the Nazca Ridge, south-east Pacific Ocean.

Gadidae

Comb Rockling *Gaidropsarus novaezelandiae*

A fairly small (up to 40 cm), elongate fish with long low dorsal and anal fins that reach to the rounded caudal fin; dark reddish brown above, purplish-grey below; dorsal fin preceded by a row of short filaments and a longer ray on the nape; pectoral fins with 20–21 rays; two barbels on snout (from anterior nostrils) and one on chin. Juveniles and small adults (<20 cm) are common in rock-pools and in shallow subtidal areas at all islands; larger adults are found down to at least 50 m. Pre-juveniles (<30 mm) are silvery and probably pelagic. It is a cryptic predator that feeds on crustaceans and small fishes. **Distribution**: Tristan, Nightingale, Inaccessible and Gough; also the west coast of South Africa, Amsterdam and St Paul Islands, Australia, New Zealand, Nazca Ridge and Bromley Plateau (31°S, 34°W).

Exocoetidae

Small-head Flying-fish *Cheilopogon pinnatibarbatus*   Flying Fish

A large flying-fish, up to 50 cm long; pectoral fins greatly enlarged, reaching past base of anal fin; pelvic fins also enlarged, reaching past origin of anal fin; body dark iridescent blue above, silvery white below; pectoral fins dusky, with narrow pale transverse band and pale rear margin. Flying fish are common around the Tristan islands in summer (November–April) when sea temperatures >16°C. They are commonly eaten by Snoek; sometimes land aboard ship at night. **Distribution**: Tristan, Nightingale, Inaccessible; also eastern North Atlantic, South Atlantic (including South Africa, St Helena, Brazil) and southern Indian Ocean (including Amsterdam and St Paul Islands, and near Marion Island); appears to occur close to land and generally avoids tropical latitudes. A single specimen of another flying fish, *Hirundichthyes rondeletii*, has been collected at Gough.

Macrorhamphosidae

Round Bellowsfish *Notopogon lilliei*   Piper

A strangely-shaped orange fish with silvery white patches up to 25 cm long; has a small, toothless mouth at the end of a long, tube-like snout; body strongly compressed; scales microscopic, lanceolate and erect, giving the body a velvety feel; adults have a patch of short bristles above operculum; soft dorsal, caudal and anal fins have white bands. Common >50 m at all islands; often caught in lobster traps up to 200 m; preyed upon by Wreckfish (Steambras). It is sometimes found washed up on beaches after storms. Juveniles drift in the pelagic zone until they reach a suitable place to settle. **Distribution**: Tristan, Nightingale, Inaccessible, Gough; also South Africa, New Zealand and South Australia. **Banded Piper** *Centriscops obliquus*, is slightly smaller with distinctive bands across its body (oblique in male, vertical in female).

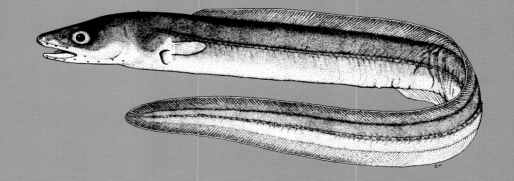

▲ **(1) Hairy Conger** *Bassanago nielseni*
▼ **(2) Comb Rockling** *Gaidropsarus novaezelandiae*

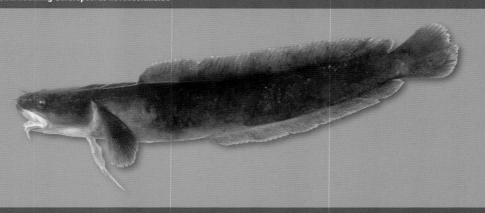

▼ **(3) Flying-fish sp.** ▼ **(4) Round Bellowsfish** *Notopogon lillei*

Scorpaenidae

Soldier *Helicolenus mouchezi*

A distinctive, bull-headed fish with conspicuous small, dark brown spots on head, body and fins; ground colour variable, from brown to pale red; belly white. Dorsal fin with 12 spines, 12–13 rays; anal fin with three strong spines, 5–6 rays; head spiny; pectoral fin rays 18–20, the upper part of fin truncate, the lower eight rays unbranched and thickened with the tips free. Inhabits deeper water (40–200 m) than False Jacopever and smaller size classes are not found close to shore; because of its preference for deeper water, it is less commonly caught. It is ovoviviparous and highly fecund (300,000 embryos in a 40 cm fish), spawning during summer (October–April). Larvae released at 3–4 mm long. It feeds almost exclusively on other fishes. **Distribution**: Tristan, Nightingale, Inaccessible, Gough; also Amsterdam and St Paul Islands, and Austral and Sapmer Seamounts in the south-west Indian Ocean.

False Jacopever *Sebastes capensis*   Soldier

Superficially similar to Soldier *Helicolenus mouchezi*, but is less boldly spotted and has 3–6 white spots on the back below the dorsal fin; maximum length 46 cm; colour variable, ranging from gold, through orange to red; dorsal fin with 13 spines, 13–14 rays; anal fin with three strong spines, six rays; head spiny; pectoral fin wedge-shaped with 18–19 rays, the lower 9–10 unbranched. This is the second most abundant fish (after Five-finger) caught at Tristan. Small individuals (<20 cm) occur in rock-pools and shallow subtidal habitats to about 10 m; adults are found in deeper water up to 150 m (rare >100 m). Highly territorial, even as juveniles, with individuals occupying caves and crevices. It is ovoviviparous and highly fecund (>200,000 embryos in a 40 cm fish). The embryos hatch inside the ovary and are released as 3–4 mm free-swimming larvae. It is an ambush predator, feeding mainly on small fish, but will also take benthic invertebrates. **Distribution**: Tristan, Nightingale, Inaccessible and Gough; range elsewhere unclear due to confusion about species limits; either this species or very close relatives occur in Chile, Argentina and South Africa.

Polyprionidae

Wreckfish *Polyprion oxygeneios*   Steambras

A distinctly bicoloured fish; dark bluish-grey above, whitish below; maximum length 150 cm. Body oblong, somewhat compressed, covered with small, strongly ctenoid scales; dorsal fin with 11–12 strong spines, 11–12 soft rays; anal fin with three spines, 8–10 rays; pectoral fins shorter than pelvics; caudal fin truncate; head scaly, except for snout. Found on rough, rocky bottoms from 80–200 m. It is seldom caught by local fishermen, and juveniles <50 cm are rarely encountered. Juveniles are pelagic until at least 30 cm and often associate with floating objects. Probably spawns in late summer (February–April). It feeds mainly on fish and lobsters. **Distribution**: Tristan, Nightingale, Inaccessible and Gough; widespread along shelf edges throughout the temperate and subtropical southern hemisphere.

Carangidae

Giant Yellowtail *Seriola lalandi*   Yellowtail, Cape Mackerel

A sleek, pelagic predator with distinctive olive-yellow fins and tail; body bluish above, shading to silvery-white below; maximum length 1.9 m. Caudal fin forked; first dorsal fin with seven spines (first minute), second dorsal with one spine, 30–35 rays; anal fin with two small spines preceding fin, a slender spine bound to first ray, and 19–22 rays; pectoral fins shorter than pelvics; caudal peduncle with a low fleshy keel on each side. Until recently this species was thought to be a rare subtropical visitor to Tristan waters, but is now known to occur year round. Diet mainly small fish and squid; also some crustaceans. **Distribution**: Tristan, Nightingale and Inaccessible; widespread in subtropical waters.

Southern Horse Mackerel *Trachurus longimanus*   Mackerel

A pelagic fish up to 50 cm long with a distinctively kinked row of large lateral scales; body dark bluish-green above, silvery white below, with a small black spot on the upper rear margin of the operculum. Caudal fin forked; first dorsal fin with eight spines, second dorsal with one spine, 31–34 rays; anal fin with two distinct spines preceding fin, a slender spine bound to first ray, and 26–29 rays; last ray of dorsal and anal fins enlarged, connected by membrane to penultimate ray but 50% farther apart than other rays; pectoral fins with 22–23 rays (top two unbranched). Fairly common, found in schools from the surface to about 50 m. It spawns October–March. It uses its long gill-rakers to catch planktonic organisms such as amphipods and small pelagic fish. **Distribution**: Tristan, Nightingale, Inaccessible and Gough; also Vema Seamount, St Paul Island, Austral Seamount, and Walters Shoal in the south-west Indian Ocean.

▲ (1) False Jacopever *Sebastes capensis* (top)
and Soldier *Helicolenus mouchezi* (bottom)

▼ (2) Giant Yellowtail *Seriola lalandi*

▲ (3) Wreckfish *Polyprion oxygeneios*
▼ (4) Southern Horse Mackeral *Trachurus longimanus*

Cheilodactylidae

Five-finger *Acantholatris monodactylus*

A common, bream-like fish with 5–6 dark brown or blackish vertical bars on the upper parts starting at the front of the dorsal fin; remainder of body usually bronze (colour varies from silver to orange); sides of head and body have numerous small black spots; maximum length 65 cm. Caudal fin forked; dorsal fin with 16–18 spines, 24–27 rays; anal fin with three spines, 11–12 rays; pectoral fins with 14–15 rays, the upper two rays and the lower 5–6 rays unbranched, the other rays branched. The Five-finger is the dominant species in terms of biomass on the shelf areas, and is the species most frequently caught for food and bait. There is a minimum size limit of 25 cm for fish caught from boats. It occurs in a wide range of habitats from 1–150 m, favouring areas with algal cover in shallower waters. It is an opportunistic carnivore, feeding on benthic invertebrates, planktonic salps, amphipods, and smaller fish. It normally occurs within 10 m of the seabed. Larval and small juvenile stages are compressed, silvery and pelagic, while larger juveniles are usually seen swimming in shoals of up to 15 individuals within 2 m of the bottom. Adults often rest on the bottom in caves and crevices. Tagging studies at Tristan show that larger individuals are territorial, with relatively small home ranges. It is slow growing; large adults are >25 years old. Spawns in summer from February–April. **Distribution**: Tristan, Nightingale, Inaccessible and Gough; also Vema Seamount, and Amsterdam and St Paul Islands, and Austral Seamount and Walters Shoal in the south-west Indian Ocean.

Latridae

Striped Trumpeter *Latris lineata*   Funnyfish

A deep-water species up to 1 m long; head and body dark olive green above, with three silvery bands from head to tail; belly silvery yellow; fins greenish yellow. Body elongate, compressed; caudal fin forked; dorsal fin with 18 spines, 34–36 rays, the fin divided almost to the base between spiny and soft-rayed parts; anal fin with three spines, 25–28 rays; pectoral fins with 17–18 rays, the lower 8–9 unbranched. Seldom caught, perhaps living at depths greater than those normally fished by island fishermen. **Distribution**: Tristan, Nightingale, Inaccessible and Gough; also Amsterdam and St Paul Islands, Australia, New Zealand, and the sub-Antarctic Auckland Islands.

Mendosoma lineatum

A fairly small, nondescript fish, bluish-green above, fading to silver-yellow below; fins pale yellow, the caudal fin darker yellow; maximum length 30 cm. Body elongate, moderately compressed; caudal fin forked; dorsal fin with 22–24 spines, 24–27 rays; anal fin with three spines, 17–21 rays; pectoral fin rays 16–18, the upper two and lower 6–8 unbranched, but not thicker or longer than other rays; mouth very protrusile, the upper jaw with one row of small conical teeth; no teeth on lower jaw. Common; occurs in schools of similar-sized individuals. Adults are epibenthic below 20 m, but juveniles occur close to the surface where they are easy prey for birds. Small groups of juveniles occasionally become trapped in rock-pools. The pelagic juveniles are compressed and silvery. It is mainly planktivorous, but also feeds on small pelagic fishes. It is an important prey item for Snoek and is eaten occasionally by Rockhopper Penguins. **Distribution**: Tristan, Nightingale, Inaccessible and Gough; also Chile, Amsterdam and St Paul Islands, Tasmania, New Zealand and the sub-Antarctic Auckland Islands.

Labridae

Tristan Wrasse *Nelabrichthys ornatus*   Concha

A fairly small, long, slender fish; changes sex with age and is sexually dimorphic. Juveniles are mainly yellow-orange. Small adults (<16 cm) are female: body olive-brown with azure lateral stripes; both juveniles and females have three black spots: one at leading edge of dorsal fin, one between the last three dorsal fin rays, and one at the base of the tail. Larger animals (>17 cm) are male; head and body brownish with violet or red lines running along length of body; dorsal fin purple-brown, with three violet longitudinal stripes and a black spot at the leading edge; tail fin rounded, reddish yellow, with concentric violet stripes. Dorsal fin with nine spines, 12–13 rays; anal fin with three slender spines, 11–12 rays; pectoral fin rays 12–14; cheeks scaly. This is the most abundant fish in shallow waters around the northern islands. It occurs close to the bottom in water 1–50 m deep, favouring areas with plentiful cover, either in the form of rocky reefs or kelp beds. Its diet is mainly epiphytic organisms. All fish begin life as females, but some change to males; the mechanism is not well understood, but is thought to be related to body size. Males establish territories about 2 m in diameter each evening during the spawning season (November–March) in open areas surrounded by adequate cover. Larger males occupy more desirable sites close to shelter. Males display vigorously at any female moving into the territory. If a female accepts a male's advances, the pair swim rapidly upwards and spawn in mid-water. **Distribution**: Tristan, Nightingale, Inaccessible and Gough; also Vema Seamount, Amsterdam and St Paul Islands.

▲ **(1) Five-finger** *Acantholatris monodactylus*

▲ **(2) Striped Trumpeter** *Latris lineata*

▲ **(3)** *Mendosoma lineatum*

▼ **(4) Tristan Wrasse** *Nelabrichthys ornatus*, male

▼ **(5) Tristan Wrasse** *Nelabrichthys ornatus*, female

Bovichtidae

Klipfish *Bovichtus diacanthus*

A small, unscaled, bull-headed fish resembling a blenny or goby; maximum length 25 cm; dorsal colour usually olive or blackish-green, but can vary from reddish-brown to blackish to match its habitat; belly and lower fins edged whitish. Body elongate, subcylindrical; first dorsal fin with 8–9 spines; second dorsal fin with 20–21 rays; 15–16 anal fin rays; dorsal and anal fin-rays unbranched; 14–15 pectoral fin rays; pelvic fins anterior to pectoral fins, with one spine, five rays; a single nostril on each side of snout. Extremely common in rock-pools and subtidal areas down to 20 m. It is able to withstand a wide temperature range, including sun-warmed pools of up to 27°C. Larvae pelagic, developing into a silvery post-larval stage that occurs in large schools that are important prey for predatory fish such as Snoek. Juveniles settle in shallow water when 5–6 cm long. Feeds mainly on epiphytic fauna and amphipods. Adults move into deeper water February–March to spawn. **Distribution**: Tristan, Nightingale, Inaccessible and Gough; endemic. Related species occur at the Antarctic Peninsula and the southern coasts of South America, Amsterdam and St Paul Islands, Australia and New Zealand.

Gempylidae

Snoek *Thyrsites atun*

A long, slender, barracuda-like pelagic predator, up to 1.3 m long; silvery with iridescent purplish hue when fresh; fins dark grey. Body distinctly elongated and compressed, with a large mouth and fearsome teeth; lateral line bends down abruptly in mid-body; caudal fin forked; dorsal fin divided, with 18–21 spines followed by a short fin of 10–12 rays and 5–7 separate finlets; anal fin of 2–3 minute spines, 8–11 rays and 5–7 finlets; pelvic fins small, with one spine and five rays; pectoral fin rays 14–15; no fleshy keels on caudal peduncle or belly; two nostrils on each side of snout. Occurs year round; the population appears to be self sustaining with larvae, juveniles and breeding adults present. Spawning occurs in shallow water in summer (October–April). Adults feed mainly on fish, including flying fish and pelagic juvenile Klipfish and *Mendosoma lineatum*. **Distribution**: Tristan, Nightingale, Inaccessible and Gough; occurs close to shore throughout temperate waters of the southern hemisphere.

Stromateidae

Southern Butterfish *Hyperoglyphe antarctica*   Bluefish

A stout-bodied fish up to 1 m long with a large, mainly unscaled head and huge eyes; dark blue-grey above fading to grey below; fins dusky. Dorsal fin divided; front part low with 7–8 short stout spines, less than half height of rear dorsal fin, which has one hidden spine and 17–20 rays; anal fin with three spines, 14–16 rays; pectoral fin long and falcate with 19–22 rays. Arguably the best eating fish at the islands; target of fisheries at seamounts around the islands. Occurs year round in water 40–150 m deep. Juveniles are pelagic, but fish >45 cm long occur in schools above the bottom. It feeds mainly on cephalopods and colonial salps, but also some fish. Matures at about 80 cm long; spawns during January–February. **Distribution**: Tristan, Nightingale, Inaccessible and Gough; occurs widely in temperate waters of the southern hemisphere.

Oval Driftfish *Schedophilus velaini*   Stumpnose

Superficially similar to Bluefish, but with more rounded 'nose' and undivided dorsal fin; maximum length 75 cm; olive green above, silvery on sides and below. Dorsal fin has 6–8 weak spines followed by 26–29 rays; anal fin with three spines, 19–21 rays; pectoral fin elongate and pointed in adults, with 21–22 rays. Relatively common; often caught amongst Bluefish. Usually found just above the seabed in waters >40 m deep, but occasionally feeds higher up in the water column; stomach contents include planktonic salps, cephalopods and small fish. Spawning occurs in late summer. Post-larvae and small juveniles pelagic, associated with flotsam and pelagic jellyfishes in the open ocean. **Distribution**: Tristan, Nightingale and Inaccessible; widespread in south temperate and subtropical waters, including at St Helena, Vema Seamount and South Africa.

▲ (1) Klipfish *Bovichtus diacanthus*

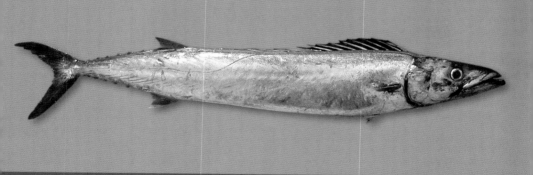

▲ (2) Snoek *Thyrsites atun*

▼ (3) Southern Butterfish *Hyperoglyphe antarctica*　　　▼ (4) Oval Driftfish *Schedophilus velaini*

CARTILAGINOUS FISHES Chondrichthyes

At least seven species of cartilaginous fishes have been recorded from Tristan waters, including six sharks and one ray. Most are rarely encountered, but the following three sharks are fairly common. Regular sight records of Great Hammerhead *Sphyrna mokarran* suggest this species is common in Tristan waters in summer.

Hexanchidae

Broadnose Sevengill Shark *Notorynchus cepedianus*   Rock Shark

The most common shark at the islands, with only one dorsal fin and seven pairs of gill slits; up to 2.5 m long; pale grey above, white below; dorsal surface of body and fins speckled with black spots; six rows of large teeth on each side of lower jaw. Frequently caught and used for bait. The local population is probably self sustaining, as all size ranges occur. Feeds predominantly on fish and squid. **Distribution**: Tristan, Nightingale, Inaccessible and Gough; occurs in relatively shallow, temperate coastal waters worldwide, except the North Atlantic.

Carcharhinidae

Blue Shark *Prionace glauca*   Bottlenose Shark

A distinctive, slender pelagic shark up to 2.5 m long with two dorsal fins and extremely long pectoral fins; brilliant dark blue above, white below; fades to grey after death; five pairs of gill slits; pectoral fins long and falcate; lower tail lobe distinctly smaller than upper; teeth strongly serrated and broadly curved in upper jaw; lower teeth narrower. Commonly caught; occurs around the islands year round, from the surface to at least 150 m. **Distribution**: Widespread in tropical and temperate waters; most common in 12–16°C waters.

Lamnidae

Shortfin Mako *Isurus oxyrinchus*   Bottlenose Shark

A fast-swimming, pelagic shark, up to 3 m long with two dorsal fins; dark blue above, white below; lower lobe of caudal (tail) fin almost as big as upper lobe; five pairs of gill slits; pectoral fins short (less than distance from snout to base of pectoral fin). A heavier bodied shark than the Blue Shark. Makos are reputed to be common in Tristan waters. Although seldom caught, they are occasionally seen leaping from the water, and are known to display aggressive behaviour towards boats. **Distribution**: Worldwide in tropical and temperate waters, both inshore and in the open ocean.

OTHER MARINE LIFE

Sea squirts Ascidiacea

Adult sea squirts are sessile filter-feeders that pump water through a mesh-like filter to extract food particles. They may be solitary or form small colonies. Although they bear little resemblance to vertebrates, the tadpole-like larval stage has a primitive backbone and nerve cord, showing that they are closely related to vertebrates. Six species have been identified from Tristan waters, the commonest being *Corella eumyota*, a coldwater, southern hemisphere species. A very small, bright orange sea squirt grows on vertical rocks in the subtidal at several sites around Tristan.

Crustaceans Crustacea

Crabs, lobsters and relatives Decapoda

There are remarkably few species of large crustacean at the islands, but the **Tristan Rock Lobster** or Crayfish *Jasus tristani* is extremely abundant, and the basis for a productive fishery. They occur from intertidal pools to more than 200 m deep, favouring rocky areas with crevices. They can jack-knife rapidly backwards to escape capture. Small lobsters are abundant in shore rock-pools and channels, where they hide amongst dense seaweeds, but many are washed ashore by storms, or are eaten by octopus. Larger animals occur in deeper waters, reaching lengths of at least 50 cm. *Jasus* is a southern hemisphere temperate genus, occurring in South Africa, St Paul and Amsterdam Islands, South Australia, New Zealand and Juan Fernandez Islands. *J. tristani* is confined to the Tristan archipelago, Gough and Vema Seamount, 650 km west of South Africa.

▲ (1) Broadnose Sevengill Shark *Notorynchus cepedianus*
▼ (2) Blue Shark *Prionace glauca*

▼ (3) Shortfin Mako *Isurus oxyrinchus*

▼ (4) Sea squirt sp.

▼ (5) Tristan Rock Lobster *Jasus tristani*

The commercial fishery for rock lobster started in the 1950s, and is run by a single concession holder. Fishing at Tristan is conducted from small boats operated by islanders, whereas that at the other islands takes place from a factory ship which sets lines of traps, as well as from small boats. There are minimum size limits (70 mm carapace length at Tristan and Nightingale, 68 mm at Inaccessible and 75 mm at Gough) and total catch quotas are set annually for each island. Despite problems with occasional poachers, the resource is in a generally healthy condition. Fishing is best in spring, after the lobster have moulted and reproduced. Traps are baited with fish heads imported from Cape Town, although in the past local fish and even penguins have been used for bait.

The **Three-spot Swimming Crab** *Ovalipes trimaculatus* inhabits exposed sandy seabeds around Tristan, especially around Seal Bay and Sandy Point. It has a purple carapace up to 8.6 cm across, with three darker spots. The hind pair of legs end in paddles, for rapid swimming. It has a wide distribution in the southern hemisphere. In other parts of its range it feeds on molluscs, but larger molluscs are in short supply on Tristan. It is preyed upon by fish, including Five-fingers.

Another crab, very similar to the Rock or Red Bait Crab *Plagusia chabrus*, lives on Tristan and Nightingale, inhabiting the zone of maximum surf action. Live specimens have a handsome dark blue carapace, but those washed up on the shore are red-brown. *Plagusia chabrus* is widespread in South Africa, South Australia, New Zealand and Chile, but was not recorded for Tristan by early expeditions, so the identification of this crab awaits confirmation. It may well be a recent arrival.

Other crustaceans

Several groups of small crustaceans are inconspicuous and often go unnoticed, unless they are present in larger numbers like amphipods or 'sandhoppers' which gather amongst piles of drift seaweed. Collectively they are extremely important, breaking down and recycling drift seaweed and other marine debris, and providing an important food for small-mouthed young fish. Around Tristan and Gough amphipods, isopods and tanaids are common among seaweeds and other marine growths in deeper water. Small crustaceans also play a key role in the zooplankton in oceanic waters around the islands. They include copepods, which are the main prey of Broad-billed Prions, the most abundant seabird breeding at the islands.

Amphipods Amphipoda

Amphipods are small, laterally flattened crustaceans, that are often abundant under stones and amongst seaweeds. They are a relatively diverse group, with around 30 species recorded from shallower Tristan waters, although 10 of these are widely dispersed oceanic species. At least 12 species have been identified from Gough seashores. Some species are unusual in that they occur in terrestrial systems at the islands (see page 117). Caprellids are a distinctive group of amphipods with a thin elongated body, known as skeleton shrimps. Looking rather like a mini praying mantis less than 1 cm long, skeleton shrimps perch on seaweeds and other marine growth, catching passing prey with their large claws.

Isopods Isopoda

Isopods are small, dorsally-flattened crustaceans including some terrestrial species known as woodlice (see page 117). 26 species have been reported from Tristan waters, and eight from Gough shores. Most are small, but the endemic *Paridotea apposita* is a veritable giant amongst isopods, with males growing up to 4.5 cm long. Despite its large size, it is very difficult to spot as its colour matches the seaweeds on which it lives, varying from light brown to dark red or deep green.

Tanaids Tanaidacea

Tanaids are small cylindrical crustaceans, <1 cm long, with distinctive strong nippers. They are abundant at Tristan, living in tubes which they build amongst seaweeds, hydroids or bryozoans. Tanaids do not have free-swimming larvae; the eggs are carried in a brood pouch beneath the female and hatch as miniature adults.

Barnacles Cirripedia

Barnacles are sessile crustaceans which anchor themselves by their heads, encase their bodies in protective shells, and use their legs to filter food particles. They are abundant on most temperate rocky seashores, forming conspicuous zonal bands, but these are entirely lacking at Tristan and Gough. A large species of *Austromegabalanus* up to 2 cm high is found as scattered individuals in the intertidal at all islands. **Goose barnacles** *Lepas* sp. are common on drift wood and other marine litter which is often washed ashore at the islands. They have fleshy stems or 'necks' and bivalve-like white shells encasing the body of the barnacle. These shells are often found in regurgitations of Tristan Skuas, and the planktonic larvae of goose barnacles appear to be the main prey of the enigmatic Grey-backed Storm Petrel.

Sea spiders Pycnogonida

Five species of pycnogonids or sea spiders have been reported from Tristan, one of which is apparently endemic to Tristan, and one endemic to Tristan and Gough. The others are found in colder waters of the southern hemisphere.

(1) Amphipod sp.

(3) Isopod sp.

▲ (2) Three-spot Swimming Crab *Ovalipes trimaculatus*

▲ (3) Isopod sp.

▼ (4) Rock Crab cf. *Plagusia chabrus*

▼ (5) Isopod *Paridotea apposita*

▼ (6) Barnacle *Austromegabalanus* sp.

▼ (7) Goose barnacles *Lepas* sp.

▼ (8) Sea spider or pycnogonid

Mollusca
Compared to other regions, the molluscs of Tristan are, with a few notable exceptions, sparse in both species and numbers. Many species are very small and are easily overlooked.

Chitons Polyplacophora
Chitons are distinctive flattened molluscs with shells consisting of eight overlapping plates, surrounded by a leathery and often bristly margin. *Ischnochiton bergotii* is common at all the islands, being found on bare open rock on the shore, and under stones in rock pools. At up to 20 mm long, it is one of the more conspicuous intertidal creatures, resembling a baby's cradle when dislodged. It grazes algal spores and broods its young. Larger chitons, up to 50 mm long, are found on open rock.

Limpets and snails Gastropoda
Limpets are ubiquitous grazers on temperate seashores, but true limpets are absent from the islands. The small limpet-like siphonariid *Kerguelenella lateralis* is abundant on upper and mid shores on Gough, and a similar siphonariid is present, but much rarer, at the northern islands. They differ from true limpets in being air-breathing. Keyhole limpets (Fissurellidae), with a small hole at the top of the shell, and slipper limpets (*Crepidula* spp.), with an internal shelf so that the empty shell resembles a slipper, also are found on the islands.

Only one marine snail is big and abundant enough to be conspicuous on the islands – the whelk *Argobuccinium tristanensis* has a solid shell up to 8 cm long, with a characteristic ridge on opposite sides of each whorl. It is common in rock pools and on subtidal rocks, and dead shells are often washed ashore. It is a predator on other marine animals; some *Argobuccinium* species have acid secretions enabling them to bore into the protective calcareous tubes of other molluscs and of polychaete worms.

A few other much smaller marine snails live amongst seaweeds and other marine animals. *Marinula tristanensis* is a small snail characteristic of damp crevices and pools on the upper shore; it is abundant on Gough but apparently rare at the northern islands. It has a distinctive tooth in the middle of the shell opening and grows to 1 cm long.

The Violet Bubble Snail *Janthina janthina* is commonly washed up on Tristan shores, often with Bluebottles *Physalia physalis* on which it feeds. This ocean drifter secretes a raft of bubbles, and hangs upside down from it at the sea surface. It has a beautiful but fragile violet-blue shell up to 3 cm across, and secretes a purple ink when disturbed. The smaller *Janthina exigua*, with a shell up to 15 mm across, also is stranded on Tristan shores.

Sea slugs and nudibranchs Opisthobranchia
Sea slugs lack an external shell. Some sea slugs are herbivorous, but the majority of nudibranchs are carnivorous, often specialising on one species of sponge, hydroid, bryozoan or other sedentary animal. Several beautiful nudibranchs have been found on Gough and Tristan in seashore pools, but remain unidentified.

Bivalves Pelecypoda
Seventeen bivalve species are known from the Tristan group. Most are tiny (<5 mm across), but they are locally abundant. The small pink mussel *Lasaea rubra* is common in upper shore crevices and seaweed turfs, and the tiny bivalves *Verticipronus tristanensis* and *Philobrya* sp. are numerous in coralline seaweed turfs. The only large bivalve is *Tawera philomela*, a relative giant with shells up to 30 mm long. It occurs subtidally, but its white shells with their distinctive concentric ridges are sometimes found washed ashore.

Shipworms Teredinidae
Worm-like bivalves with bodies up to 20 cm long with small, paired rasp-like shells at one end that they use to bore deep into wood. The animals may be long-dead in stranded driftwood, with only the chalk-lined burrows and small paired shells remaining.

Octopus, cuttlefish and squid Cephalopoda
A large number of squid species occur in oceanic waters around the islands, forming the bulk of the diet of many species of seabirds breeding at the islands. Beaks of these squid are sometimes found in pellets of indigestible material regurgitated by albatrosses and petrels. However, the only inshore, shallow-water cephalopod is the bottom-dwelling **Common Octopus** *Octopus vulgaris* which is frequent around the islands, occurring from intertidal pools to >100 m deep. Some have tentacles >1 m long, presumably thriving on a diet of abundant crayfish. They are sometimes caught in lobster traps, and form a valuable bycatch for the lobster fishery, or are used as bait.

▲ (1) Chitons *Ischnochiton* sp.
▼ (4) *Marinula tristanensis*

▲ (2) Siphonariid limpet
▼ (5) Whelk *Argobuccinium tristanensis*

▲ (3) Slipper limpet *Crepidula* sp.
▼ (6) Violet Bubble Snail *Janthina janthina*

▲ (7) Sea slug sp.
▼ (10) Shipworms

▲ (8) Sea slug sp.
▼ (11) Common Octopus *Octopus vulgaris*

▲ (9) Small bivalves

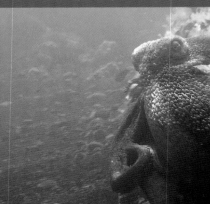

Starfish, sea urchins and sea cucumbers Echinodermata

The echinoderm fauna in shallow waters around the islands is extremely species-poor, with only one species of urchin and one starfish seen commonly. A few other species occur in deeper waters. No sea cucumbers (holothurians) have so far been found on the islands. The echinoderm fauna has affinities with that of the Magellanic region, but also some links with South Africa; four species are apparently endemic to Tristan.

Starfish and brittlestars Asteroidea

The only starfish commonly seen in shallow water is *Henricia simplex*, a pale purple or pink species up to 6 cm long. It is also found at Marion and the Crozet Islands and is probably widespread in the South Atlantic and adjacent sub-Antarctic. The small white brittlestar *Amphipholis squamata* is relatively common amongst seaweeds. It has been found in the holdfasts of floating Giant Kelp, which may be how it drifted to the islands originally. Several other small starfish and brittlestars have been recorded from the islands, including the viviparous brittlestar *Amphiura capensis* which is also found in South Africa.

Sea urchins Echinoidea

The urchin *Arbacia crassispina* is abundant around the islands, occurring from intertidal pools to water >40 m deep. It grows up to 7 cm across and has reddish brown spines, usually with five radiating spineless patches. Some individuals have reduced, flattened spines on the dorsal side. Its test (shell) is a greenish, flattened sphere, often found washed up on beaches. Grazing by *Arbacia* is probably responsible for the generally bare appearance of many of the more level rocky sea-beds around the island. *A. crassispina* is endemic to Tristan and Gough, but closely related to the South American *A. dufresnii*. A smaller urchin, *Notechinus magellanicus*, occurs in rock pools on Tristan and Gough. *Notechinus* is a coldwater, southern hemisphere genus.

Flatworms Turbellaria

Flatworms are small, relatively simple worms that glide rapidly on small hairs or cilia. Two species have been found in pools and under stones on Gough shores; unidentified turbellarians also have been found at Tristan.

Bristle worms Polychaeta

Polychaetes are a large and diverse group of marine worms, their bodies divided into many segments, characteristically with various types of bristles. Almost 50 species have been reported from shallow waters around the islands, with seven endemic to Tristan and Gough, half of the remainder known only from cold southern waters, and the rest found in many parts of the world. Only 15 species have been reported from Gough seashores, but sampling has been less extensive than at Tristan.

Common polychaetes include tiny **spirorbid worms** *Spirorbis* sp. that live in individual hard, coiled, calcareous tubes. Although each white tube is only a few millimetres across, they are conspicuous by their sheer numbers in some habitats, for example when growing on the fronds of Giant Kelp. Here they settle in rows, following the longitudinal grooves of the frond. On rippled sandy seabeds, the white tubes of dead spirorbid worms accumulate in the dips, forming an obvious contrast to the black volcanic sand. **Filigree worms** *Salmacina dysteri* live in fine creeping calcareous tubes forming colonies spreading out over the rocks, or small coral-like clumps. Both filigree and spirorbid worms feed by holding a crown of stiff bristles into the current, withdrawing quickly into their tubes if threatened.

Other polychaetes include small **spionid worms** (Spionidae) that live in colonies of non-calcareous tubes, often bored into calcareous algae or inside bryozoans and other sedentary animals, each worm holding out two tentacles to feed. **Terebellid worms** (Terebellidae) live buried in sediment, or in rock crevices, sending out a bunch of long tentacles to search for food. Many polychaete worms are free-living, mainly carnivorous, and inhabit a wide variety of habitats.

Ribbon or bootlace worms Nemertea

Nemerteans are unsegmented, externally relatively featureless worms, with a tongue-like proboscis that can be everted rapidly to capture prey. Six species have been recorded from Gough seashores, and nemerteans also occur on Tristan.

▲ (1) Starfish *Henricia simplex*

▲ (2) Sea urchin *Arbacia crassispina*

▲ (3) Bristle worm sp.

▲ (4) Spirorbid worms *Spirorbis* sp. on kelp

▲ (5) Filigree worms *Salmacina dysteri*

▼ (6) Spionid worms

▼ (7) Terebellid worm

▼ (8) Ribbon worm

Sea mats or moss animals Bryozoa

Bryozoans are small colonial animals, forming much-branched, bushy growths (looking superficially like hydroids), or encrusting mats on rocks, seaweeds and drifting litter. Thirty-seven species have been identified from Tristan waters, making the bryozoan fauna relatively diverse compared to other animal groups, probably reflecting the ease with which they reach the islands on floating debris. The most conspicuous species in the subtidal is a bushy orange bryozoan up to 10 cm high which is abundant where there is strong water movement on underwater reef crests and the tops of cliffs. Thirteen species have been reported from shallow waters around Tristan, nearly all of which occur elsewhere in the South Atlantic. Of the 37 species of bryozoans recorded from all depths at Tristan, 12 also occur in South Africa, 11 in New Zealand and nine in South America; none is endemic to Tristan.

Hydroids, jellyfish, anemones, soft corals, sea fans Cnidaria

All these animals have tentacles armed with stinging cells with which they capture their prey, usually other small animals; some species have symbiotic relationships with algae and obtain much of their energy from photosynthesis.

Hydroids or sea firs Hydrozoa

Colonial animals attached to the seabed with creeping stolons, from which arise fine main stems branched in various ways, bearing tiny feeding polyps, each with a ring of tentacles and a central mouth. Two small species are common in shallow water around Tristan. A sea fir with main axes less than 3 cm long, and many neat side branches resembling a white feather, is abundant on underwater reef crests, where the wave surge is strong. Sea firs less than 1 cm high, with unbranched uprights, grow on the fronds of Giant Kelp around Gough and Tristan, their stolons following the grooves in the kelp frond. Several other small species grow on vertical rocks, and larger, bushy species grow on the edges of cliffs in water >40 m deep.

Siphonophores Siphonophora

Colonial, jellyfish-like animals made up of individuals with different functions: feeding, reproduction, defence and flotation. The Portuguese Man-of-War or Blue-bottle *Physalia physalis* is often washed ashore. This bright blue, ocean-going siphonophore has a gas-filled float with an upturned 'prow' that is supposed to resemble old-style Portuguese caravelle ships, hence its common name. The float keeps the animal at the sea surface and acts as a sail, propelling it around the oceans, trailing long and very poisonous tentacles. It can sting even after being washed up on the shore, and should not be touched.

Corals, anemones and sea fans Anthozoa

The anthozoans comprise a diverse group of sessile cnidarians. Those found at Tristan are mainly sub-Antarctic in distribution.

Stoloniferans (Stolonifera) and soft corals (Alcyonacea) are related to hard corals but do not have a hard skeleton. They have many small polyps, each with eight tentacles with side-branches, with which they feed. Soft corals form erect colonies while stoloniferans have polyps arising from a creeping base. One species, probably a stoloniferan, is common on Tristan. It has a pink base with white polyps, and forms colonies up to 10 cm across on underwater rocks and kelp holdfasts.

Sea fans (Gorgonacea) are colonial animals with many small polyps and a flexible, horny skeleton. They are often branched in one plane, hence their common name. Around Tristan they appear to be confined to deeper water; only one species has been seen by divers, always below 40 m. They were found growing out from the rock face on the edge of deep drop-offs, where there is probably enhanced current for feeding.

Colonial anemones (Zoantharia) have polyps that are joined at the base. The beautiful trumpet anemone *Parazoanthus hertwigi*, apparently endemic to Tristan, is common on underwater rocks around Tristan, growing in clumps especially on the upper parts of cliffs. The column and disc of this anemone is brownish orange to yellow, and the column is often encrusted with small black sand fragments. The disc has faint radial markings, and the tentacles and mouth are paler. When retracted the polyps become small orange knobs, and the connecting tissue between them can be clearly seen.

Sea anemones (Actiniaria) are common in the rock pools on Tristan shores, and in some places in deeper waters. Particularly abundant is a small white or pale-coloured anemone, probably a species of *Anthothoe*, that emits sticky threads (acontia) when disturbed. Hundreds of these little anemones (up to 2 cm across) stud the shady walls of lava channels on rocky shores. They also grow on Giant Kelp holdfasts. At one site north of Tristan, large areas of seabed at 35–40 m are covered with white anemones. A distinctive orange anemone with gravel attached to warts on its column inhabits crevices in seashore pools. Other small, unidentified anemones have been recorded from the seashores and subtidal of the islands.

▲ (1) Bryozoan (sea mat) sp.   ▲ (2) Bryozoan (sea mat) sp.

▲ (3) Hydroid sp.   ▲ (4) Hydroid sp.   ▲ (5) Portuguese Man-of-War
Physalia physalis

▲ (6) Soft coral sp.   ▲ (7) Sea fan sp.   ▲ (8) Trumpet Anemone
Parazoanthus hertwigi

▼ (9) Anemone sp.   ▼ (10) Anemone sp.   ▼ (11) Anemone sp.

Knobbed-tentacled anemones (Corallimorpharia) are represented at Tristan by Jewel Anemones *Corynactis annulata* which have small knobs on the ends of the tentacles, and are identical in structure to the polyps of hard corals. Mostly <1cm across, there are two common colour varieties, pink and orange, often with a thin coloured line and a zig-zag white line around the outer part of the disc. Jewel anemones reproduce by splitting into two identical individuals, forming 'clone' patches of identical colour. There are extensive patches of these anemones, which seem to be resistant to urchin grazing, on underwater rocks in the most exposed places around Tristan. *Corynactis annulata* also occurs in South Africa.

Sponges Porifera

Porifera means 'hole bearer'; the bodies of sponges are riddled with holes, and they feed by pumping water through them, filtering out any nutritious particles. Sponges generally thrive in wave-exposed places, and Tristan is no exception. The shallow-water sponges are mainly encrusting forms, hugging the rock, and brightening up the scenery with a variety of textures and colours. Compared to other marine invertebrate groups, the sponges of Tristan are relatively diverse, with at least 10 common species mainly found on vertical rocks. They are particularly abundant on the rugged sides of lava flows. Particularly common on Tristan are two with a 'spiky' texture, one blue, the other bright pink. Other common forms are pale crusts and hemispheres, smooth grey mounds with rows of holes, and stalked white blobs.

SEAWEEDS Algae

In contrast to most other groups of marine organisms, the seaweeds of Tristan are remarkably diverse, with more than 120 species described. Only some 40 species have been reported from Gough, but sampling here has been mainly confined to the intertidal; subtidal collections will undoubtedly add more species. However, there are major differences between Gough and the northern islands; Gough is more sub-Antarctic in nature due to its position south of the Subtropical Front, while Tristan has affinities with both South African and South American seaweed floras. Only a small selection of the seaweed flora is covered here, concentrating on common species that can be easily seen on the sea-shore, washed up from below, or are major components of the subtidal.

Green seaweeds Chlorophyta

Green seaweeds are most conspicuous on upper shore rocks and pools, or in damp runnels. The **Sea Lettuce** *Ulva lactuca* forms small rosettes on open rock, or larger flat sheets in rock pools and the subtidal, while tubular *Ulva* sp. (previously *Enteromorpha* sp.) line upper shore pools. Both species have bright green fronds that grow quickly and can colonise boulders during calm periods. A spongy layer of blackish-green *Codium adhaerens* grows on some shady, vertical rocks in the mid-shore. Species of *Cladophora*, a much-branched, finely filamentous green seaweed, are common in some places, particularly on rocks affected by sand.

Brown seaweeds Phaeophyta

Large brown seaweeds collectively known as kelps are abundant around Tristan and Gough, dominating rocky areas down to 30 m depth. **Giant Kelp** *Macrocystis pyrifera* grows to more than 30 m long, and is easily identified by its big branched holdfast and long, slender, flexible stipes bearing strap-shaped blades, each supported by a gas-filled bladder. It forms a distinct zone around most of the islands, often discernible as a patch of smoother water. **Pale Kelp** *Laminaria pallida* is usually less than 2 m high, has a single stout stipe and fan-shaped blade. **Bull Kelp** *Durvillaea antarctica* is not a true kelp, but is distinctive enough to be classified in its own group. It is a typically sub-Antarctic species, forming a distinct band on exposed lower shores around Gough, but is absent from the northern islands.

Smaller brown algae are both abundant and zone-forming on Tristan shores, including the yellow-brown **Dead Man's Fingers** *Splachnidium rugosum*, with its distinctive bunches of turgid fronds, and the dark brown filamentous *Halopteris funicularis*, while the flat, dichotomous *Dictyota liturata* is frequent; none of these are known from Gough. The convoluted, gelatinous cushions of *Colpomenia sinuosa* and the tubular *Scytosiphon lomentaria* grow on both Tristan and Gough shores. *Zonaria tournefortii*, a dark brown seaweed which grows out from vertical rock, has a curious distribution, occurring on Nightingale and Inaccessible, but so far it has not been seen on Tristan, despite being relatively conspicuous.

▲ (1) Jewel Anemones *Corynactis annulata*

▲ (2) Sponge sp.

▲ (3) Sponge sp.

▲ (4) Sponge sp.

▼ (5) Sea Lettuce *Ulva lactuca*

▼ (6) Giant Kelp *Macrocystis pyrifera*

▼ (7) Pale Kelp *Laminaria pallida*

▼ (8) *Cladophora* sp.

▼ (9) *Zonaria tournefortii*

Red seaweeds Rhodophyta

Red seaweeds are the main components of the dense seaweed turfs on the wave-washed shores of the islands. The term 'red' seaweed is a little misleading; some, especially the subtidal species, are red, but they can be a wide range of colours from yellow to brown, purple, or almost black, while the 'coralline' seaweeds are chalky pink, purple or whitish. *Porphyra tristanensis* grows as thin, shiny sheets on the highest levels of the shore, often dried to the rocks. The short, curved fronds of *Rhodoglossum revolutum* grow as a turf on the upper shore; both these species are endemic to the islands. In shaded places at the northern islands, *Bostrychia mixta* and *Gelidium* spp form a moss-like turf of short, tangled fronds, 1 cm high. Other turf-forming red seaweeds include the tough, dark purple *Gigartina stiriata*, the dark red filamentous *Streblocladia atrata*, as well as scour-tolerant seaweeds in the group Phyllophoraceae. *Iridaea* spp, with flat red fronds, are present at Tristan and Gough, but are much more abundant on Gough, where they form distinct zones. *Iridaea* spp. typically are abundant on sub-Antarctic shores, but their identification is difficult and requires further investigation.

Coralline seaweeds have chalky deposits in their cell walls, making them very hard. They are abundant in rock pools and in the subtidal, but they too are hard to identify, requiring specialist knowledge. *Corallina* spp. and other jointed coralline seaweeds often form a dense turf in the shallower seashore pools, and in a band around low water and a few metres below, while their bleached white skeletons are often washed up. Encrusting coralline seaweeds resemble pink paint, covering rock pools and subtidal rocks. Some encrusting species form knobbly growths on rocks; in the deeper subtidal, some pebbles become completely covered in these growths and are known as 'hedgehog' stones.

Many more red seaweeds live rather inaccessibly on the outermost, wave-washed reefs or on subtidal rocks, including small, inconspicuous species that form part of the red seaweed turfs on Tristan shores. Some of these can be found washed ashore on Tristan after storms, when they often bleach to lurid colours in the sun. Some of the larger and more easily identified include the narrow red straps of *Epymenia elongata*, up to 40 cm long. Species of *Plocamium* have beautiful fronds branched in one plane, with the smallest side-branches all on one side near the tips of the main branches. Several species, including *Schizoseris papenfussii*, *S. multifoliata* and *Neuroglossum multilobum,* have very thin, much-branched blades, with narrow but tough stipes. The beautiful dark pink *Pseudophycodrys pulcherrima* often turns blackish on drying. The long, feathery (but very variable) fronds of *Schimmelmannia elegans* grow up to 50 cm long on wave-washed rocks, including inside the harbour on Tristan. This species, endemic to Tristan, has been discovered recently in the turbulent outfall from an aquarium in Cape Town, and is thought to have been introduced with live crayfish from Tristan.

▼ Bull Kelp *Durvillaea antarctica*, is a brown seaweed common at Gough but absent from Tristan (see page 142)

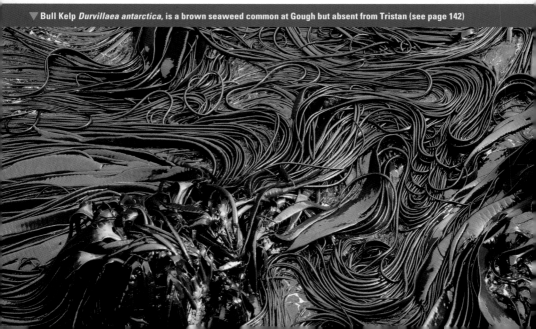

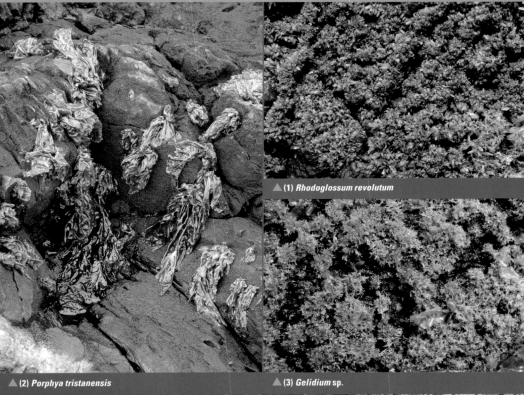

(1) *Rhodoglossum revolutum*

(2) *Porphya tristanensis*

(3) *Gelidium* sp.

(4) *Gigartina stiriata*   (5) cf. *Gymnogongrus* sp.   (6) Coralline seaweed

(7) *Epymenia elongata*   (8) *Plocamium* sp.   (9) *Pseudophycodrys pulcherrima*

VISITING TRISTAN

Tristan deserves its reputation as the most remote community in the world. It requires a fair amount of commitment to visit the islands, but it is well worth the effort. The island community has identified ecotourism as an important area for growth, which will help support conservation. Hopefully this book will encourage more tourism; this section provides a brief guide to potential visitors.

Getting there
The only way to reach Tristan is by ship. The two main ways are either to join a cruise ship that includes the islands on its itinerary or to come on one of the scheduled ships plying between the islands and Cape Town, South Africa. On average, four or five cruise ships call at the islands each year. They offer a chance to see all the islands, with landings possible at Nightingale, and sometimes Inaccessible from the smaller, natural history cruises. However, they usually spend only a few days at the archipelago, and there is always the chance that inclement weather will prevent landing. All vessels must first call at the main island of Tristan to complete immigration procedures and pick up Tristan guides before attempting to visit the outer islands. If there is only one fine day during the visit, you will get ashore at Tristan but not the other islands.

The other option is to spend more time at Tristan as an independent visitor. This offers the chance to really experience the islands, but scheduled sailings are relatively infrequent, berths are limited, and nearly all of those available are allocated well in advance for use by the Tristan community. It also requires a fair amount of time, as it takes 5–7 days each way between Cape Town and Tristan. Summer (September–April) is the best time to visit the islands, when the weather is better, numbers of seals and seabirds peak, and most plants flower. October–December is ideal for birds, but the weather is perhaps more favourable for landings later in summer. Note that the island goes on holiday from mid-December to early January, and it is difficult to arrange guides for outings during this period.

The South African supply ship *SA Agulhas* calls at Tristan *en route* to and from the weather station at Gough Island each September–October, allowing some three weeks ashore and a total trip time of five weeks. This provides the most reliable way to visit, and as a result it is quite busy on the island at this time, making it harder to arrange outings. Also, the weather is often unsettled in early spring, making boat trips around Tristan or to the outer islands problematic. Visiting later in summer offers a better chance of reaching Nightingale or Inaccessible, but one has to be prepared for unexpected changes to shipping schedules. The fishing boats that offer berths at other times of the year are quite comfortable, but their schedules may vary at short notice depending on problems with fishing gear or other issues.

Independent visitors need to apply to the Administrator stating the purpose of their visit, the duration of stay, their nationality and age. Approval is then given by the Island Council. Tourists do not require a visa, but they must have proof of medical insurance, a return ticket and pay a small landing fee. Accommodation on Tristan ranges from full board to self-catering. Many visitors elect to stay with a family on the island, which is like being adopted for the duration of your visit. The only danger is putting on too much weight from all the fine island food.

Out and about on Tristan
Part of the charm of Tristan is wandering around the village, with its small museum and gift shop, two churches, supermarket, post office, pub and swimming pool. A highlight of any visit is to attend a dance in the Prince Phillip Hall. Outside the village, visitors are free to explore the settlement plain between Pigbite and Anchorstock. There is a bus to the potato patches, and a taxi service can be arranged. There are few native animals or plants on the Settlement Plain, but a few pairs of Tristan Thrushes persist in the bottom of the deep gullies behind the patches. It is also worth checking the wetlands and garden areas for vagrant birds. Other activities include fishing, swimming on the black lava sands at Runaway Beach or a round of golf on the famous course next to Hottentot Gulch.

Trips away from the Settlement Plain must be led by a guide. There is a sliding scale of charges, depending on party size. Access to the Base is usually via one of three routes. Burntwood, west of the patches, is the easiest route, but still entails a stiff climb of around 400 m. Hottentot Gulch and the route above Pigbite to Big Green Hill climb more than 600 m and are much steeper; they are not advised for the unfit or those prone to vertigo or a fear of heights! The Base offers extensive tracts of natural vegetation as well as breeding Yellow-nosed Albatrosses, Gough Moorhens and small numbers of Tristan Thrushes, mainly in the deeper gulches. Ascending the Peak is a memorable achievement, provided the weather remains clear. It is usually reached via Hottentot Gulch, with a round trip of 8–10 hours, depending on your level of fitness. Boat trips can be arranged to land at Sandy Point, Stony Beach or The Caves. Rockhopper Penguins can be

▲ **(1) A visitor tackles Tristan's challenging greens.**

▲ **(2) Many birds appear quite confiding, but don't approach them too closely. Breeding birds are easily stressed, and if they abandon their nests, eggs and chicks are easy prey for Skuas and Starchies.**

▲ **(3) Cleaning boots and protective clothing is essential to stop new plants, fungi and microbes from reaching the islands.**

viewed at Sandy Point, and the largest concentration of fur seals is at The Caves. Some families have huts at the Caves and Stony Beach, and it may be possible to arrange a weekend away (but be prepared to walk back over the Base if the sea gets up and you can't get back by boat).

Nightingale, Inaccessible and Gough

For anyone interested in natural history, a trip to Nightingale Island is a must. Visits have to be accompanied by Tristan guides, and a small fee is payable. Depending on sea conditions, landings take place either at the huts on the east coast (Landing by the Rock), or in the channel opposite Alex Island (Around the West Side). Both sites require a level of agility, as you have to step directly onto the rock. Be especially careful on the wet rocks, which often have an extremely slippery film of algae. The main landing site at the huts is used by a large colony of Rockhopper Penguins, which breed in the dense tussock grass above the huts. The landing sites also are used by fur seals, and ledges on the adjacent cliffs have nests of Antarctic Terns and Brown Noddies. Once ashore, you are besieged by Tristan Thrushes, and Nightingale Buntings are abundant. A path cut through the dense tussock leads to the Ponds, where there are several pairs of Tristan Skuas and about 1,000 pairs of Yellow-nosed Albatrosses. Wilkins' Buntings are locally common in the *Phylica* copses. Great Shearwaters are abundant, and are seen flying over the island during the day, especially once their chicks hatch. The walk to the Ponds takes about an hour, with a short climb just before the Ponds.

The east coast of Inaccessible Island between The Waterfall and Salt Beach also can be visited by small groups of wildlife enthusiasts or researchers, provided they are accompanied by Tristan guides. Landings are on boulder beaches, and can be quite wet. The main attraction is the Inaccessible Rail, which is common in this area, but rather secretive. It is best located by its calls, and then you can wait for it to cross an open area. Spectacled Petrels and the few remaining pairs of Tristan Albatrosses are confined to the island's plateau, which is not accessible to tourists. Gough Island also is closed to tourists, but some cruise ships run inflatable boats close inshore. With luck, both the Gough Bunting and Gough Moorhen can be seen along the sheltered east coast, as well as the only breeding population of Southern Elephant Seals.

▲ (1) Elephant Seals should not be disturbed.

▲ (2) Landing at Nightingale requires timing and agilty. Beware the slippery rocks!

▲ (3) Once ashore, remain in a group with your guide. This is the north landing of Nightingale, with Alex Island in the background.

Environmental checklist for visitors

- Visitors must ensure that their clothing and equipment is free of seeds and other propagules that may introduce alien species. Scrub all shoes to remove dirt and mud, clean seeds from socks, velcro fasteners on jackets and over-trousers, turn out fluff and other debris from pockets and nooks and crannies in camera bags, back-packs and other camping equipment. Tents used elsewhere should not be taken to Tristan. Clothing and equipment should be inspected by Tristan's Agriculture and Natural Resources Department before going ashore.
- Pack all food and equipment into clean containers immediately before leaving for the outer islands. Don't leave containers standing around where a mouse or rat could stow away. Ensure that all ships and boats are rodent free.
- No fresh produce can be taken to the outer islands, because insects and other bugs are easily carried in this way.
- Remain with your Tristan guide at all times, and heed their requests regarding safe approach distances to animals so that you won't disturb them or endanger yourself (seals and seabirds bite!) Move slowly and quietly. In general, do not approach within 5 m of birds and fur seals, or 10 m of elephant seals (of course, it's alright if the birds come closer to you).
- Stay on paths. Walking of paths collapses many bird burrows and seeds of alien plants already on the islands are spread by humans.
- No animals may be killed or disturbed, and no native plants may be picked or damaged (including dead wood).
- No rocks or 'souvenirs' other than beach litter (eg fishing floats) may be collected. Relics dating to before 1950 should not be disturbed or removed.
- Fires and smoking are not permitted – tussock burns easily!
- Please do not litter. All wastes must be removed from the islands.

For further information about visiting the islands, consult the Tristan website www.tristandc.com

APPENDIX Introduced flowering plants

T = Tristan, N = Nightingale, I = Inaccessible, G = Gough

Agavaceae
Phormium tenax (New Zealand Flax) — T N I
Apiaceae
Centella asiatica (Asiatic Pennywort) — T I
Araceae
Zantedeschia aethiopica (Arum Lily, Calla Lily) — T
Asteraceae
Anthemis cotula (Stinking Chamomile) — T
Bellis perennis (Daisy) — T
Conyza bonariensis (Flax-Leaved Fleabane) — T
Conyza sumatrensis (Sumatran Fleabane) — T I
Cotula australis (Australian Brass Buttons) — T N
Crepis capillaris (Smooth Hawksbeard) — T
Gnaphalium purpureum (Purple Cudweed) — T
Hypochaeris glabra (Smooth Catsear) — T G
Lactuca serriola (Prickly Lettuce) — T G
Leontodon taraxacoides (Lesser Hawkbit) — T
Leucanthemum vulgare (Oxeye Daisy) — T
Pseudognaphalium luteo-album
(Muckweed, Jersey Cudweed) — T I
Senecio vulgaris (Groundsel) — T
Sonchus asper (Prickly Sowthistle) — T G
Sonchus oleraceus (Common Sowthistle,
Annual Sowthistle) — T N I G
Taraxacum officinale (Dandelion) — T
Vellereophyton dealbatum (White Cudweed) — T
Boraginaceae
Lithospermum sp. (Gromwell) — T
Myosotis collina (Forget-me-not) — T
Myosotis discolor (Changing Forget-me-not) — T
Brassicaceae
Brassica juncea (Mustard) — T
Brassica rapa (Rape Seed) — T I
Capsella bursa-pastoris (Shepherd's Purse) — G
Coronopus didymus (Lesser Swinecress) — T
Nasturtium officinale (Watercress) — T
Raphanus sativus (Garden Radish) — T I
Caryophyllaceae
Cerastium fontanum (Common Mouse-ear) — T I G
Cerastium glomeratum (Sticky Mouse-ear) — T
Polycarpon tetraphyllum (Four-leaved Allseed) — T
Sagina apetala (Annual Pearlwort) — T
Sagina procumbens (Procumbent Pearlwort) — T G
Saponaria officinalis (Soapwort) — T
Scleranthus annuus (Annual Knawel) — T
Silene alba (White Campion) — T
Silene gallica (Common Catchfly) — T
Spergula arvensis (Corn Spurrey) — T
Stellaria media (Common Chickweed) — T G
Chenopodiaceae
Chenopodium album (Fat Hen) — T
Chenopodium murale (Nettle-leaved Goosefoot) — T
Crassulaceae
Crassula pellucida (Stonecrop) — T
Cyperaceae
Cyperus esculentus (Nutgrass, New Bull Grass) — T
Cyperus longus (Galingale) — T
Cyperus tenellus (Tiny Flat-sedge) — T
Mariscus congestus (Clustered Flat-sedge, Old Bull Grass) — T I
Euphorbiaceae
Euphorbia peplus (Petty Spurge, Milkweed) — T

Fabaceae
Lotus corniculatus (Birdsfoot Trefoil) — T
Medicago polymorpha (Toothed Medick) — T
Medicago sativa (Lucerne) — T
Trifolium dubium (Lesser Trefoil) — T
Trifolium micranthum (Slender Trefoil) — T
Trifolium pratense (Red Clover) — T
Trifolium repens (White Clover) — T
Trifolium spp. (Clover) — T
Trifolium subterraneum (Burrowing Clover) — T
Ulex europaeus (Gorse) — T
Fumariaceae
Fumaria sp. (Fumitory) — T
Geraniaceae
Geranium dissectum (Cut-leafed Cranesbill) — T
Iridaceae
Romulea rosea var. *australis* (Sand Crocus, Onion Grass) — T
Juncaceae
Juncus bufonius (Toad Rush) — T
Juncus effusus (Soft Rush) — T
Juncus tenuis (Slender Rush) — T
Lamiaceae
Leonitis leonurus (Dwarf Lion's Tail) — T
Mentha sp. (Mint) — T
Prunella vulgaris (Selfheal) — T
Lobeliaceae
Lobelia erinus (Lobelia) — T
Malvaceae
Malva parviflora (Least Mallow) — T
Moraceae
Ficus carica (Fig) — T
Myrtaceae
Eucalyptus viminalis (Manna Gum) — T
Metrosideros excelsa (New Zealand Christmas Tree) — T
Onagraceae
Oenothera indecora (Evening Primrose) — T
Oxalidaceae
Oxalis corniculata (Procumbent Yellow-sorrel) — T I
Oxalis purpurea (Purple Woodsorrel) — T
Pinaceae
Pinus caribaea (Bahamas Pitch Pine) — I
Pinus spp. (Pine) — T
Plantaginaceae
Plantago lanceolata (Narrowleaf Plantain) — T G
Plantago major (Greater Plantain) — T I G
Poaceae
Agrostis castellana (Highland Bent) — T G
Agrostis gigantea (Black Bent, Red Top) — T I
Agrostis lachnantha (South African Bentgrass) — G
Agrostis stolonifera (Creeping Bent) — T I G
Agrostis tenuis (Common Bent, Brown Top) — T G
Aira caryophyllea (Silvery Hair-grass) — T I
Anthoxanthum odoratum
(Vanilla Grass, Sweet Vernalgrass) — T
Arrhenatherum elatius (False Oat-grass) — G
Avenella flexuosa (Wavy Hair Grass) — T
Bromus willdenowii (Rescue Grass) — T I
Cynodon dactylon (Bermuda Grass) — T I
Cynosurus cristatus (Crested Dog's-tail) — T
Dactylis glomerata (Cocksfoot) — T G
Digitaria sanguinalis (Hairy Finger-grass) — T

Echinochloa crus-galli (Cockspur Grass) — T
Eleusine indica (Goosegrass) — T
Festuca arundinacea (Tall Fescue) — T
Festuca rubra (Red Fescue) — T
Holcus lanatus (Farm Grass, Common Velvet Grass, Yorkshire Fog) — T N I G
Hordeum glaucum (Wall Barley) — T
Hordeum leporinum (Hare Barley) — T
Lolium multiflorum (Italian Rye-grass) — T
Lolium perenne (Perennial Rye-grass) — T
Lolium rigidum (Annual Rye-grass) — T
Lolium x *hybridum* (Short Rotation Rye-grass) — T
Paspalum dilatatum (Water Grass) — T
Pennisetum clandestinum (Kikuyu Grass) — T
Phalaris tuberosa (Bulbous Canary Grass) — T
Poa annua (Annual Meadow-grass, Annual Blue-grass) — T N I G
Poa infirma (Early Meadow-grass) — T
Poa pratensis (Smooth Meadow-grass) — T G
Poa trivialis (Rough Meadow-grass) — T
Polypogon monspeliensis (Annual Beard-grass) — T
Sporobolus africanus (Ratstail Grass, Dropseed) — T
Vulpia bromoides (Squirrel-tail Fescue) — T I

Polygonaceae
Polygonum aviculare (Knotgrass) — T
Rumex acetosella ssp. *angiocarpus* (Sorrel Dock, Sour Grass) — T I G
Rumex crispus (Curled Dock) — T
Rumex obtusifolius (Braid-leaved Dock) — T N I G
Rumex steudelii — T

Primulaceae
Anagallis arvensis (Scarlet Pimpernel) — T

Ranunculaceae
Ranunculus repens (Creeping Buttercup) — T

Rosaceae
Malus domestica (Apple) — T N I G
Prunus persica (Peach) — T
Rosa rubiginosa (Sweet Briar) — T
Rosa spinosissima (Scotch Rose) — T
Rubus saxatilis (Stone Bramble) — T
Rubus spp. (Bramble) — T

Rubiaceae
Galium aparine (Common Cleavers) — T

Salicaceae
Salix babylonica (Weeping Willow) — T I
Salix spp. (Willow) — T

Scrophulariaceae
Verbascum virgatum (Twiggy Mullein) — T
Veronica agrestis (Green Field Speedwell) — T
Veronica serpyllifolia (Thyme-leaved Speedwell) — T I

Solanaceae
Physalis peruviana (Goldenberry) — T I
Solanum nigrum (Black Nightshade, Tristan Blackberry) — T I
Solanum tuberosum (Potato) — T N I G

Valerianaceae
Centranthus ruber (Red Valerian) — T

Verbenaceae
Verbena bonariensis (Tall Vervain) — G
Verbena officinalis (Vervain) — T

Based on the following references and unpublished data.

Christophersen E (1944) New phanerogams from Tristan da Cuhna. *Res. Norw. Sci. Exped. Tristan da Cunha 1937–1938* 11: 1–15.

Christophersen E (1968) Flowering plants from Tristan da Cuhna. *Res. Norw. Sci. Exped. Tristan da Cunha 1937–1938* 55: 1–29.

Groves E W (1981) Vascular plant collections from the Tristan da Cunha group of islands. *Bull. Br. Mus. Nat. Hist. (Bot.)* 8: 333–420.

Hooper S S (1968) Cyperaceae from Tristan da Cunha. *Res. Norw. Sci. Exped. Tristan da Cunha 1937–1938* 54: 1–9.

Roux J P, Ryan P G, Milton S J and Moloney C L (1992) Vegetation and checklist of Inaccessible Island, central South Atlantic Ocean, with notes on Nightingale Island. *Bothalia* 22: 93–109.

Wace N M (1967) Alien plants in the Tristan da Cunha Islands. *Int. Union Conserv. Nat. Publ. New Ser.* 9: 46–59.

Wace N M and Dickson J H (1965) The terrestrial botany of the Tristan da Cunha islands. *Phil. Trans. R. Soc. Lond.* B 249: 273–360.

References

General information

Baker P E, Gass I G, Harris P G and le Maitre R W (1964) The volcanological report of the Royal Society Expedition to Tristan da Cunha, 1962. *Phil. Trans. R. Soc. Lond.*, A 256: 439–578.

Brander J (1940) *Tristan da Cunha 1506–1902*. Allen & Unwin, London.

Crawford A B (1982) *Tristan da Cunha and the roaring forties*. Charles Skilton, Edinburgh and London.

Glass J and Green A (2003) *A Short Guide to Tristan da Cunha*. Whitby Press, Whitby, UK.

Jones A G, Chown S L, Ryan P G, Gremmen N J M and Gaston K J (2003) A review of conservation threats on Gough Island: a case study for terrestrial conservation in the Southern Oceans. *Biol. Conserv.* 113: 75–87.

Munch P A (1945) Sociology of Tristan da Cunha. *Res. Norw. Sci. Exped. Tristan da Cunha 1937–1938* 13: 1–331.

Ollier C D (1984) Geomorphology of the South Atlantic volcanic islands. Part I: the Tristan da Cunha group. *Z. Geomorphol.* 28: 367–382.

Preece R C, Bennett K D and Carter J R (1986) The Quaternary palaeobotany of Inaccessible Island (Tristan da Cunha group). *J. Biogeogr.* 13: 1–33.

Stoltenhoff F and Stoltenhoff G (1873) Two years on Inaccessible Island. *Cape Monthly Mag.* 7 (Dec): 321–337.

Wace N M (1969) The discovery, exploitation and settlement of the Tristan da Cunha islands. *Proc. R. Geogr. Soc. Austr.* 70: 11–40.

Wace N M and Holdgate M W (1976) Man and nature in the Tristan da Cunha Islands. *International Union for the Conservation of Nature and Natural Resources Monograph* 6: 1–114.

Plants

See also Appendix, page 151

Arnell S (1958) Hepatics from Tristan da Cunha. *Res. Norw. Sci. Exped. Tristan da Cunha 1937–1938* 42: 1–76.

Dean W R J, Milton S J, Ryan P G and Moloney C L (1994) The role of disturbance in the establishment of indigenous and alien plants at Inaccessible Island, South Atlantic Ocean. *Vegetatio* 113: 13–23.

Dennis R W G (1955) Ascomycetes from Tristan da Cunha. *Res. Norw. Sci. Exped. Tristan da Cunha 1937–1938* 36: 1–10.

Dixon H N (1960) Mosses of Tristan da Cunha. *Res. Norw. Sci. Exped. Tristan da Cunha 1937–1938* 48: 1–49.

Jorgensen P M (1977) Foliose and fruticose lichens from Tristan da Cunha. *Norske Videnskaps-Akademi (Naturv. Klasse Skrifter)* 36: 1–40.

Jorgensen P M (1979) The phytogeographical relationships of the lichen flora of Tristan da Cunha, South Atlantic Ocean (excluding Gough Island). *Can. J. Bot.* 57: 2279–2282.

Milton S J, Ryan P G, Moloney C L, Cooper J and Medeiros A C Jr (1993) Disturbance and demography of *Phylica arborea* (Rhamnaceae) on the Tristan-Gough group of islands. *Bot. J. Linn. Soc.* 111: 55–70.

Roux J P (1993) The genus *Asplenium* L. (Aspleniaceae: Pteridophyta) in the Tristan-Gough island group. *Kew Bull.* 48: 79–97.

Roux J P (1993) *Elaphoglossum* Schott ex J. Smith (Lomariopsidaceae: Pteridophyta) in the Tristan da Cunha, Gough and Marion Island groups. *Bot. J. Linn. Soc.* 112 203–222.

Wace N M (1961) The vegetation of Gough Island. *Ecol. Monogr.* 31: 337–367.

Wace N M and Holdgate M W (1958) The vegetation of Tristan da Cunha. *J. Ecol.* 46: 595–620.

Birds

Cuthbert R J (2004) Breeding biology of the Atlantic Petrel, *Pterodroma incerta*, and a population estimate of this and other burrowing petrels on Gough Island, South Atlantic Ocean. *Emu* 104: 221–228.

Cuthbert R J (2005) Breeding biology, chick growth and provisioning of Great Shearwaters (*Puffinus gravis*) at Gough Island, South Atlantic Ocean. *Emu* 105: 305–310.

Cuthbert R J and Sommer E S (2004) Population size and trends of four globally threatened seabirds at Gough Island, South Atlantic Ocean. *Mar. Ornith.* 32: 97–103.

Cuthbert R J, Phillips R A and Ryan P G (2003) Separating Tristan Albatrosses and Wandering Albatrosses using morphometric measurements. *Waterbirds* 26: 338–344.

Cuthbert R J, Ryan P G, Cooper J and Hilton G (2003) Demography and population trends of the Atlantic Yellow-nosed Albatross *Thalassarche chlororhynchos*. *Condor* 105: 439–452.

Cuthbert R J, Sommer E S, Ryan P G, Cooper J and Hilton G (2004) Demography and conservation status of the Tristan Albatross *Diomedea [exulans] dabbenena*. *Biol. Conserv.* 117: 471–481.

Elliott H F I (1957) A contribution to the ornithology of the Tristan da Cunha group. *Ibis* 99: 545–586.

Fraser M W, Ryan P G and Watkins B P (1988) The seabirds of Inaccessible Island, South Atlantic Ocean. *Cormorant* 16: 7–33.

Fraser M W, Dean W R J and Best I C (1992) Observations on the Inaccessible Island Rail *Atlantisia rogersi*: the world's smallest flightless bird. *Bull. Br. Orn. Club* 112: 12–22.

Fraser M W, Ryan P G, Dean W R J, Briggs D J and Moloney C L (1994) Biology of the Tristan Thrush *Nesocichla eremita*. *Ostrich* 65: 14–25.

Hagen Y (1952) The birds of Tristan da Cunha. *Res. Norw. Sci. Exped. Tristan da Cunha 1937–1938* 20: 1–248.

Richardson M E (1984) Aspects of the ornithology of the Tristan da Cunha group and Gough Island, 1972–1974. *Cormorant* 12: 122–201.

Rowan M K (1951) The Yellow-nosed Albatross *Diomedea chlororhynchos* Gmelin at its breeding grounds in the Tristan da Cunha group. *Ostrich* 22: 139–155.

Rowan M K (1952) The Greater Shearwater *Puffinus gravis* at its breeding grounds. *Ibis* 94: 97–121.

Ryan P G (1991) The impact of the commercial lobster fishery on seabirds at the Tristan da Cunha islands, South Atlantic. *Biol. Conserv.* 57: 1–12.

Ryan P G and Moloney C L (1991) Prey selection and temporal variation in the diet of Subantarctic Skuas at Inaccessible Island, Tristan da Cunha. *Ostrich* 62: 52–58.

Ryan P G, Bloomer P, Moloney C L, Grant T and Delport W (2007) Ecological speciation in South Atlantic island finches. *Science* 315: 1420–1423.

Ryan P G, Dorse C and Hilton G M (2006) The conservation status of the Spectacled Petrel *Procellaria conspicillata*. *Biol. Conserv.* 131: 575–583.

Ryan P G, Moloney C L and Hudon J (1994) Color variation and hybridization among *Nesospiza* buntings on Inaccessible Island, Tristan da Cunha. *Auk* 111: 314–327.

Swales M K (1965) The sea-birds of Gough Island. *Ibis* 107:17–42, 215–229.

Watkins B P and Furness R W (1986) Population status, breeding and conservation of the Gough Moorhen. *Ostrich* 57: 32–36.

Mammals

Best P B (1988) Right Whales *Eubalaena australis* at Tristan da Cunha – a clue to the 'non-recovery' of depleted stocks? *Biol. Conserv.* 46: 23–51.

Bester M N (1987) The Subantarctic Fur Seal *Arctocephalus tropicalis* at Gough Island (Tristan da Cunha Group). In: Proceedings of the Fur Seal Workshop, Cambridge, April 1984. NOAA Tech. Rep. NMFS 51: 57–60.

Bester M N, Möller H, Wium J and Enslin B (2001) An update on the status of Southern Elephant Seals at Gough Island. *S. Afr. J. Wildl. Res.* 31: 68–71.

Bester M N, Wilson J W, Burle M-H and Hofmeyr G J G (2006) Population trend of Subantarctic Fur Seals at Gough Island. *S. Afr. J. Wildl. Res.* 36: 191–194.

Bester M N (1982) Distribution, habitat selection and colony types of the Amsterdam Island Fur Seal *Arctocephalus tropicalis* at Gough Island. *J. Zool., Lond.* 196: 217–231.

Cuthbert R J and Hilton G (2004) Introduced house mice *Mus musculus*: a significant predator of threatened and endemic birds on Gough Island, South Atlantic Ocean? *Biol. Conserv.* 117: 483–489.

Jones A G, Chown S L and Gaston K J (2003) Introduced house mice as a conservation concern on Gough Island. *Biodiv. & Conserv.* 12: 2107–2119.

Wilson J W, Burle M-H and Bester M N (2006) Vagrant Antarctic pinnipeds at Gough Island. *Polar Biol.* 29: 905–908.

Terrestrial invertebrates

Beier M (1955) Pseudoscorpione von Tristan da Cunha. *Res. Norw. Sci. Exped. Tristan da Cunha 1937–1938* 35: 1–4.

Brink P (1948) Coleoptera of Tristan da Cunha. *Res. Norw. Sci. Exped. Tristan da Cunha 1937–1938* 17: 1–123.

China W E (1958) Hemiptera of Tristan da Cunha. *Res. Norw. Sci. Exped. Tristan da Cunha 1937–1938* 43: 1–8.

Clay T (1957) Mallophaga from Tristan da Cunha. Part I. *Res. Norw. Sci. Exped. Tristan da Cunha 1937–1938* 40: 1–5.

Hackman W (1959) On the genus *Scaptomyza* Hardy (Diptera, Drosophilidae). *Acta Zool. Fenn.* 97: 3–73.

Holdgate M W (1959) The fresh water fauna of Gough Island (South Atlantic). *Proc. Linn. Soc., Lond.* 172: 8–24.

Holdgate M W (1965) The fauna of the Tristan da Cunha islands. *Phil. Trans. R. Soc. Lond.* B 249: 361–424.

Jeekel C A W (1954) Diplopoda of Tristan da Cunha. *Res. Norw. Sci. Exped. Tristan da Cunha 1937–1938* 32: 1–9.

Jones A G, Chown S L, Webb TJ and Gaston K J (2003) The free-living pterygote insects of Gough Island, South Atlantic Ocean. Syst. & Biodiv. 1: 213–273.

Kensley B (1994) Redescription of *Iais elongata* Siverten & Holthuis, 1980, from the South Atlantic Ocean (Crustacea: Isopoda: Asellota). *Proc. Biol. Soc. Wash.* 107: 274–282.

Kuschel G (1962) The Curculionidae of Gough Island and the relationships of the weevil fauna of the Tristan da Cunha group. *Proc. Linn. Soc., Lond.* 173: 69–78.

Lawrence R F (1955) Chilopoda of Tristan da Cunha. *Res. Norw. Sci. Exped. Tristan da Cunha 1937–1938* 39: 1–13.

Morison G D (1958) Thysanoptera of Tristan da Cunha. *Res. Norw. Sci. Exped. Tristan da Cunha 1937–1938* 47: 1–5.

Rapoport E H (1970) Collembola of Tristan da Cunha, Nightingale and Inaccessible Islands. *Nytt. Mag. Zool.* 18: 23–32.

Viette P E L (1952) Lepidoptera. *Res. Norw. Sci. Exped. Tristan da Cunha 1937–1938* 23: 1–19.

Marine life

Andrew T G and Hecht T (1992) The feeding biology of *Acantholatris monodactylus* (Pisces: Cheilodactylidae) at Tristan da Cunha and Gough Island, South Atlantic Ocean. *S. Afr. J. Antarct. Res.* 22: 41–49.

Andrew T G, Hecht T, Heemstra P C and Lutjeharms J R E (1995) The fishes of the Tristan da Cunha Group and Gough Island, South Atlantic Ocean. *Ichthyol. Bull. J.L.B. Smith Inst.* 63: 1–43.

Baardseth E (1941) The marine algae of Tristan da Cunha. *Res. Norw. Sci. Exped. Tristan da Cunha 1937–1938* 9: 1–173.

Carlgren O (1941) Corallimorpharia, Actiniaria, and Zooantharia. *Res. Norw. Sci. Exped. Tristan da Cunha 1937–1938* 8: 1–12.

Chamberlain Y M (1965) Marine algae of Gough Island. *Bull. Br. Mus. (Nat. Hist.) Bot.* 3: 175–232.

Chamberlain Y, Holdgate M W and Wace N (1985) The littoral ecology of Gough Island, South Atlantic Ocean. *Tethys* 11: 302–319.

Day J H (1954) The Polychaeta of Tristan da Cunha. *Res. Norw. Sci. Exped. Tristan da Cunha 1937–1938* 29: 1–35.

Holthuis L B and Sivertsen E (1960) The Crustacea Decapoda, Mysidacea and Cirripedia of the Tristan da Cunha archipelago. *Res. Norw. Sci. Exped. Tristan da Cunha 1937–1938* 52: 1–55.

Millar R H (1960) Ascidians from the Tristan da Cunha group of islands. *Res. Norw. Sci. Exped. Tristan da Cunha 1937–1938* 53: 1–15.

Mortensen T (1940) Echinoderms of Tristan da Cunha. *Res. Norw. Sci. Exped. Tristan da Cunha 1937–1938* 7: 1–12.

Pollock D E (1981) Population dynamics of rock lobster *Jasus tristani* at the Tristan da Cunha group of islands. *Fish. Bull. S. Afr.* 15: 49–66.

Roscoe M J (1979) Biology and exploitation of the rock lobster *Jasus tristani* at the Tristan da Cunha islands, South Atlantic, 1949–1976. *Investl Rpt Sea Fish. Branch S. Afr.* 118: 1–47.

Sivertsen E and Holthuis L B (1980) The marine isopod crustacea of the Tristan da Cunha archipelago. *Gunneria* 35: 1–128.

Soot-Ryen T (1960) Pelecypods from Tristan da Cunha. *Res. Norw. Sci. Exped. Tristan da Cunha 1937–1938* 49: 1–47.

Stephensen K (1949) The Amphipoda of Tristan da Cunha. *Res. Norw. Sci. Exped. Tristan da Cunha 1937–1938* 19: 1–61.

Stock J H (1954) Pycnogonida from Tristan da Cunha. *Res. Norw. Sci. Exped. Tristan da Cunha 1937–1938* 33: 1–13.

Vigeland I (1958) Bryozoa of Tristan da Cunha. *Res. Norw. Sci. Exped. Tristan da Cunha 1937–1938* 44: 1–17.

Wiborg K F (1960) Marine copepods of Tristan da Cunha. *Res. Norw. Sci. Exped. Tristan da Cunha 1937–1938* 51: 1–44.

Photograph credits

Page iv
©**Peter Ryan**

Facing page 1
©**Peter Ryan**

Page 5
©**Peter Ryan** (Plates 1–4)

Pages 6 and 7
©**Peter Ryan** (Plates 1,2)
©**James Glass** (Plate 3)

Page 9
©**Peter Ryan** (Plates 1,4)
©**Niek Gremmen** (Plates 2,3,5)
©**Cliff Dorse** (Plate 6)

Pages 10 and 11
©**Peter Ryan** (Plates 1,4)
©**Crown Copyright** (Plate 2)
©**James Glass** (Plate 3)

Pages 12 and 13
©**Richard Cuthbert** (Plate 1)
©**James Glass** (Plates 2–4)

Page 14
©**Cliff Dorse**

Page 17
©**Angel/Wanless** (Plates 1,7)
©**Niek Gremmen** (Plates 2,3,9)
©**Cliff Dorse** (Plate 4)
©**Peter Ryan** (Plates 5,6,8)

Page 19
©**Gerhard Jakubowsky** (Plates 1,3,5)
©**Peter Ryan** (Plates 2,4,6)

Page 21
©**Gerhard Jakubowsky** (Plates 1,3)
©**Peter Ryan** (Plates 2,8)
©**Angel/Wanless** (Plate 4)
©**Cliff Dorse** (Plate 5)
©**Niek Gremmen** (Plates 6,7)

Page 23
©**Gerhard Jakubowsky** (Plates 1,2)
©**Angel/Wanless** (Plates 3,7–9)
©**Niek Gremmen** (Plates 4,5)
©**Peter Ryan** (Plate 6)
©**Cliff Dorse** (Plates 10)

Page 25
©**Niek Gremmen** (Plates 1,2,7)
©**Cliff Dorse** (Plate 3)
©**Peter Ryan** (Plate 4–6)

Page 27
©**Peter Ryan** (Plates 1,7,10)
©**Niek Gremmen** (Plates 2–6)
©**Cliff Dorse** (Plate 8)
©**Angel/Wanless** (Plate 9,11,12)

Page 29
©**Niek Gremmen** (Plates 1,3,9,10)
©**Cliff Dorse** (Plates 2,4,5)
©**Peter Ryan** (Plate 6)
©**Angel/Wanless** (Plates 7,8)

Page 31
©**Peter Ryan** (Plates 1,5)
©**Niek Gremmen** (Plates 2,6)
©**Cliff Dorse** (Plate 3)
©**Christine Hänel** (Plate 4)

Page 33
©**Niek Gremmen** (Plates 1,6)
©**Cliff Dorse** (Plate 2)
©**Angel/Wanless** (Plate 3)
©**Gerhard Jakubowsky** (Plates 4,5,7)

Page 35
©**Gerhard Jakubowsky** (Plates 1,3,4)
©**from Groves (1981)** (Plate 2)

Page 37
©**Gerhard Jakubowsky** (Plates 1,2,6)
©**Peter Ryan** (Plates 3,4)
©**Niek Gremmen** (Plate 5)
©**Angel/Wanless** (Plate 7)

Page 39
©**Niek Gremmen** (Plates 1,2)
©**Cliff Dorse** (Plate 3)
©**Angel/Wanless** (Plates 4,5,7)
©**Peter Ryan** (Plate 6)

Page 41
©**Cliff Dorse** (Plate 1)
©**Angel/Wanless** (Plates 2,3,5,6)
©**Peter Ryan** (Plate 4)
©**Gerhard Jakubowsky** (Plate 8)
©**from Christophersen (1944)** (Plate 9)

Page 43
©**Christine Hänel** (Plate 1)
©**Peter Ryan** (Plate 2)
©**Niek Gremmen** (Plates 3,4)

Page 45
©**Peter Ryan** (Plate 1)
©**Angel/Wanless** (Plates 2,4,6)
©**Niek Gremmen** (Plate 3)
©**Koos Roux** (Plate 5)

Page 47
©**Peter Ryan** (Plates 1,4,7)
©**Angel/Wanless** (Plate 2)
©**Koos Roux** (Plate 3)
©**Niek Gremmen** (Plate 5,6)

Page 49
©**Niek Gremmen** (Plate 1)
©**Angel/Wanless** (Plates 2,3,5–7,9)
©**Koos Roux** (Plate 4)
©**Peter Ryan** (Plate 8)
©**Cliff Dorse** (Plate 10)

Page 51
©**Niek Gremmen** (Plates 1,4)
©**Angel/Wanless** (Plates 2,5)
©**Koos Roux** (Plates 3,6)

Page 53
©**Peter Ryan** (Plate 1)
©**Niek Gremmen** (Plates 2,3,5)
©**Angel/Wanless** (Plate 4)

Page 55
©**Niek Gremmen** (Plates 1–6)

Page 57
©**Niek Gremmen** (Plates 1–6)

Page 59
©**Niek Gremmen** (Plates 1–9)
©**Angel/Wanless** (Plates 10,11)
©**Bart van de Vijer** (Plate 12)

Page 60
©**Peter Ryan**

Page 63
©**Peter Ryan** (Plates 1–6)

Page 65
©**Peter Ryan** (Plates 1,3,4)
©**Angel/Wanless** (Plate 2)

Page 67
©**Peter Ryan** (Plates 1–7)

Page 69
©**Peter Ryan** (Plates 1–7)

Page 71
©**Peter Ryan** (Plates 1–5)

Page 73
©**Peter Ryan** (Plates 1–7)

Page 75
©**Peter Ryan** (Plates 1–3,5)
©**Marie-Helene Burle** (Plate 4)

Page 77
©**John Graham** (Plate 1)
©**Peter Ryan** (Plates 2–5)
©**Barrie Rose** (Plate 6)

Page 79
©**Hadoram Shirihai*** (Plates 1,3)
©**Peter Ryan** (Plates 2,5,7,8)
©**Marie-Helene Burle** (Plates 4,6)

Page 81
©**Peter Ryan (** Plates 1,2,4,5)
©**Marie-Helene Burle** (Plate 3)

Page 83
©**Peter Ryan** (Plates 1–4,6,7)
©**Marie-Helene Burle** (Plate 5)

Page 85
©**Hadoram Shirihai*** (Plate 1)
©**Marie-Helene Burle** (Plate 2)
©**Peter Ryan** (Plates 3–5)
©**Dick Forsman** (Plate 6)

Page 87
©**Peter Ryan** (Plates 1–4)

Page 89
©**Peter Ryan** (Plates 1–6)

Page 91
©**Peter Ryan** (Plates 1–3)
©**Marie-Helene Burle** (Plate 4)

Page 93
©**Peter Ryan** (Plates 1–6)

Page 95
©**Tui De Roy** (Plate 1)
©**Peter Ryan** (Plates 2–6)

Page 97
©**Peter Ryan** (Plates 1,4,5,6)
©**Nik Huin** (Plate 2)
©**Graeme Searle** (Plate 3)

Page 98
©**Peter Ryan**

Page 101
©**Peter Ryan** (Plates 1–4)

Page 103
©**Marie-Helene Burle** (Plates 1,4,5)
©**Peter Ryan** (Plates 2,3)

Page 105
©**Yvonne Kamp** (Plate 1)
©**John Graham** (Plate 2)
©**Peter Ryan** (Plates 3,4)
©**Trevor Hardaker** (Plate 5)
©**Barrie Rose** (Plate 6)

Page 107
©**Trevor Hardaker** (Plates 1,2)
©**Peter Ryan** (Plates 3,4,7)
©**John Graham** (Plates 5,6)

Page 109
©**Sue Daly** (Plate 1)
©**Marie-Helene Burle** (Plate 2)
©**Peter Ryan** (Plate 3)

Page 110
©**Marie-Helene Burle**

Page 115
©**Christine Hänel** (Plates 1–4,7,8,11)
©**Paul Tyler** (Plate 5)
©**Tristan Island Government**
(Plates 6,9,10)

Page 119
©**Christine Hänel** (Plates 1–8,10)
©**August Brinkmann** (Plate 9)

Page 120
©**Sue Scott**

Page 123
©**Sue Scott** (Plates 1–6)

Page 125
©**Elaine Heemstra** (Plate 1)
©**Tim Andrew** (Plates 2,4)
©**Peter Ryan** (Plate 3)

Page 127
©**Paul Tyler** (Plates 1,4)
©**Sue Scott** (Plate 2)
©**Tim Andrew** (Plate 3)

Page 129
©**Sue Scott** (Plate 1)
©**Tim Andrew** (Plate 2)
©**Paul Tyler** (Plates 3–5)

Page 131
©**Sue Scott** (Plate 1)
©**Tim Andrew** (Plates 2,3)
©**Elaine Heemstra** (Plate 4)

Page 133
©**Sue Scott** (Plates 1,5)
©**Jeremy Stafford-Deitsch** (Plates 2,3)
©**Paul Tyler** (Plate 4)

Page 135
©**Sue Scott** (Plates 1–8)

Page 137
©**Sue Scott** (Plates 1–10)
©**Paul Tyler** (Plate 11)

Page 139
©**Sue Scott** (Plates 1–4,6,7)
©**Paul Tyler** (Plates 5,8)

Page 141
©**Sue Scott** (Plates 1,3,5,8–10)
©**Paul Tyler** (Plates 2,4,6,7,11)

Page 143
©**Sue Scott** (Plates 1–9)

Page 144
©**Peter Ryan**

Page 145
©**Sue Scott** (Plates 1–9)

Page 146
©**James Glass**

Page 148
©**Peter Ryan** (Plates 1–3)

Page 149
©**Peter Ryan** (Plates 1–3)

*photographs by Hadoram Shirihai are taken from the forthcoming *Albatrosses, Petrels and Shearwaters of the World* by Shirihai *et al.*, A & C Black, London.

Index of scientific names

Index of common names